LEGENDARY LOCALS

OF

FALMOUTH

MASSACHUSETTS

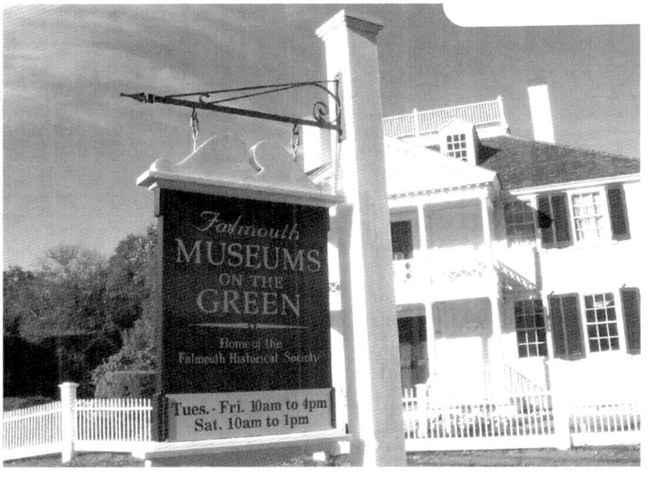

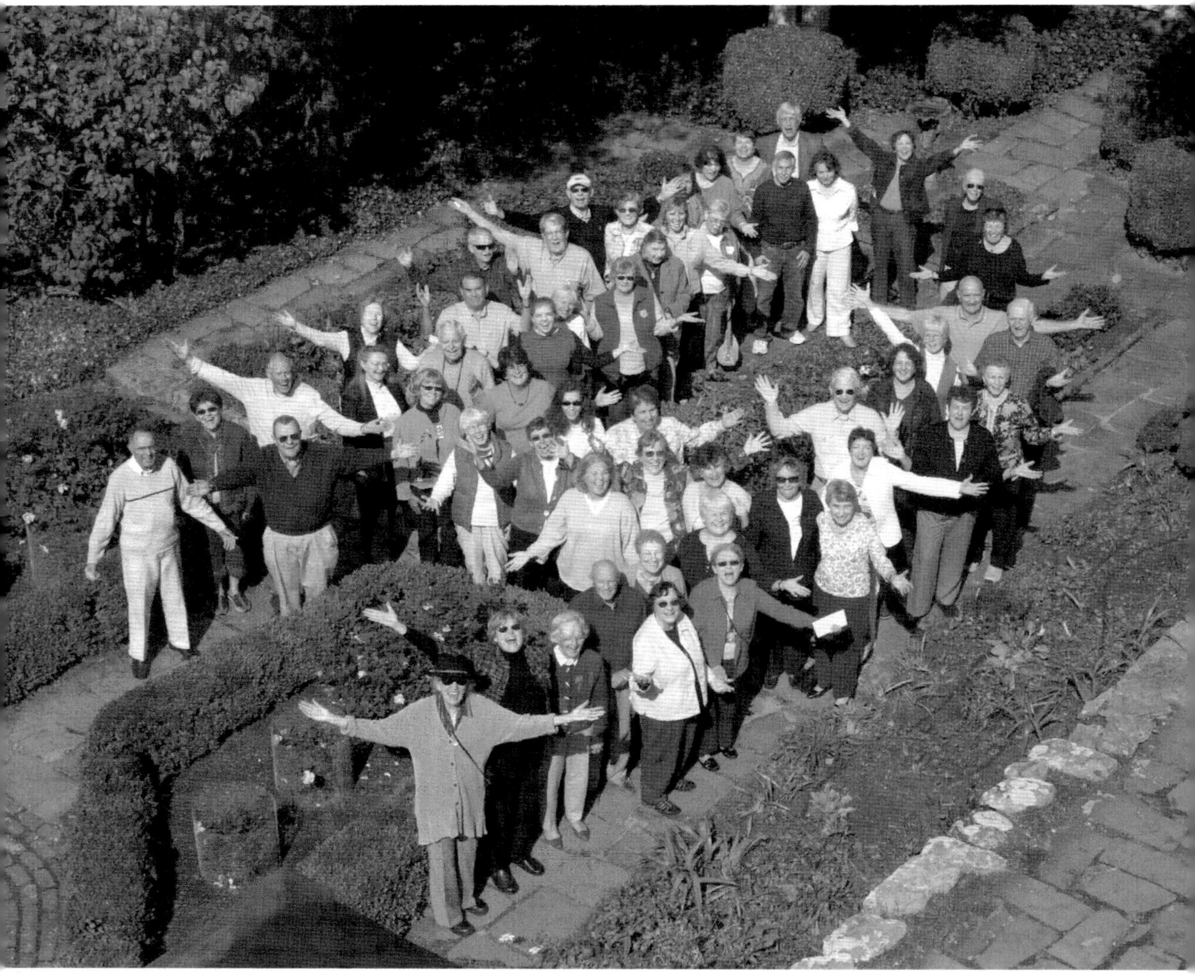

Volunteers of the Falmouth Historical Society

The Falmouth Historical Society depends on the support of an army of loyal volunteers. Here are a few of the historical society's volunteers standing by the gardens at the Museums on the Green. Professional photographer Amy Rader took this photograph from the widow's walk on the Wick's House. (Courtesy Amy Rader.)

Page 1: Dr. Francis Wicks House

Pictured is the entrance to the Dr. Francis Wicks House, Museums on the Green, Falmouth Historical Society. (Courtesy Mary Sicchio.)

LEGENDARY LOCALS

OF

FALMOUTH

MASSACHUSETTS

FALMOUTH HISTORICAL SOCIETY

LEGENDARY LOCALS

ISBN 978-1-4671-0043-4

Legendary Locals is an imprint of Arcadia Publishing
Charleston, South Carolina

Printed in the United States of America

Library of Congress Control Number: 2012943459

For all general information, please contact Arcadia Publishing:
Telephone 843-853-2070
Fax 843-853-0044
E-mail sales@arcadiapublishing.com
For customer service and orders:
Toll-Free 1-888-313-2665

Visit us on the Internet at www.arcadiapublishing.com

Dedication

This book is dedicated to the archivists of the Falmouth Historical Society who created and maintained an extraordinary collection: Rev. H.H. Smythe, Amelia Lawrence, Charlotte Price, Dorothy Svenning, and Mary Sicchio.

On the cover: From left to right:
(TOP ROW) Gus T. Canty, director, Falmouth Recreation Center (Courtesy Tom Canty; see page 94), G.W. Swift, Civil War soldier (Courtesy Falmouth Historical Society, see page 56), Kitty Baker, journalist (Courtesy Falmouth Historical Society; see page 100), James H. Fisher, whale man (Courtesy Falmouth Historical Society; see page 47), George Hampson, scientist (Courtesy Falmouth Historical Society; see page 101).
(MIDDLE ROW) Cynthia Augusta Botelho, librarian and Strawberry Queen (Courtesy Falmouth Historical Society; see page 87), Tony Andrews, farmer (Courtesy Falmouth Historical Society; see page 84), Elijah Swift, early entrepreneur (Courtesy Falmouth Historical Society; see page 26), Dana Miskell, lumber businessman (Courtesy Miskell family; see page 35), Katharine Lee Bates, teacher and poet (Courtesy Falmouth Historical Society; see page 92).
(BOTTOM ROW) Judith Stetson, activist and editor (Courtesy Amy Radar; see page 104), Henry D. Swift and D. Wheeler Swift, Quaker brothers and businessmen (Courtesy Falmouth Historical Society; see page 28), Mary Chipman Lawrence, sea captain's wife (Courtesy Falmouth Historical Society; see page 46), Albert Marks, strawberry grower (Courtesy Falmouth Historical Society; see page 85), Rev. H.H. Smyth, pastor, St. Barnabas Church (Courtesy Falmouth Historical Society; see page 78).

CONTENTS

ACKNOWLEDGMENTS

First and foremost, we acknowledge the collections of the Falmouth Historical Society and the citizens of Falmouth who have donated their papers and photographs to the Falmouth Historical Society. We also need to thank Len Miele, Meg Costello, and T. Rich Miner Jr. for their support in compiling this publication. Special thanks to the following individuals and organizations: Amy Rader, WHOI/MBL archives, Woods Hole Historical Museum, Mount Holyoke Archives, Connecticut College, Len Miele, Tom Canty, Margaret Hough Russell, Nate Ellis, Fred Lawrence, Les Garrick, Beach Rose Inn, T. Rich Miner Jr., Nickerson Archives, Cape Cod Community College, Doug Rugh, and Hilary Osborn. For the rare and generous gift of editing, we acknowledge Len Miele, Erin Vosgien, and Laura Saylor. Unless otherwise noted, photographs in this book are courtesy the Falmouth Historical Society.

INTRODUCTION

Let us begin with our wily founder, Jonathan Hatch, who knew somehow that Mill Road, by the coastline and not far from Woods Hole, would be the perfect place to begin his search for independent living. He is matched by his descendant Allen Hatch, who found Hatchville, on the opposite end of Falmouth, to be his Garden of Eden more than 300 years later.

Many of these early souls exhibited courage and became tipping points, defining the nature of Falmouth. The tolerance of Isaac Robinson set a peaceful space in the early wilderness of Falmouth in the 1600s. Early Quaker families contributed their industry and religious fervor to the mix in their West Falmouth settlement. The West Falmouth Swift family moved from the occupation of blacksmiths to entrepreneur inventors in two generations. Some of our most enduring heroes are represented in the early militia of the town. Gen. Joseph Dimmick, who stood up to British privateers, is the subject of a Depression-era mural at the Falmouth Village Post Office. Weston Jenkins's defiance is legendary in the War of 1812. Generations of Civil War, World War I, and World War II veterans are commemorated in monuments located in front of the public library.

The Falmouth Historical Society has a large collection of mariner images because their founders were largely descendants of seamen. Among them were Lewis Lawrence and Amelia Lawrence. Their stories are sometimes chilling—often death defying—and say something about a tradition of toughness and daring. Whaling wives were among these durable salts, who birthed their babies in the South Seas and kept logbooks. Elijah Swift capitalized on his carpentry and made his dizzying rise to whaling fleet owner, live oak lumber dealer, and state legislator. It was Silas Jones who encountered aborigines in the South Seas and returned with a prized war club. It is this artifact that has been used in part to help pay for the new education center at the Museums on the Green.

Falmouth's history is marked by pageantry: Gosnold's tercentenary, the US bicentennial, Falmouth's tercentenary, and the reenactment of the Battle of Falmouth. All these anniversaries and celebrations were good sources for photographs as well as civic pride.

Two chapters are allotted to the newcomers settling Falmouth in the 20th and 21st centuries. The waves of migration included: wealthy Bostonians and Worcester developers, Portuguese and Azorean mariners and farmers looking for relief from the mills of New Bedford, the scientists of Woods Hole, and the summer tourists. It was a mixing of cultures that was not always easy but created the cosmopolitan culture of Falmouth.

Beginning in 1890, the summer people came to Falmouth led by Joseph Story Fay and James Madison Beebe. These Boston merchant princes changed the landscape of Falmouth, adding fabulous mansions, yachts, Romanesque churches, and progress. A collection gifted to the Falmouth Historical Society by Margaret Hough Russell can be seen in the chapter on the history of agricultural development in Falmouth, including cranberry and strawberry growers. Farmers from Brava, the Azores, and St. Michael's appear with their stories of hardship and belief in the land. The Festival of Strawberries recognizes an important cash crop for the town.

While looking for images of the people of Falmouth, I often found entire lineages of families who came to Falmouth and mostly stayed. These families included the Swifts, the Lawrences (both Teaticket and seafaring lines), the Miskells, and the Ellises. At the turn of the century, the town fathers emerged as a congenial group looking out for the interests of the town, envisioning roads, and public planning.

The scientists of Woods Hole arrived in 1880 with the beginning of the Marine Biological Laboratory (MBL) and the Woods Hole Oceanographic Institute (WHOI). Beginning with Cornelia Clapp and continuing through Rachael Carson, these persons of vision and science have added a world importance to this village. The genius and research of Albert Szent-Györgyi and Robert Ballard have brought attention to Woods Hole beyond its quaint seaside location. A visit from the Japanese emperor in 1975 was taken in stride by this village.

One of the more remarkable stories of philanthropy and social consciousness is found in Josiah K. Lilly, who adopted Falmouth and made it the recipient of many civic capital improvements.

The artists and creative people of Falmouth are represented by Katharine Lee Bates, who attained national fame with her poem "America the Beautiful." Marine artist E.F. Lincoln, abstract artist William Littlefield, and silversmith Gladys Panis were among those in Falmouth who lived by the tradition of the arts. There are group photographs that depict the town's great tradition of organizing. Temperance groups, garden clubs, and veterans' organizations all helped define the nature of Falmouth.

With the changing fortunes of the town, place and street names changed to reflect its citizens of means and influence: Gus Canty of the Gus Canty Recreation Building, Peg Mullen of the Mullen Hall School, Frances A. Crane of the Frances A. Crane Wildlife Sanctuary, Peg Noonan of Peg Noonan Park, Harvey Clauson of Clauson's Corner, and Rev. Samuel Palmer of Palmer Avenue. The theory that self-interest undermines the common good is not shown in many of the stories told here. As success came to many of these people, they spread their influence throughout the town as committee members and as town officials.

Finally, there are the unique individuals who win our affection through the power of their personalities, including columnist writer Kitty Baker, baseball enthusiast Al Irish, and road race runner Tommy Leonard.

I hope these photographs are enlightening and entertaining and begin a conversation about what it means to live in Falmouth and how the town has evolved from our first lawless, runaway founder, Jonathan Hatch. Although incomplete and imperfect, I submit that this book is a history, local in scope, but significant, singular, and meaningful to our place in US history.

—Mary Sicchio
August 2012

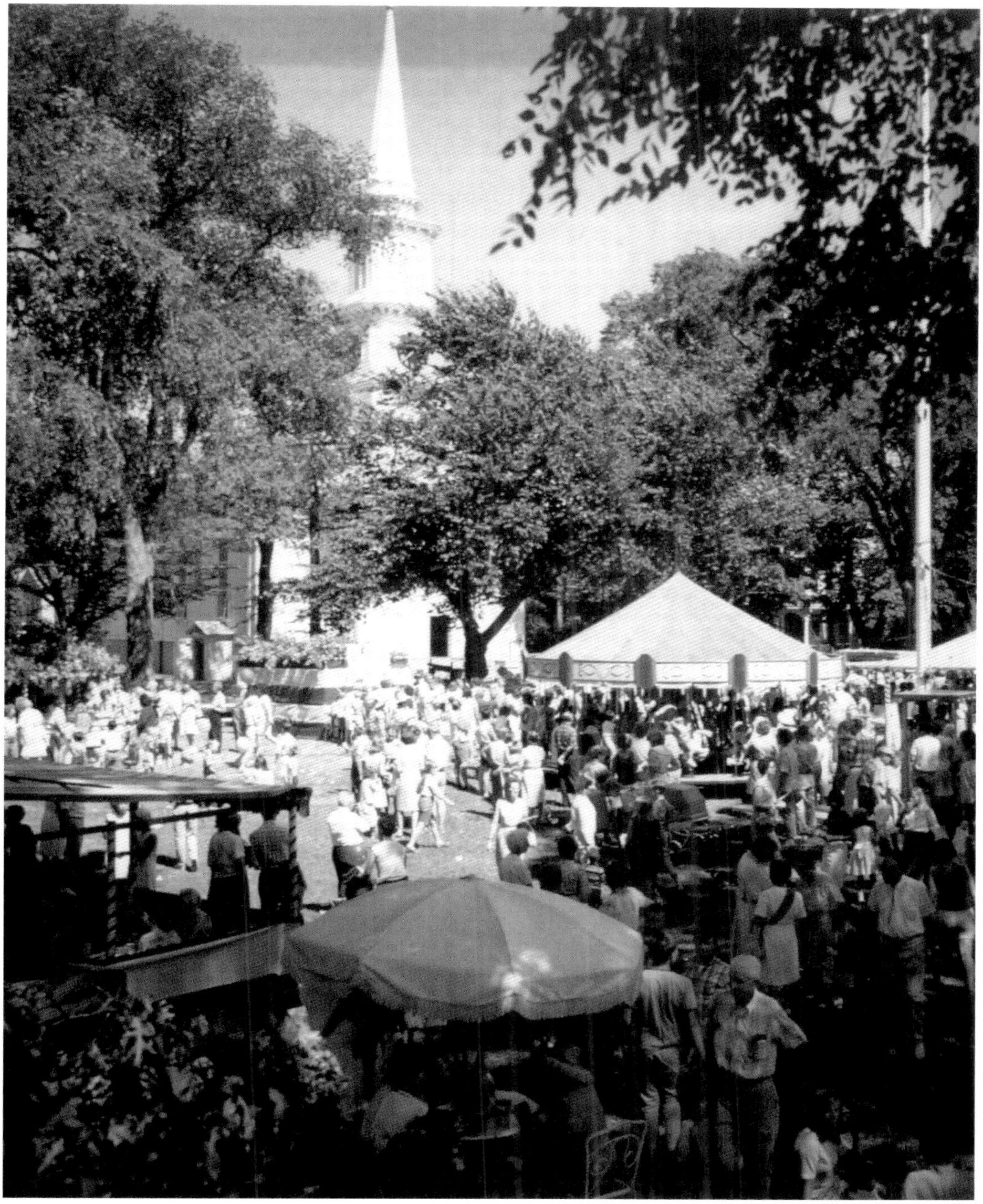

Nursing Fete

The steeple of the Congregational church is visible in this photograph of the Nursing Fete, which was held annually from 1919 to 1986, supporting the Falmouth Nursing Association. The merry-go-round, games of chance, and tea tent were set up on the Village Green and were a rallying point of civic pride. Many locals remember this August event as a highlight of their summers. The Falmouth Nursing Association eventually became part of the Visiting Nurses of Cape Cod, but for a time, it was a strictly local public health group with local funding.

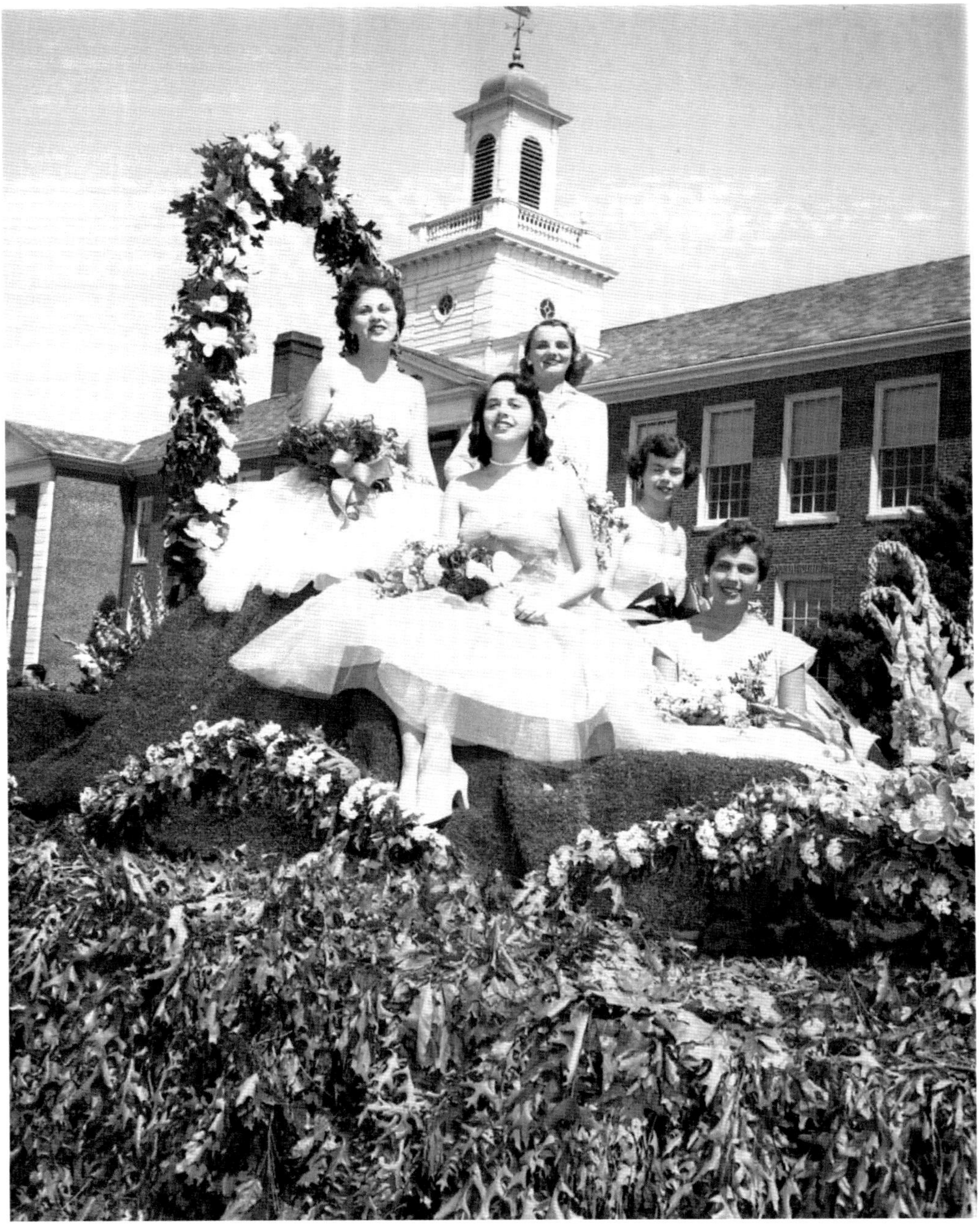

Strawberry Queen

This photograph shows the Strawberry Queen and her court for the 1954 Falmouth Festival of Strawberries parade. In the background are the Mullen Hall School buildings as the parade heads to Main Street. The festival would only last one more year but remains a sweet memory for all those who participated, especially all the Strawberry Queens and members of their courts. The parade was part of several days of events, including strawberry picking, strawberry eating, dancing, and promotion of the strawberry trade.

CHAPTER ONE

Runaway Founders, Proprietors, and Heroes

O beautiful for heroes proved / In liberating strife

—Katharine Lee Bates, "America the Beautiful"

This chapter begins with the bedrock citizens of Falmouth history—the founders and defenders whose stories are told and retold, commemorated, reenacted and honored—including an early explorer, first families, a Revolutionary hero, and a champion of the War of 1812.

A Quaker sympathizer and a much-loved reverend helped set Falmouth's compass, and some of the early physicians and their visions of health care are recalled. The town encountered real and serious military force from the British twice in its early history but managed to survive and prevail.

The Battle of Falmouth and the attacks of the HMS *Nimrod* are illustrated and the stories of the makeshift militia are told. The monuments posted around Falmouth record stories of its early history including the Mariners Memorial Rock, the First Settlement stone, the post office WPA mural, and the gravestone epitaphs. Reenactments, painted portraits, daguerreotypes, silhouettes, and engravings are part of this discovery of those who came first.

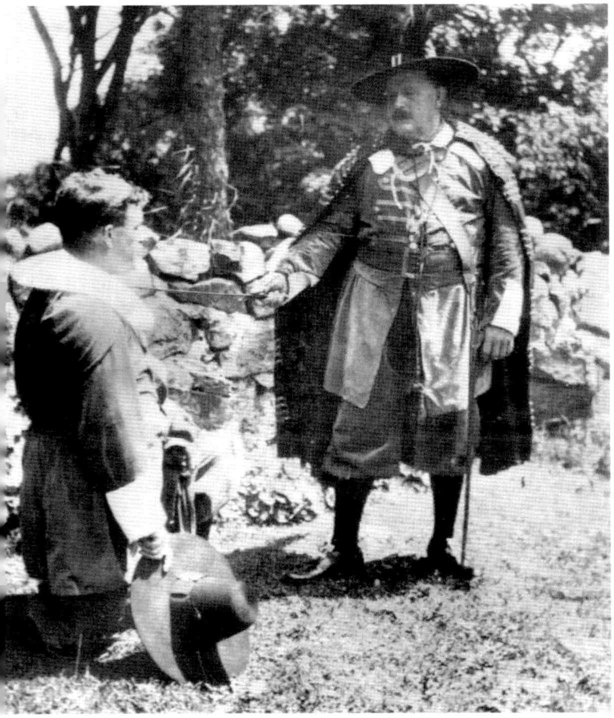

Bartholomew Gosnold (1572–1607)
Bartholomew Gosnold provides a direct connection between Falmouth, England, and Falmouth, Massachusetts. His voyage on the ship *Concord* in 1602, setting out from Falmouth, England, sealed Falmouth's connection to England before the Plymouth settlement. Besides naming Falmouth and the Elizabeth Islands, he also named Cape Cod for all the cod in the area's waters. His brief stay in Cuttyhunk and mainland landing was commemorated with the tercentenary celebration in 1907. At left, J.K.P. Purdham (right), representing Gosnold, is joined by a fellow reenactor. The Mariner Memorial Rock at Locust Street and Elm Road was unveiled at the weeklong festivities with schoolchildren presiding. Below, Marion Eldridge unveils the memorial in this historic tableau commemorating the 300th anniversary of Gosnold's Landing.

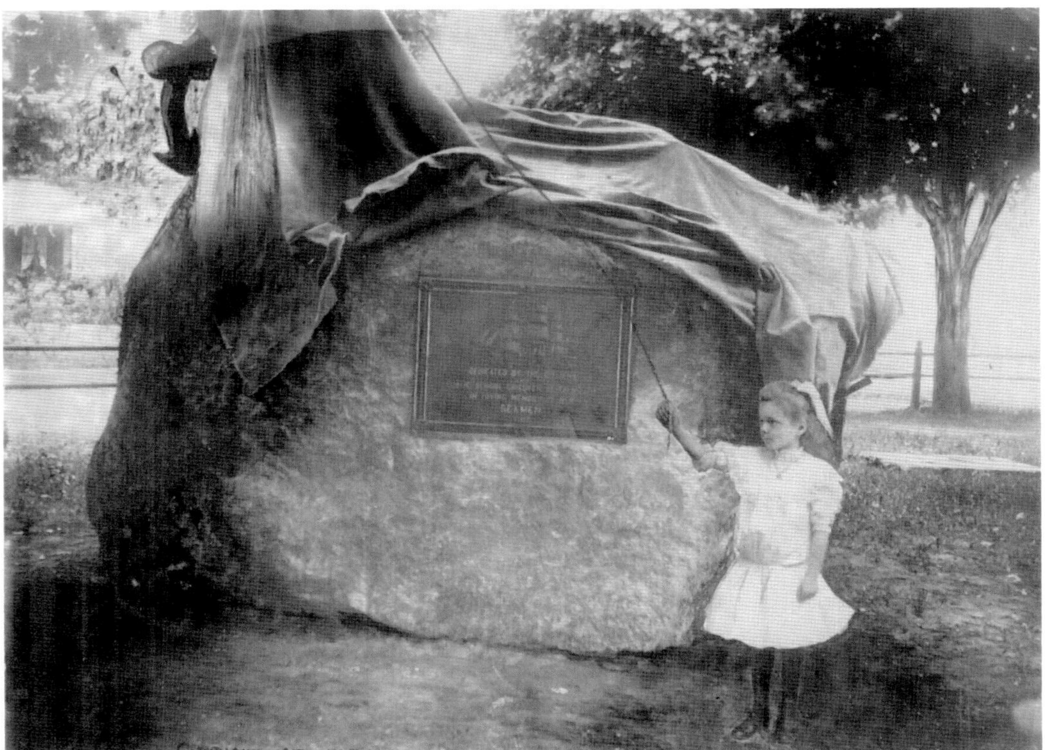

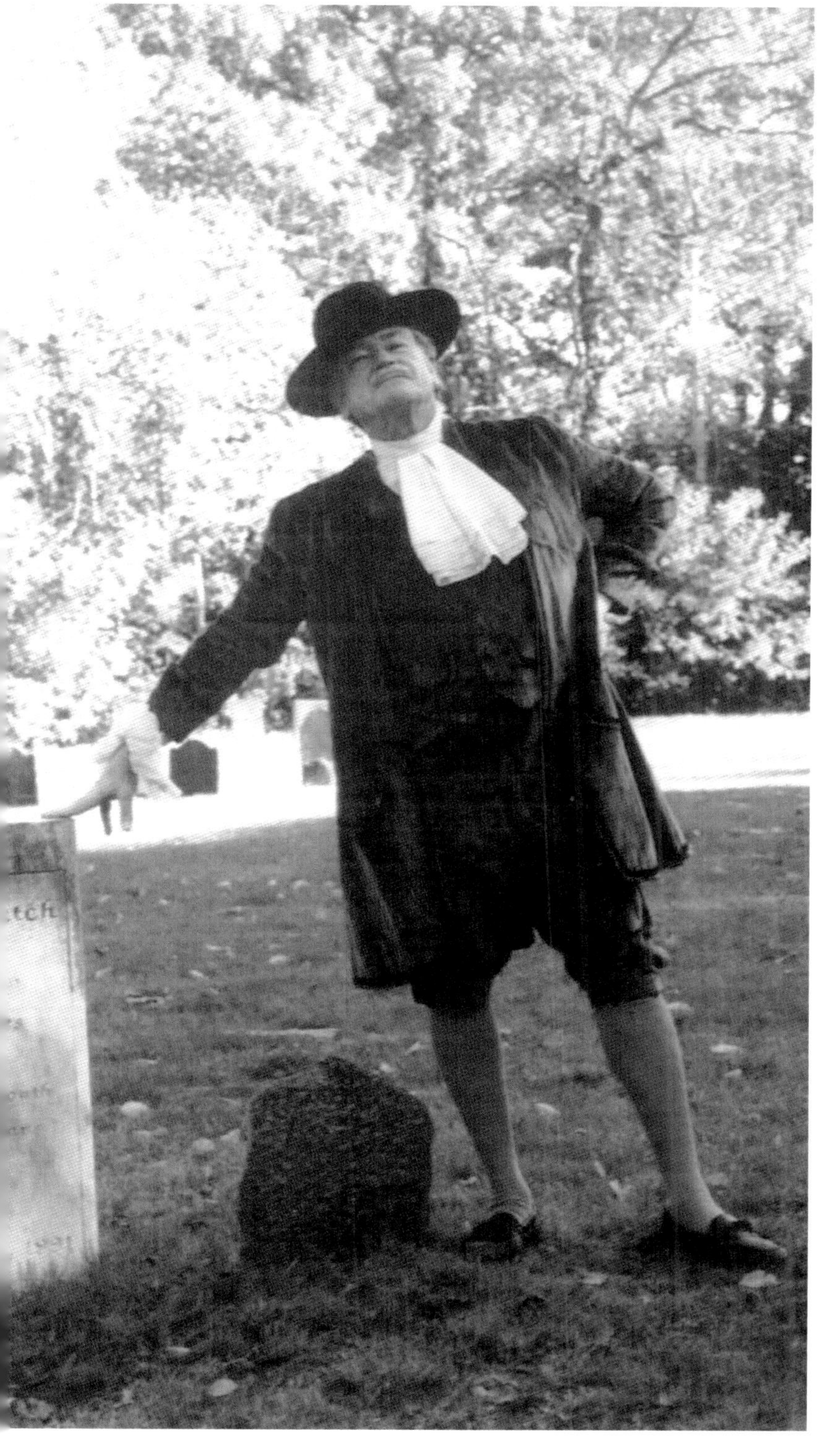

Jonathan Hatch (1624–1710)
Jonathan Hatch is an unlikely founder of a quiet Cape Cod town, but it was this runaway apprentice, ordinary, tavern owner, and father of 11 whose name appears with the first proprietors on the November 29, 1661, document incorporating Suckanesset, later known as Falmouth. He had many encounters with the courts of the Plymouth Colony. It was said that he spoke to the Native Americans in their own language and had many dealings with them. He lived a full 86 years and is buried at the Old Town Burial Ground. Here, B. Grant Willis, a persuasive local attorney and past president of the Falmouth Historical Society, portrays Falmouth's founding father in 18th-century garb by the Hatch gravesite.

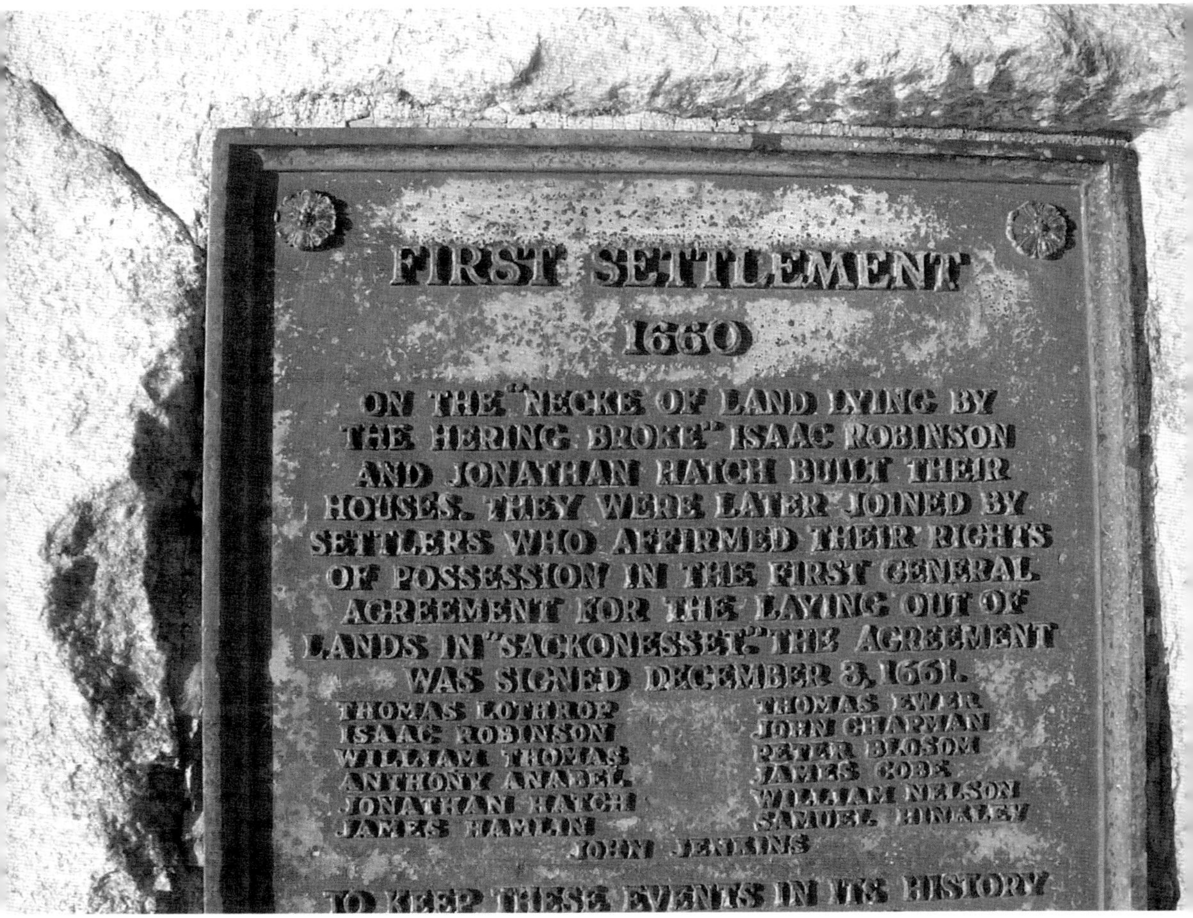

Isaac Robinson (1610–1704)

Isaac Robinson, son of the pilgrims' pastor in Leyden, is honored as a founder of Falmouth. While living in Barnstable, he was commissioned by the authorities to infiltrate the Quaker meeting, considered to be a subversive force. Instead, Robinson found that he admired the Friends, and though he never converted, he became their advocate. In retaliation, the town fathers temporarily disenfranchised him. Seeking freer air to breathe, in 1660, Robinson joined Jonathan Hatch as one of the first white men to settle in Falmouth. His presence encouraged many Quakers to follow suit. In 1664, Isaac was licensed to keep an inn for travelers to the islands. Eventually, he moved back to his daughter's home in Barnstable, where he died at the age of 93. Along Surf Drive beach, not far from Mill Road, stands the First Settlers Monument, commemorating Falmouth's first arrivals. Not all stayed in Falmouth, but important names such as Jonathan Hatch and Isaac Robinson are remembered.

Rev. Samuel Palmer (1707–1775)

Rev. Samuel Palmer was the third settled minister of the First Congregational Church on the Village Green. He received both a bachelor and master of arts degree from Harvard College in 1727–1730. Palmer resided in a large two-story house on the same site where the historical society's Conant House now stands. This location is on Palmer Avenue, which bears Reverend Palmer's name. When he was 29, he married Mercy Parker, the mother of his first six children. When she died, he married Sarah Allen (he was 44 years old) and became the father of six more children. Reverend Palmer was not only the town's religious leader, but he was the town's physician as well. Although he did not have a medical degree, he probably ministered to the physical needs of his parishioners through scripture and prayer. His greatest legacy is the meticulous church history he wrote over a period of 44 years, a history of Falmouth Colonial life from 1731 to 1775. It is a fascinating account of such social issues as racial and religious intolerance, blasphemy, alcoholism, and premarital sex. Reverend Palmer was interred at Old Town Burial Ground.

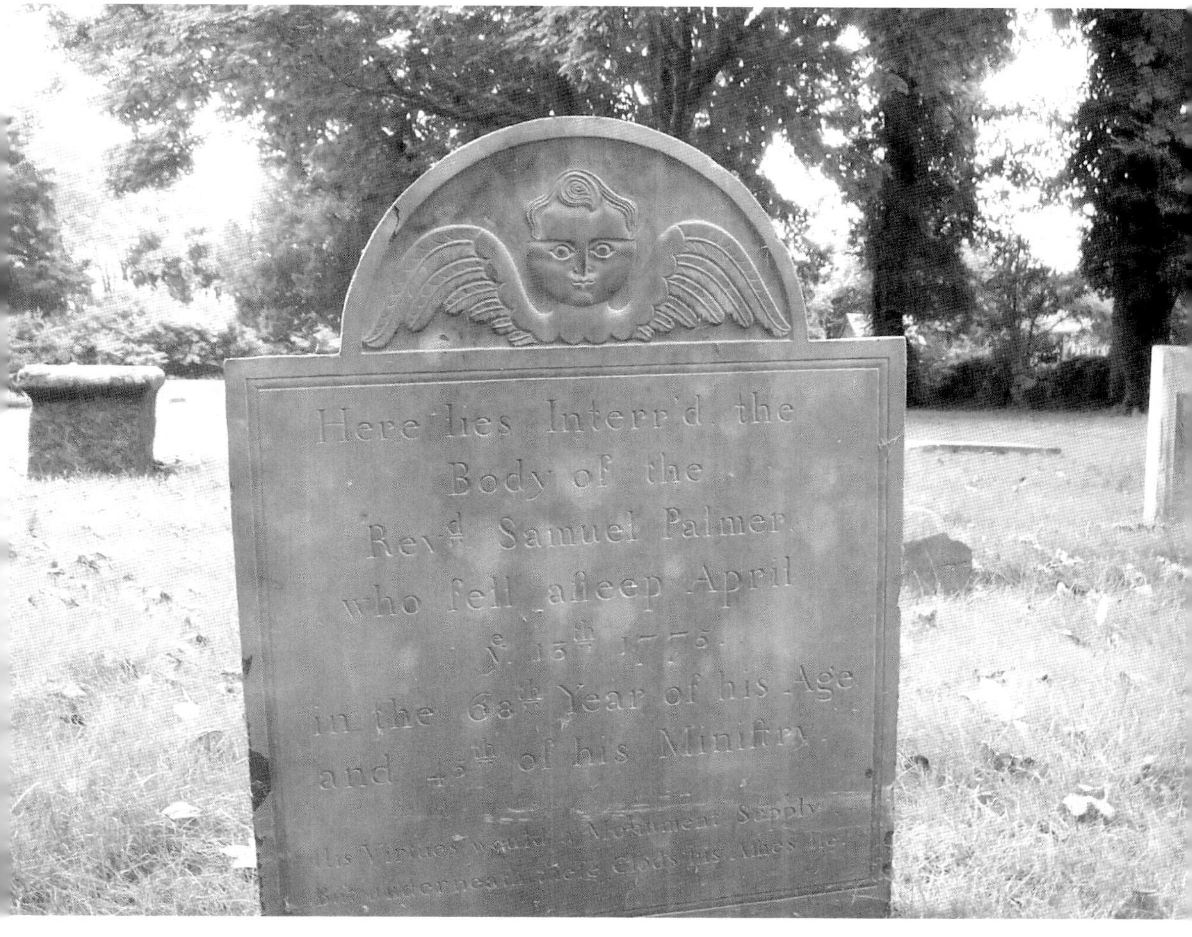

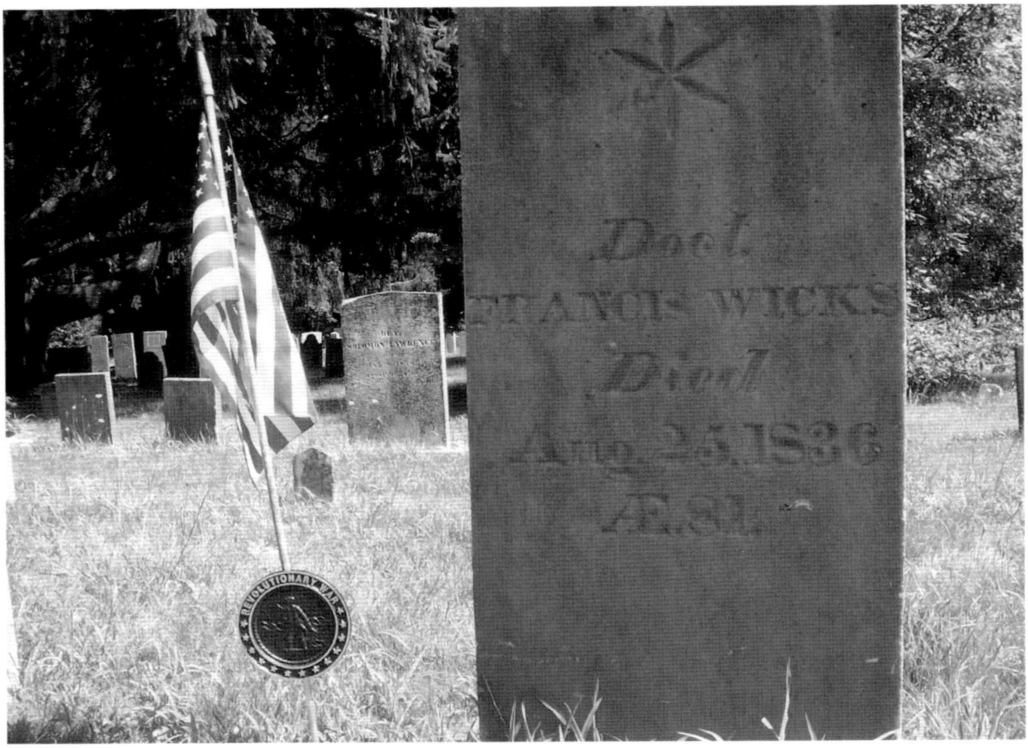

Dr. Francis Wicks (1755–1836)

Dr. Francis Wicks was a local pioneer of smallpox prevention. From 1797 to 1802, he operated an inoculation hospital at Nobska Point. Here, patients were deliberately infected with mild cases of smallpox, then quarantined till they recovered assured of future immunity. He supplied Harvard's Dr. Benjamin Waterhouse with live smallpox virus for a decisive 1802 experiment that calmed public fears about the new procedure. Wicks dispensed vaccinations and other treatments from an office in his home that is now maintained by the Falmouth Historical Society as one of its Museums on the Green. Medicine, however, was not his only pursuit. Wicks was a tireless public servant, working with other local leaders to give the town a library, school, Masonic lodge, bank, town poor house, and a renovated meetinghouse complete with a Paul Revere bell. Elected several times to the state legislature, he was also a member of Falmouth's first board of health. Almost forgotten for decades after his death, Wicks is now honored as a man who made a lasting mark on medicine and on Falmouth's community life.

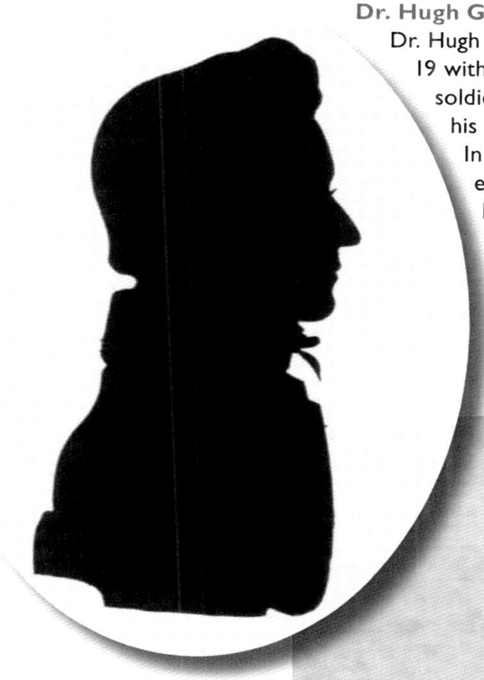

Dr. Hugh G. Donaldson (1757–1812)

Dr. Hugh G. Donaldson arrived from London at the age of 19 with ambitions to be a physician rather than a king's soldier. Family legends tell of his running away from his English home to America to pursue his dreams. In Falmouth, he apprenticed with Dr. Wicks and experimented with Dr. Jenner's smallpox vaccine. He proved the vaccine's effectiveness by inoculating his two youngest children. Dr. Donaldson was an early visionary, and his gravestone (reset in 1995) is in the Old Town Burial Ground. His descendants included M. Sylvia Donaldson.

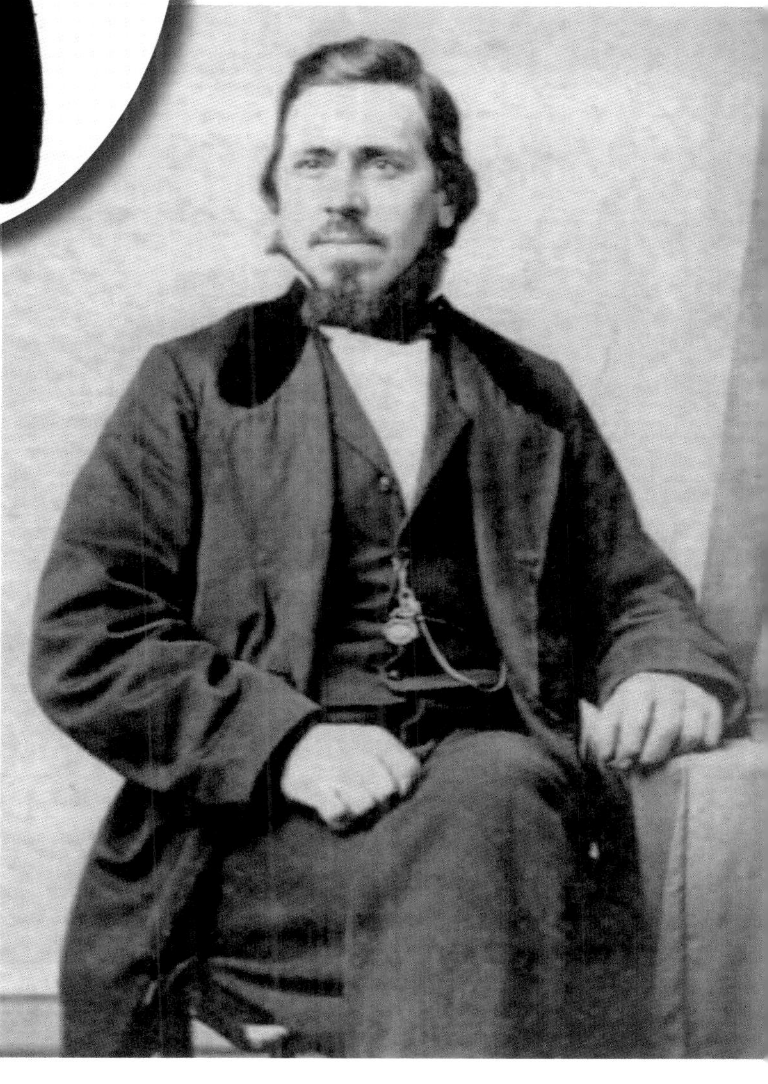

Dr. Aaron Cornish (1795–1864)

Dr. Aaron Cornish, a Harvard Medical School graduate, became a physician in Falmouth at the age of 25, serving the sick for 35 years. For most of his time in Falmouth, he lived on Palmer Avenue at the house of Dr. Wicks. He was described as a scholarly, quiet man and was universally respected. He practiced in New Bedford for a period of nine years where he died. His burial at Oak Grove Cemetery was attended by fellow Masons.

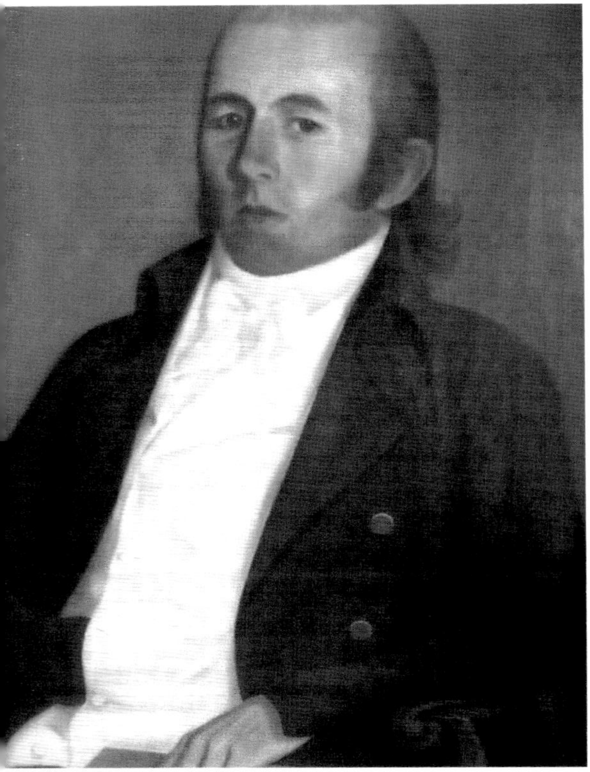

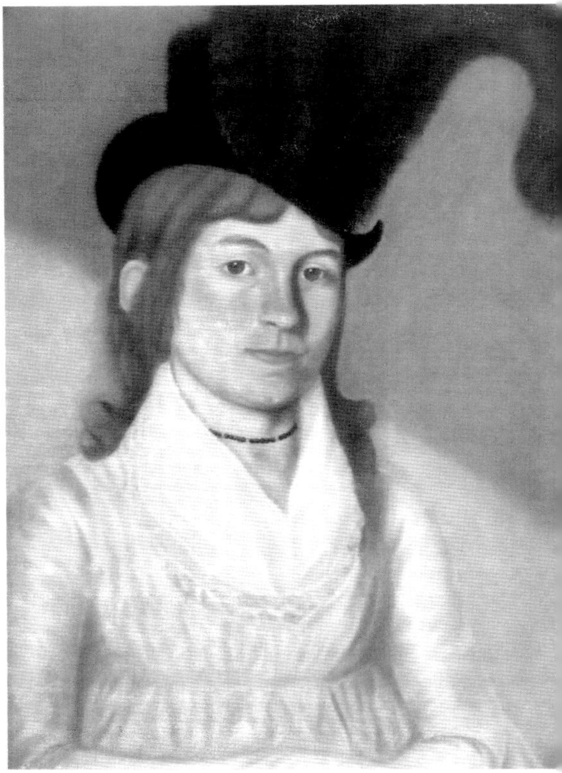

Thatcher Lewis (1772–1842) and Rebecca Lewis (1780–1806)
Thatcher Lewis was a carpenter and new member of the Falmouth Marine Lodge when this portrait was painted in 1803. Beside him is his wife, Rebecca Lewis. They lived on Locust Street in a simple Colonial house he built. Thatcher and his wife represented an upwardly mobile class of craftspeople in the growing Falmouth economy. Rebecca died at the age of 26. Her epitaph reads: "Farewell my bosom friend / Till heavenly love / Shall unite us in the world above." Their images are among the first encountered by visitors to Dr. Wicks's house at the Museums on the Green. (Both, courtesy T. Richard Miner Jr.)

Daniel Swift (1792–1879) and Hepzibah W. Hoxie Swift (1797–1858)
Quakers Daniel Swift and Hepzibah Swift married in Sandwich and came to live in West Falmouth. Their wedding certificate, signed by all 23 wedding guests, is held in the collections of the Falmouth Historical Society. Among this couple's seven children, born over their 35-year marriage, were Daniel W. Swift and Henry D. Swift. This Swift family marked the beginnings of another Falmouth family dynasty.

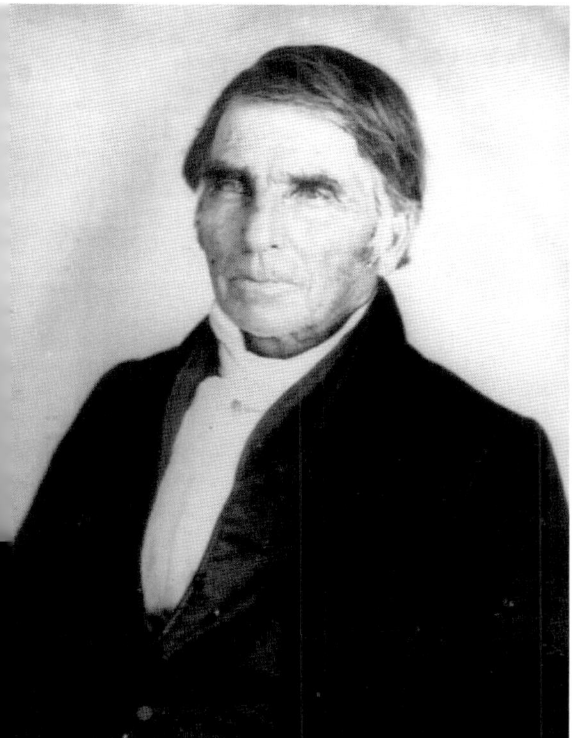

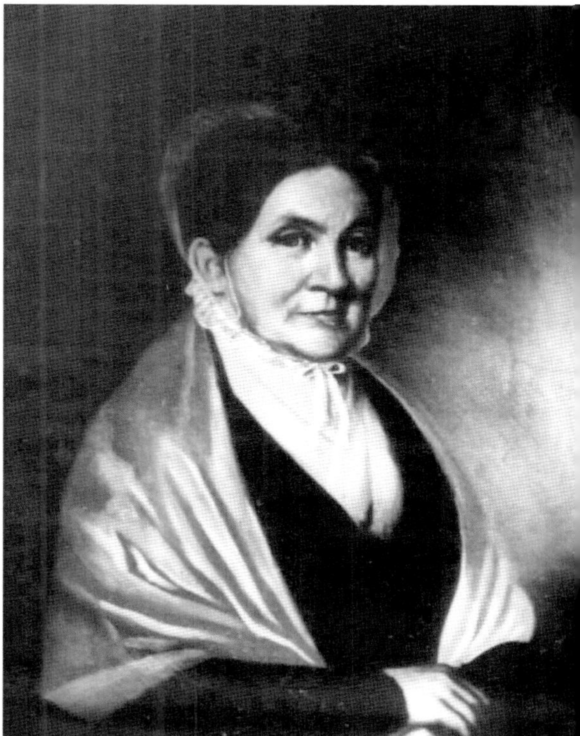

Col. Joseph Dimmick and the Battle of Falmouth (April 2, 1779) (OPPOSITE PAGE)
On April 2, 1779, two hundred citizens from Falmouth and surrounding villages stood their ground in trenches near the Old Stone Dock by Surf Drive and faced down 10 British men-of-war. The siege of cannon fire rained on the town from daybreak to dusk. The British, although inflicting some damage but no casualties, did not land and the town was not set afire. In this painting by Lewis Gifford (1854–1936), a Woods Hole artist and pictorial historian, Colonel Dimmick stands his ground in the center.

Gen. Joseph Dimmick (1734–1822)
Gen. Joseph Dimmick was a militia hero during the Revolutionary War, facing down English privateers at Tarpaulin Cove and standing in the trenches at Old Stone Dock during the Battle of Falmouth on April 2, 1779. He served as sheriff and state senator, fathered 10 children, and maintained an exceptional moral reputation. He is immortalized in the Falmouth Post Office mural *Recapture of Corn Schooner From British*, painted in 1943 by Karl Oberteuffer. General Dimmick is the tall, lanky figure on the far left.

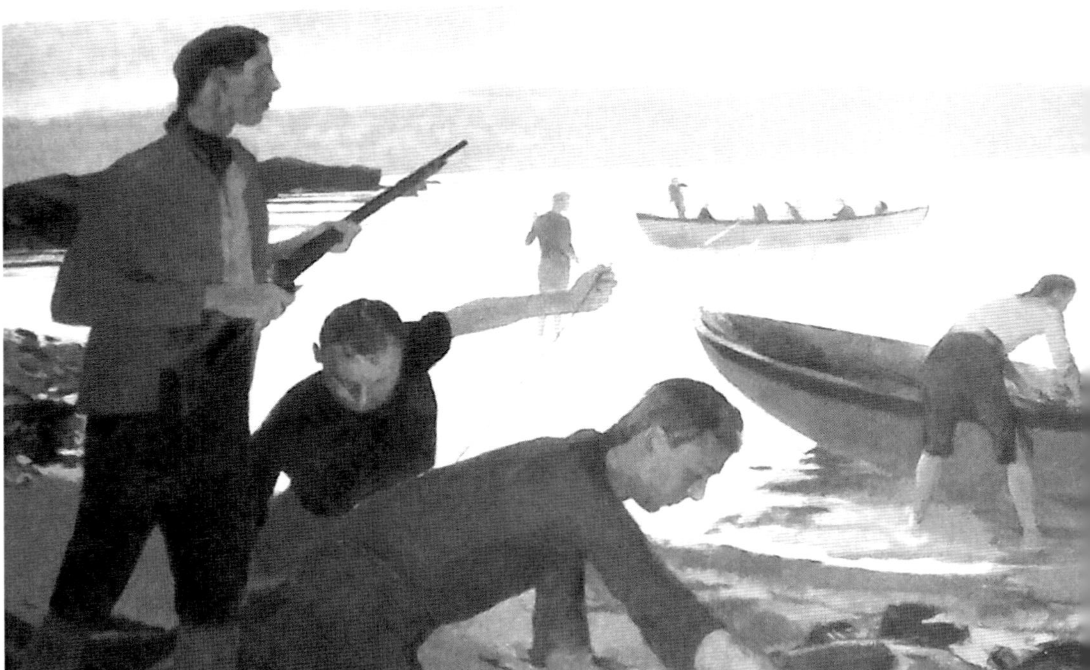

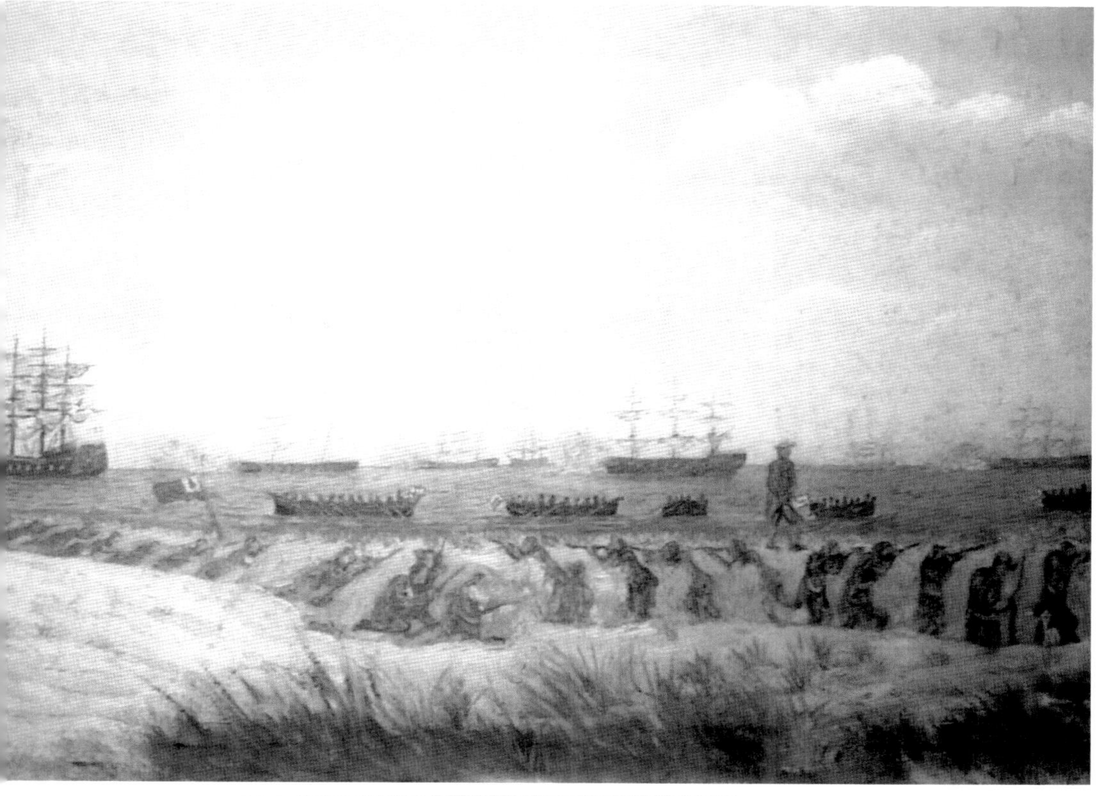

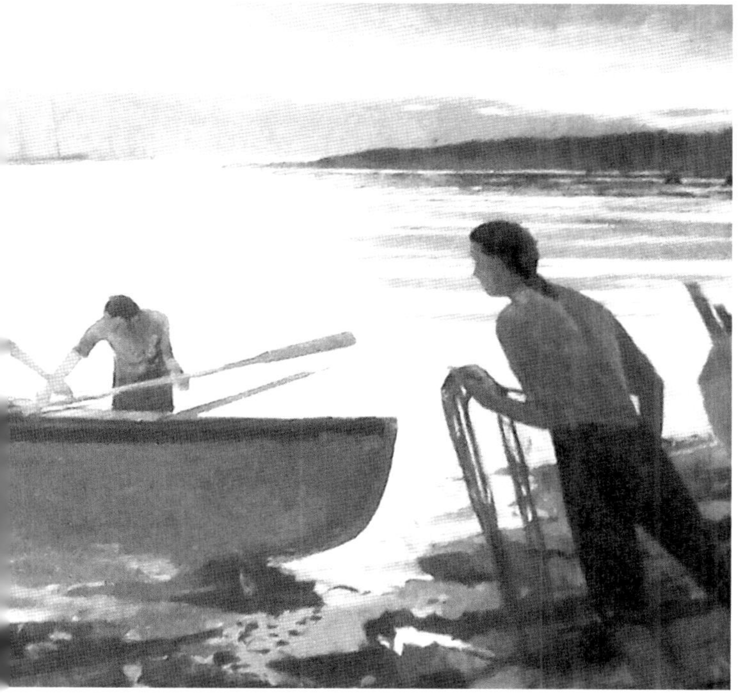

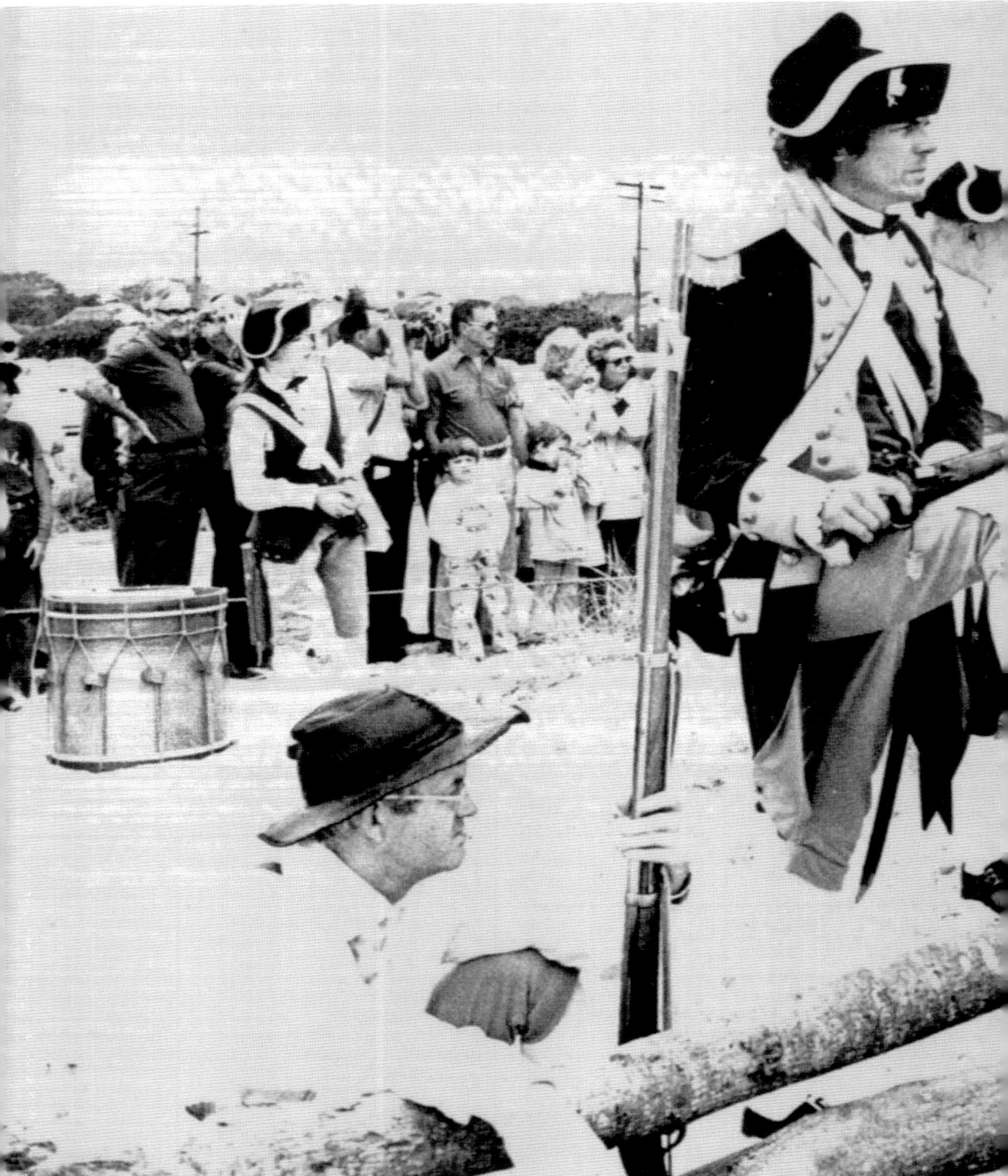

The Reenactment of the Battle of Falmouth
On June 12, 1999, the Reenactment of the Battle of Falmouth took place 220 years after the original

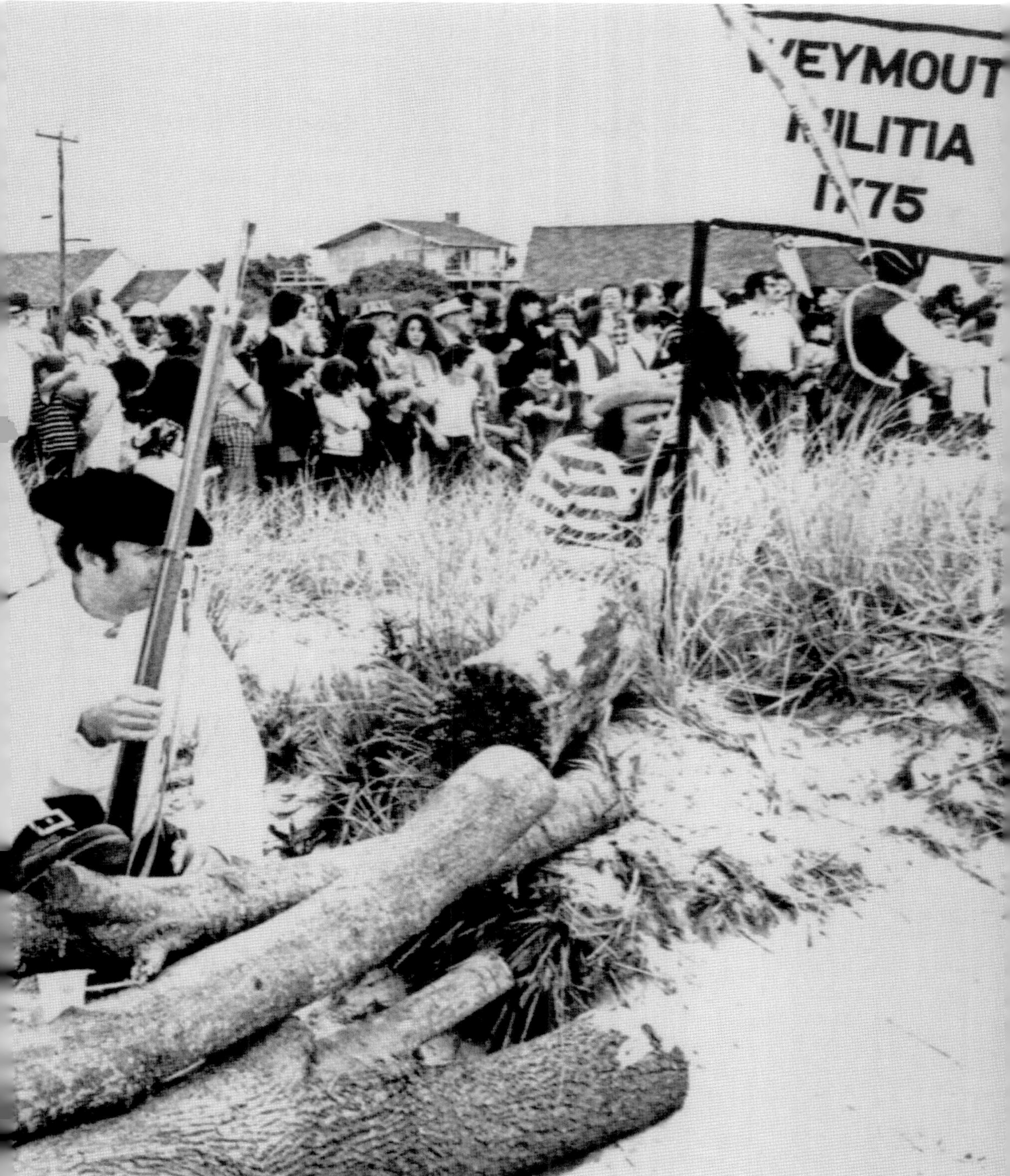

battle. The reenactment was an extravaganza created by Bob Bidwell and his committee. It included 300 British Loyalist and Colonist reenactors, fife and drum members, five tall ships, and four long boats.

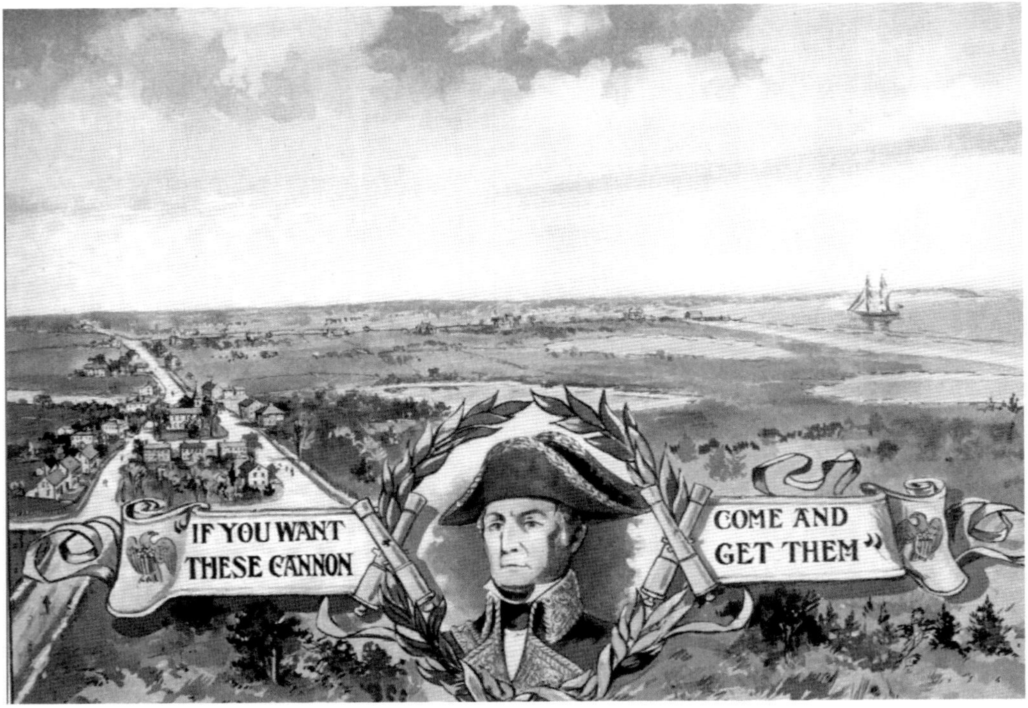

Weston Jenkins (1768–1834)
Weston Jenkins was a man to match his times. A fiery, redheaded warrior, he appeared in time to form the Falmouth Artillery Company in 1806 and protected the two brass cannons owned by the town. Falmouth never paid ransom to the British marauders in 1814 but once again took its stand. It was in January 1814 when the HMS *Nimrod* launched the cannonball attack on Falmouth that Jenkins spoke his legendary phrase: "If you want these cannon, come and take them but I'll give you what's in them first."

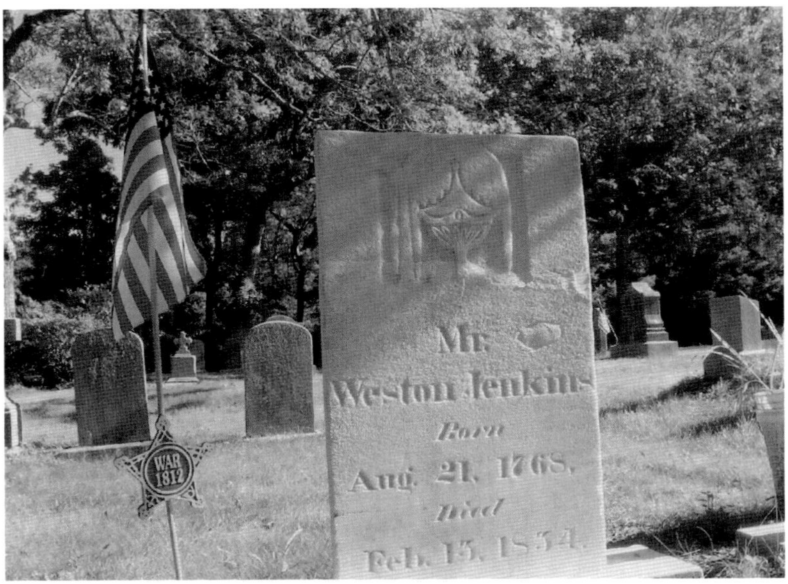

CHAPTER TWO

Dynasties and Family Histories

From the 14 families who settled on the shore of Fresh Pond in 1661 to the 2,071 voters registered in 1929.

—Theodate Geoffrey, *Suckanesset*

Individuals in this chapter came as families—generations that contributed to the character, businesses, and landmarks in Falmouth. There are three generations of Miskells, two different lines of Lawrences, and one line of Ellises with several generations named Nathan.

The dynasty of Elijah Swift and the Lawrence maritime line became linked in the economy of the town. A second Lawrence line of farmers and businessmen is noted. The lumber industry can be traced from B.B. King to the Miskell family. Several lines of town officials, such as those of the Hewin and Ellis families, are discussed.

The growing entrepreneurial and community service spirit of Falmouth is captured in these personalities from the whaling, lumber, agricultural, and construction trades. Commerce, dynasties, and family history are a part of the Falmouth tradition.

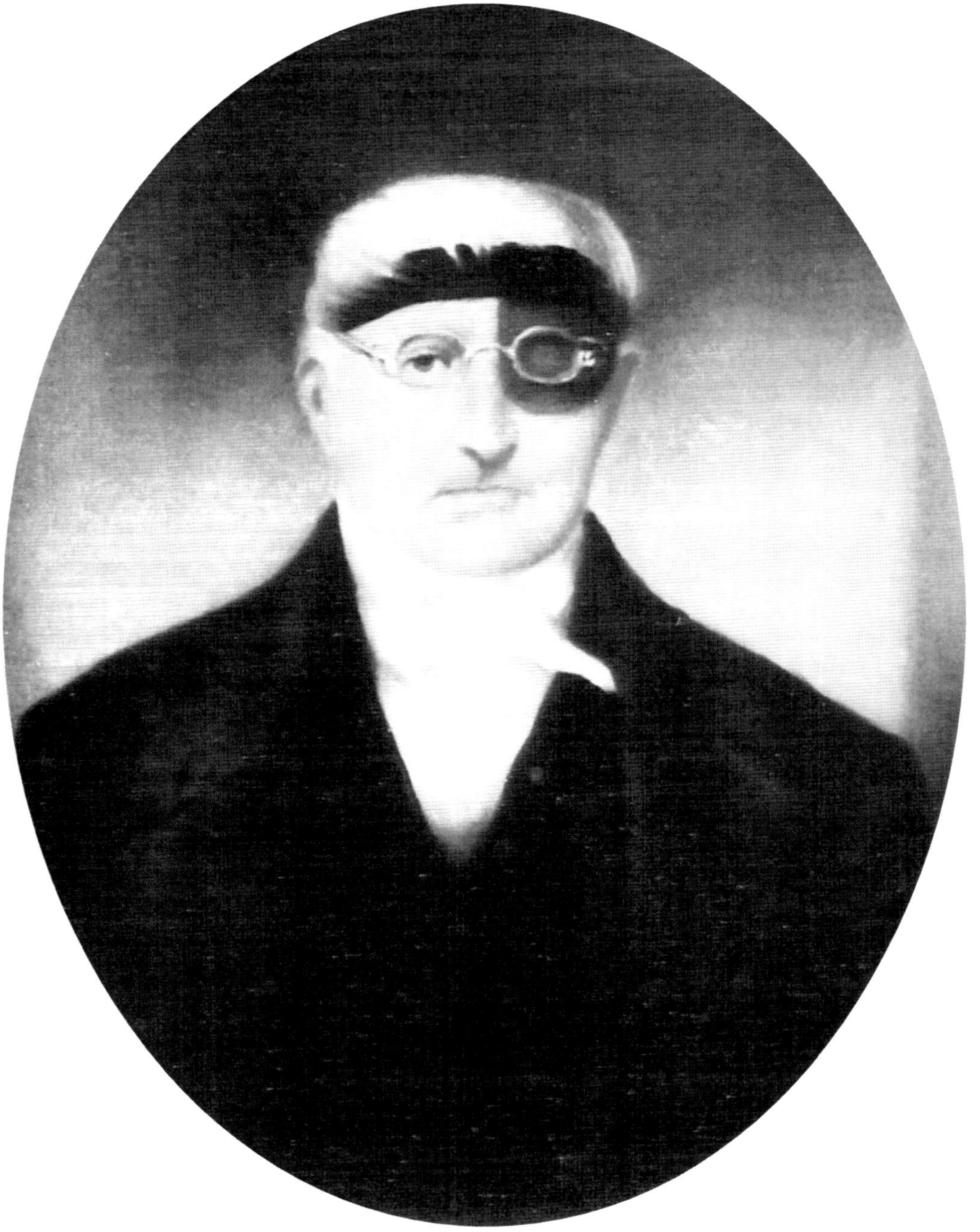

Elijah Swift (1774–1852)
Elijah Swift was born in East Falmouth and rose from a carpenter to become one of the wealthiest self-made businessmen in Falmouth. This fierce figure with an eye patch parlayed his background in carpentry to become a shipwright and together, with live oak lumber commerce, maintained controlling interest in at least eight whaling ships. He became the founder of the Falmouth National Bank. He dominated the commercial world of Falmouth in his time and left behind a Swift family maritime legacy.

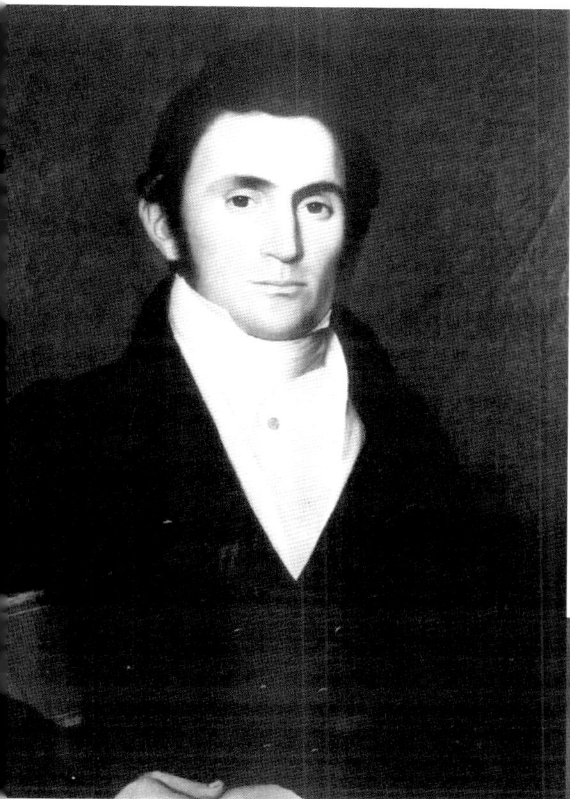

Oliver Cromwell Swift (1797–1874)
Oliver Cromwell Swift shared in his father's enterprises from a young age but in a more reserve, fastidious fashion. He controlled and outfitted the Swift ships and carried on the live oak trade in Carolina and Florida. It was under his watch, with the last voyage of the *Commodore Morris* in 1864, that it became clear that whaling was no longer a profitable enterprise. The Swift wealth became diversified in the lumber industry and briefly in a glass factory in Falmouth. He was president of the Falmouth National Bank, as was his father, and director of the Old Colony Line. The Swift fortune was left to the next generation, but the fierce drive of Elijah Swift was never again matched.

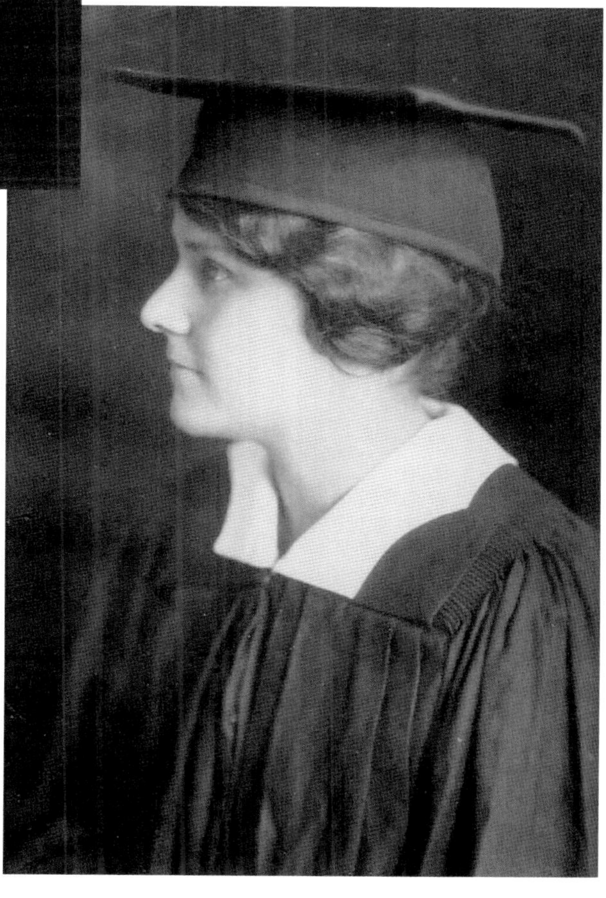

Elsy Swift Jessup (1905–2005)
Elsy Swift Jessup was a direct descendant of Elijah Swift, whaling entrepreneur, and Eugene E.C. Swift, Falmouth meat dealer and merchant entrepreneur. She proudly kept all her family's papers at her house at 98 Main Street. Her papers included accounts, Pew deeds, family portraits, wills, and property holdings from 1817 to 1907. A fire bucket marked "Elijah Swift 5" and a Civil War sword were included in her collections. Elsy graduated from Boston University in 1925, as pictured here. Her sense of history led her to leave all her accumulated papers to the Falmouth Historical Society upon her death in 2005.

Daniel Wheeler Swift (1840–1910) and Henry D. Swift (1833–1916)

The Swift brothers were birthright Quakers born in West Falmouth who earned their fortunes in Worcester, Massachusetts, with inventions including an envelope-making machine and an early clothes wringer. In 1863, Henry D. Swift became a conscientious objector to the Civil War and was saved from execution by pardon. Both brothers returned to their home in West Falmouth and are buried in the local Friends burial ground. This rare tintype image shows the brothers in their early manhood with sleeves rolled beginning their entrepreneurial ventures.

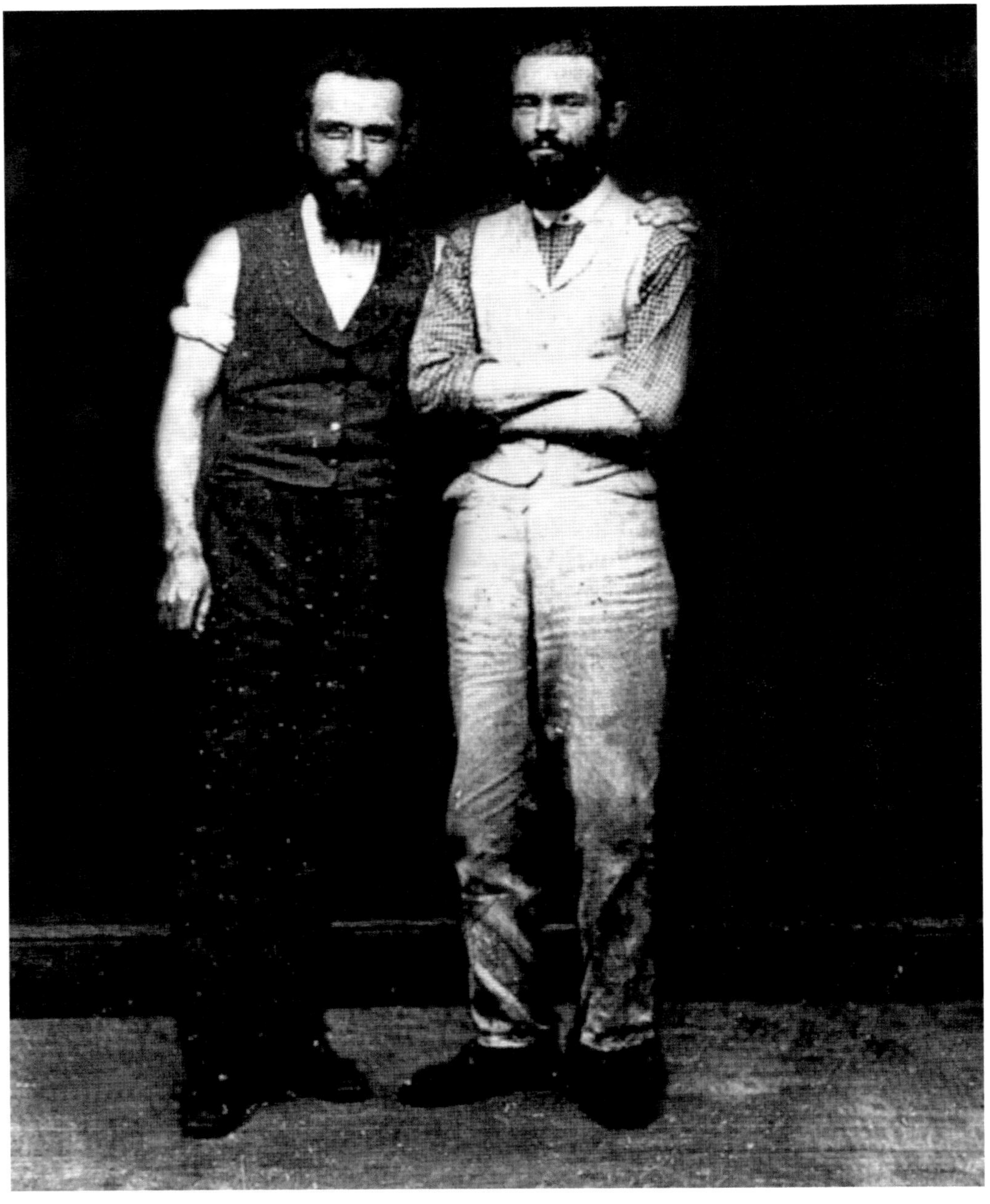

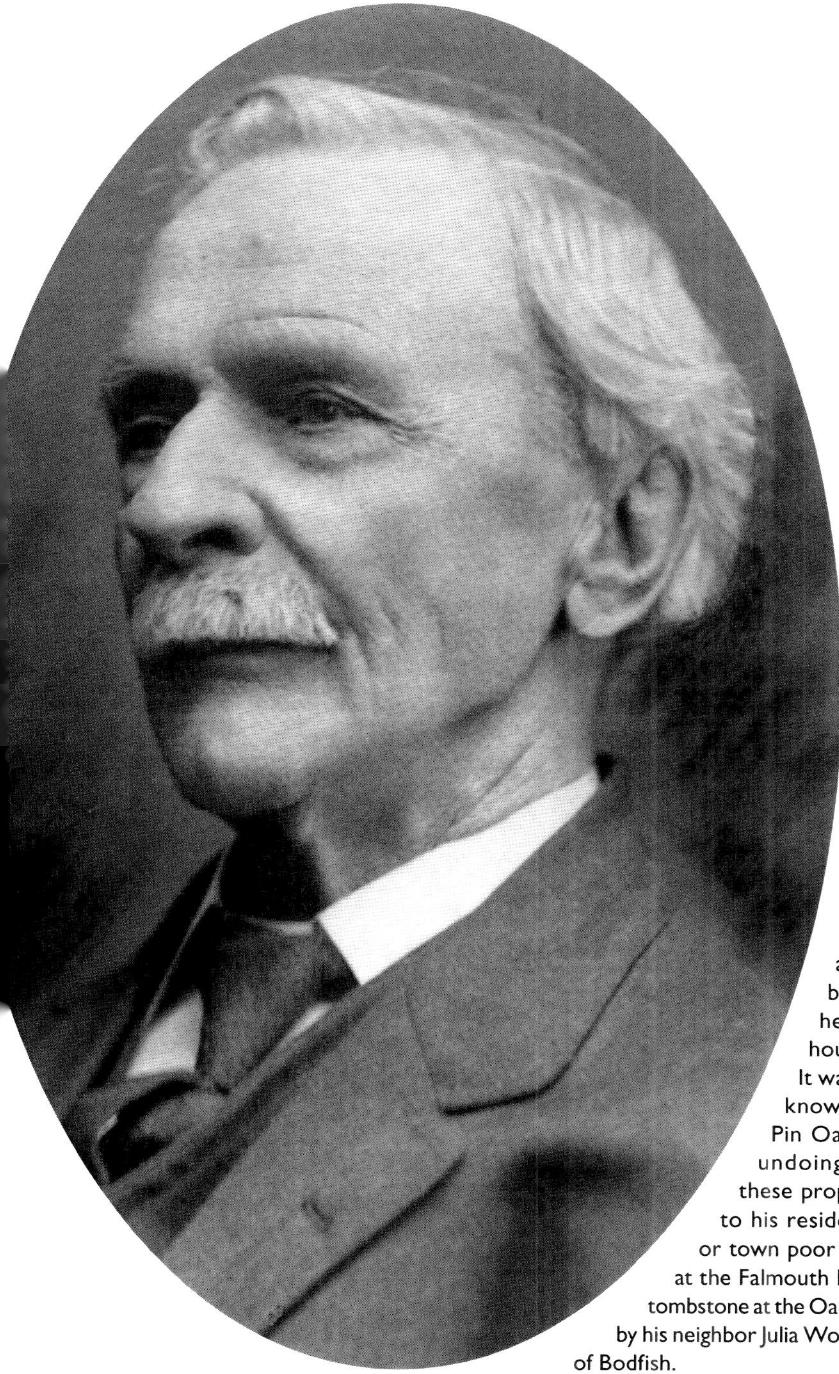

Robinson Crocker Bodfish (1818–1912) Robinson Crocker Bodfish's hard-luck story speaks to turn-of-the-century real estate woes. R.C. Bodfish was named for his ancestor Isaac Robinson and was one of the original members of the Falmouth Historical Society in 1900, acting as its first secretary. A bookkeeper by profession, he lived in the John Hatch house by the Village Green. It was his dream development known as Ocean Vista, along Pin Oak Way, that became his undoing. The foreclosure on these properties and his home led to his residence at the Alms House or town poor house. His writings, kept at the Falmouth Historical Society, and his tombstone at the Oak Grove Cemetery, paid for by his neighbor Julia Wood, are the only reminders of Bodfish.

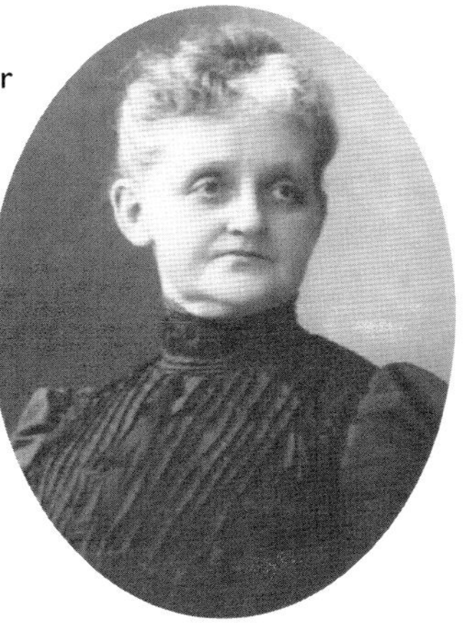

Julia Warren Wood (1849–1932)
Julia Wood died in the same room she was born, and the same newspaper that carried her obituary also discussed her will and her beautiful mansion on Palmer Avenue. Julia long wanted her house, which she inherited through her grandfather Capt. Warren Bourne and her mother, Sophia Swift, to be bequeathed to the Falmouth Historical Society. In a minor scandal of the time, due to the Depression and Julia's lengthy illness, a mortgage existed on her home. A campaign to pay her mortgage was successful under society president Arthur M. Morse, and the lovely yellow Federal icon, complete with a widow's walk, became part of the Falmouth Historical Society.

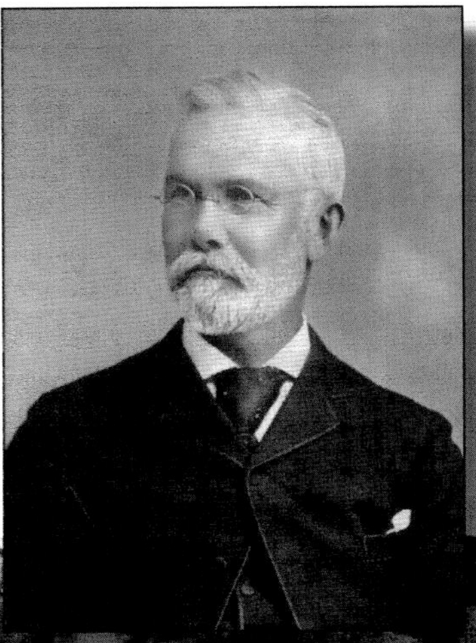

James B. Wood (1838–1900)
James Wood is a little-known naval hero of the Civil War. He enlisted as master of the steamer *Maratanza*. He was engaged in blockade services during the Civil War and assisted in the capture of the Confederate steamer *Tenser* off North Carolina in 1864. He participated in the capture of Fort Fisher, Fort Anderson, Fort Strong, and the city of Wilmington in 1865. He was married to Julia W. Swift in 1873. Although living next door to the Congregational church, both James and his wife were faithful members of St. Barnabas Church. They are buried side by side with their infant son Clifton at Oak Grove Cemetery.

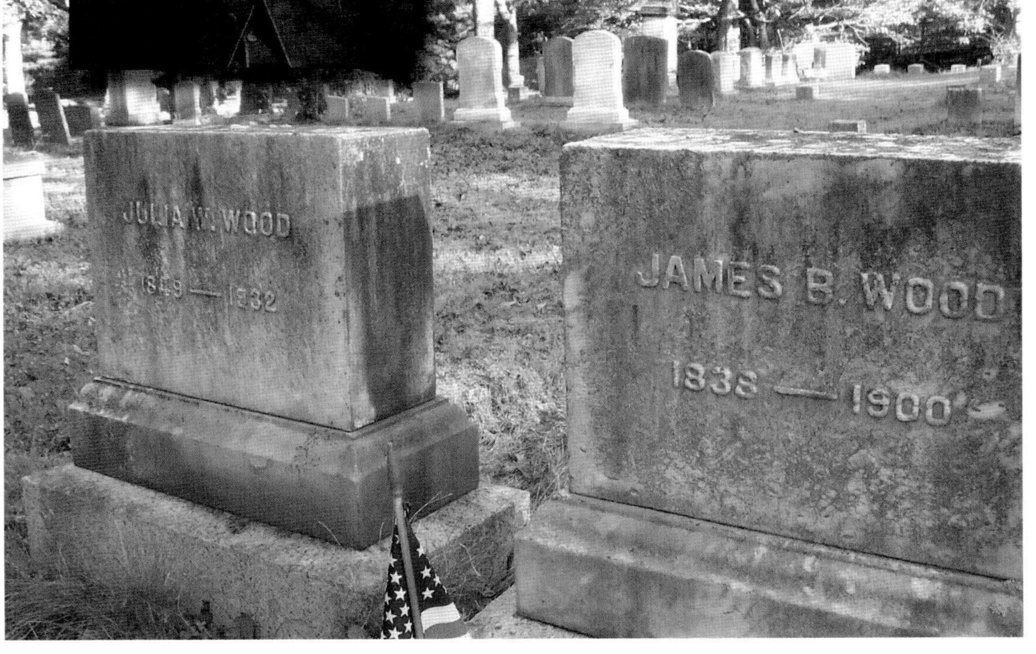

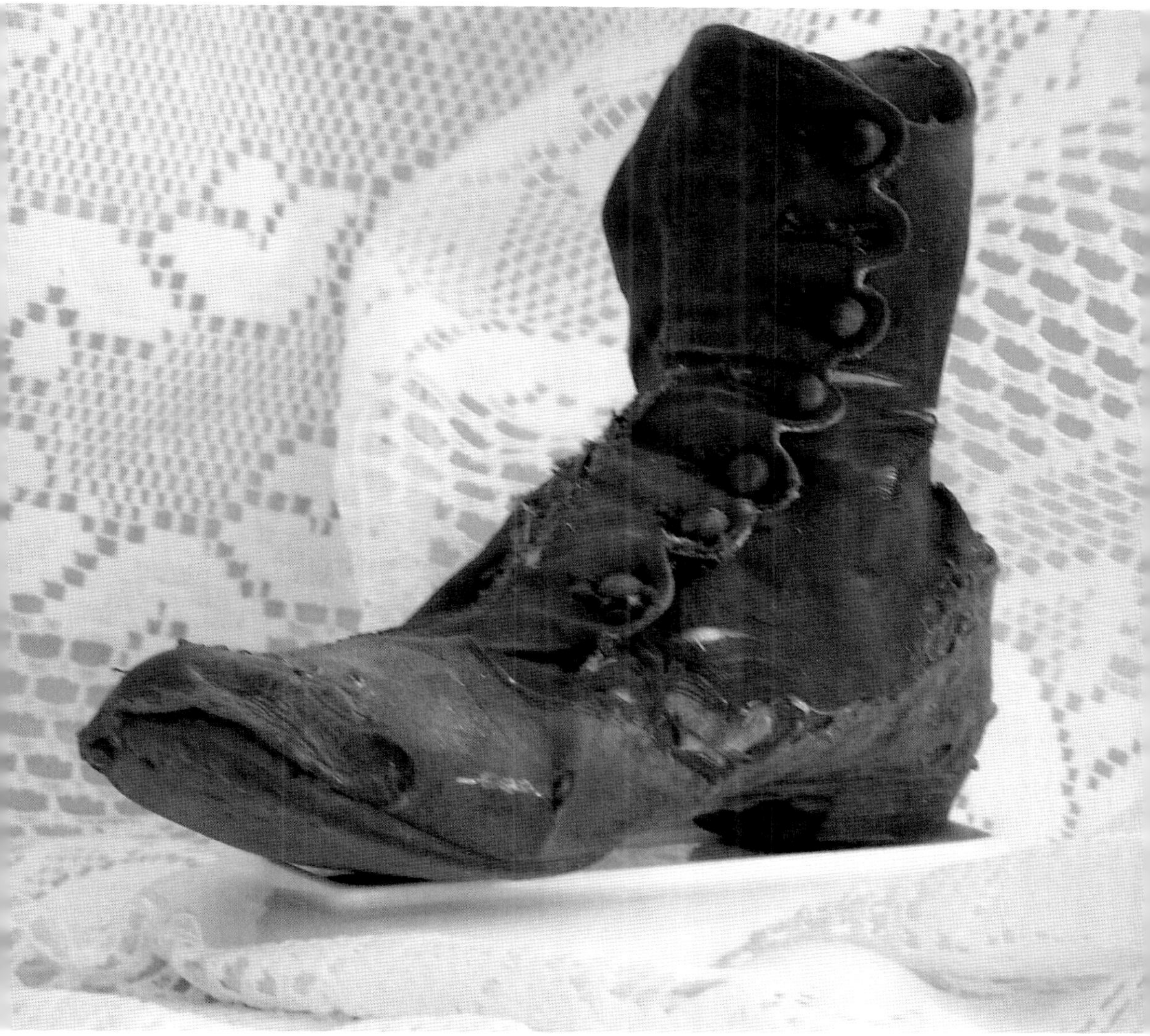

Annette "Nettie" Gifford (1872–1921)
Annette Gifford grew up in West Falmouth in the house built by her father, James Gifford, in 1863 with her mother, Charlotte Lumbert Gifford. Annette later married William W. Cooke, a chiropodist or early foot doctor, in 1898. It is ironic that in 2006, while renovated the old Gifford House (now known as the Beach Rose Inn), Nettie's childhood high-button shoe was found. Her concealment shoe was placed in the walls to ward off evil spirits. It is now displayed at the local bed and breakfast and reminds the people of Falmouth of spirits past. (Courtesy Beach Rose Inn.)

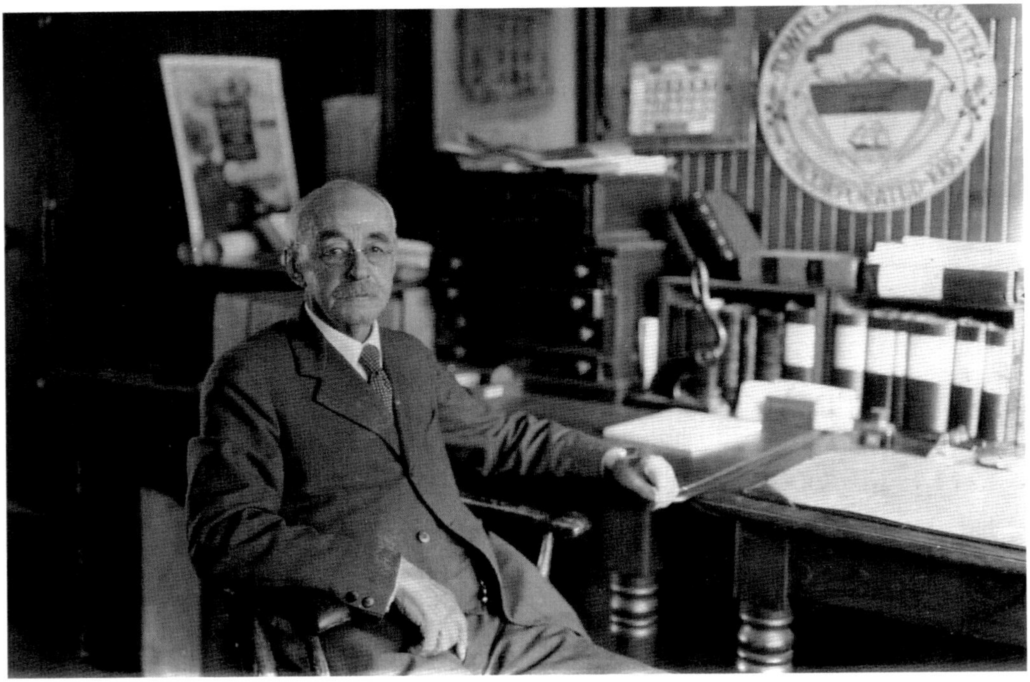

William Harrison Hewins (1840–1936)
William H. Hewins was the town clerk for Falmouth from 1884 to 1934, walking from his home on Hewins Street to nearby town hall every day. He was the second vice president of the Falmouth Historical Society and served as historian of the Masonic Order Marine Lodge. His varied business careers included manager of a dry goods business, agent of the Hartford Fire Insurance Co., and president of the Falmouth National Bank from 1918 to 1934.

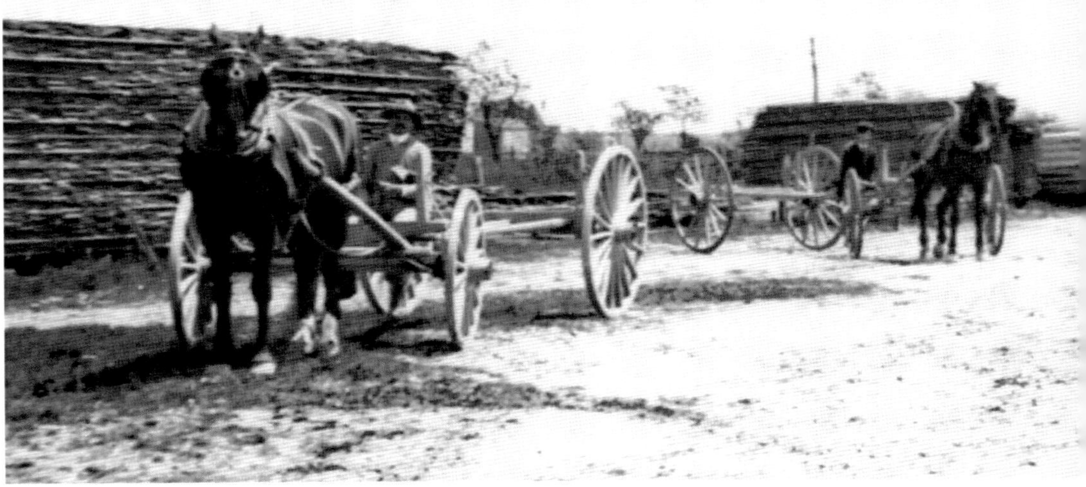

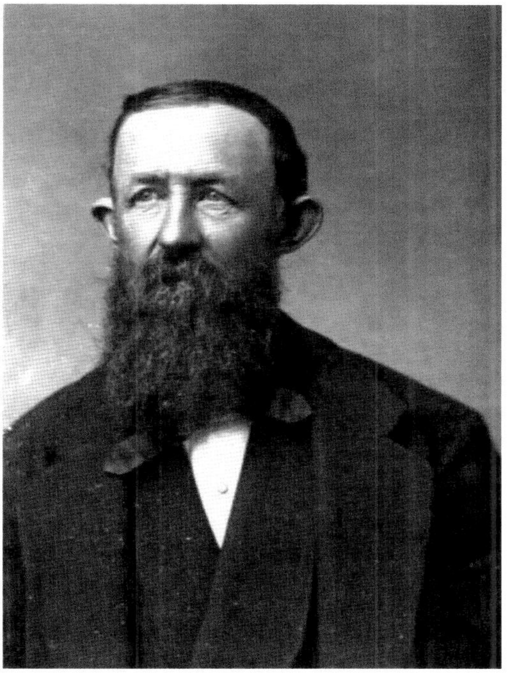

Benjamin Baylies King (1825–?)
B.B. King is pictured as the rugged individual who ran a lumberyard located off King Street. He lived there with his wife, Sarah, and children. He sold his business to James Cameron by 1890. B.B. King account books, marked with his hurried script, are kept by the Falmouth Historical Society. Cameron is shown posing in front of his lumberyard between Shore and King Streets. The lumberyard became an important business to the growing population of Falmouth.

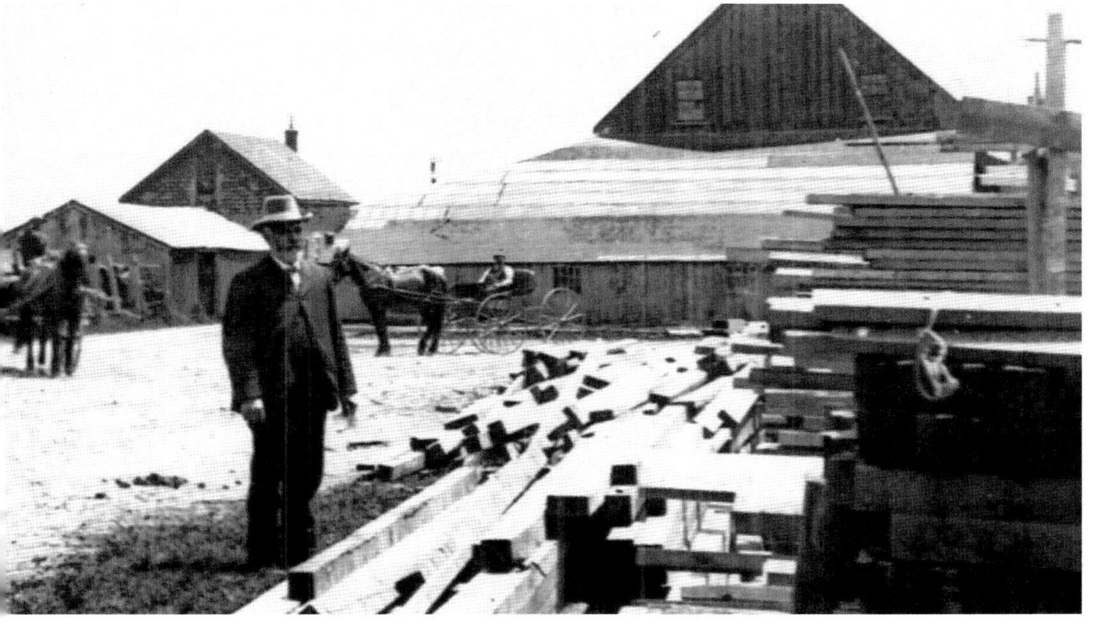

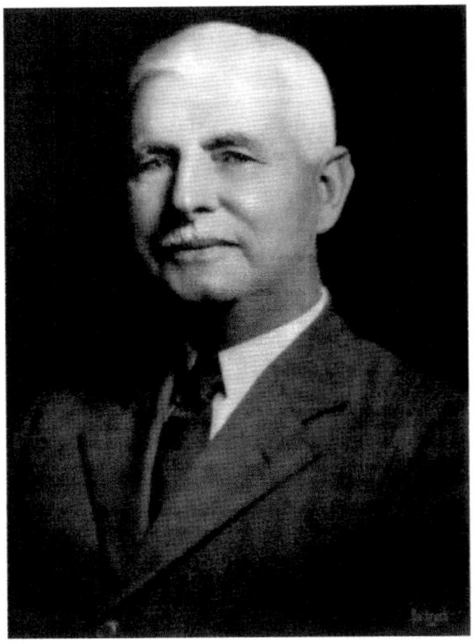

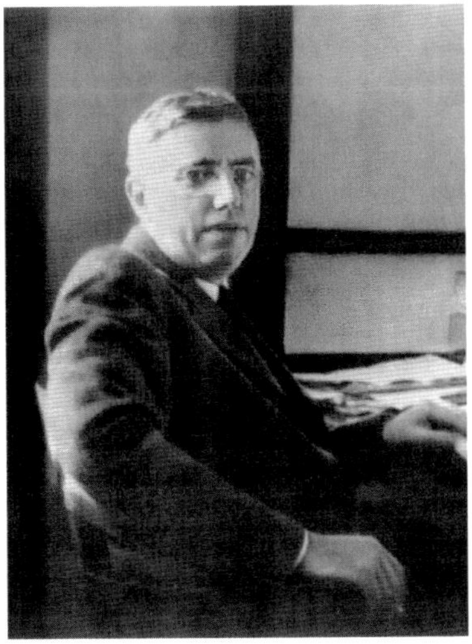

Miskell Family and the Wood Lumber Company (1912–)
Wood Lumber Company is a century-old, single-family business marking three generations and the passage of time in Falmouth. In 1912, James H. Miskell and Edmund Wood purchased the Wood Lumber Co. on Locust Street. Joseph B. Miskell (1890–1959) was sent from New Bedford to become manager of Wood Lumber Co. (1912–1957). In 1946, Joseph B. "Bud" Miskell Jr. (1921–2009) began his long command at the helm. The company survived the Great Depression, the New England Hurricane of 1938, the 1940s Camp Edwards build up, and a fire in 1968. From 1986 to the present, Dana and Eileen Miskell have managed Wood Lumber, leading the company through growth and new challenges, including a major expansion and redesign of the company's buildings. Shown here are James H. Miskell (left), Joseph B. Miskell (right), and the Wood Lumber Company in 1934. (All, courtesy Miskell family.)

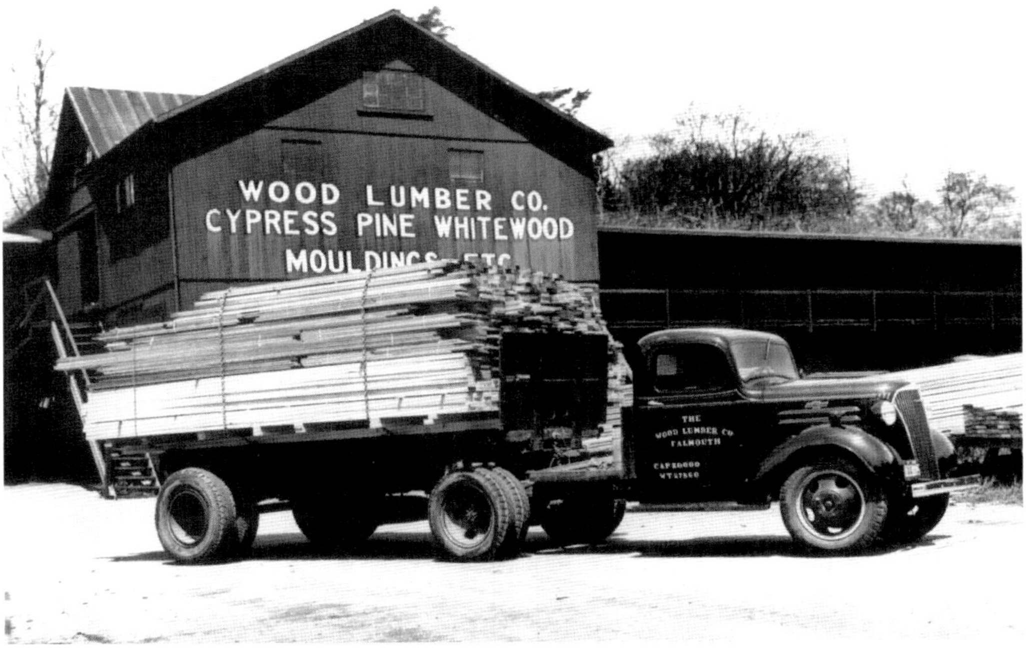

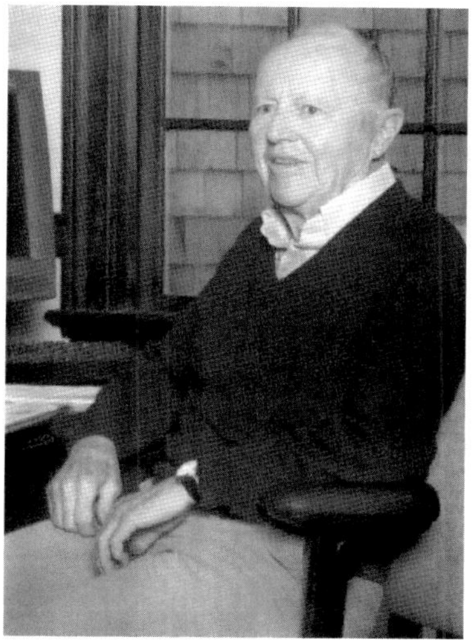

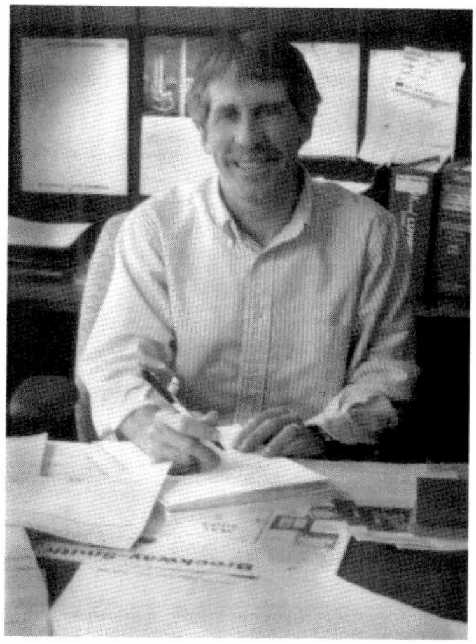

Miskell Family and the Wood Lumber Company (1912–)
On the 50th anniversary of the Wood Lumber Company in 1965, the company adopted the Cape Cod Chamber of Commerce slogan: "Cape Cod: A Wonderful Way of Life." Wood Lumber and the Miskell family became part of the building boom of retirement, summer, and year-round housing. Pictured here are Bud Miskell (left), his son Dana Miskell (right), and the new store.

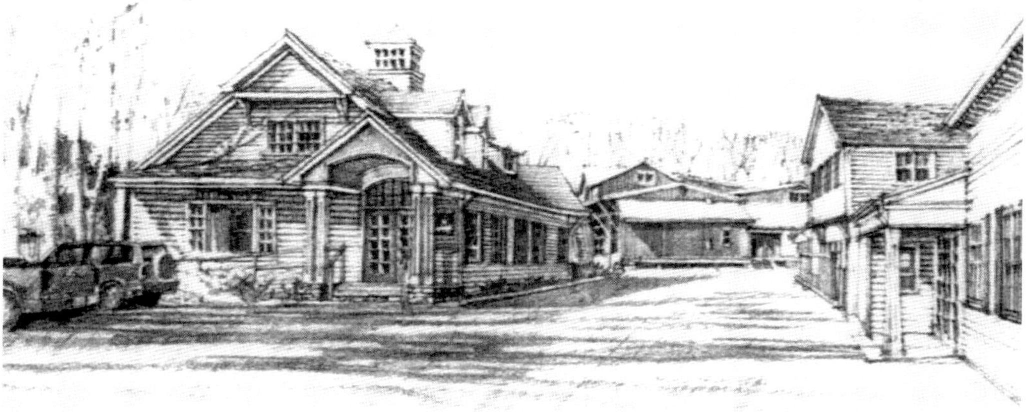

The Wood Lumber Company

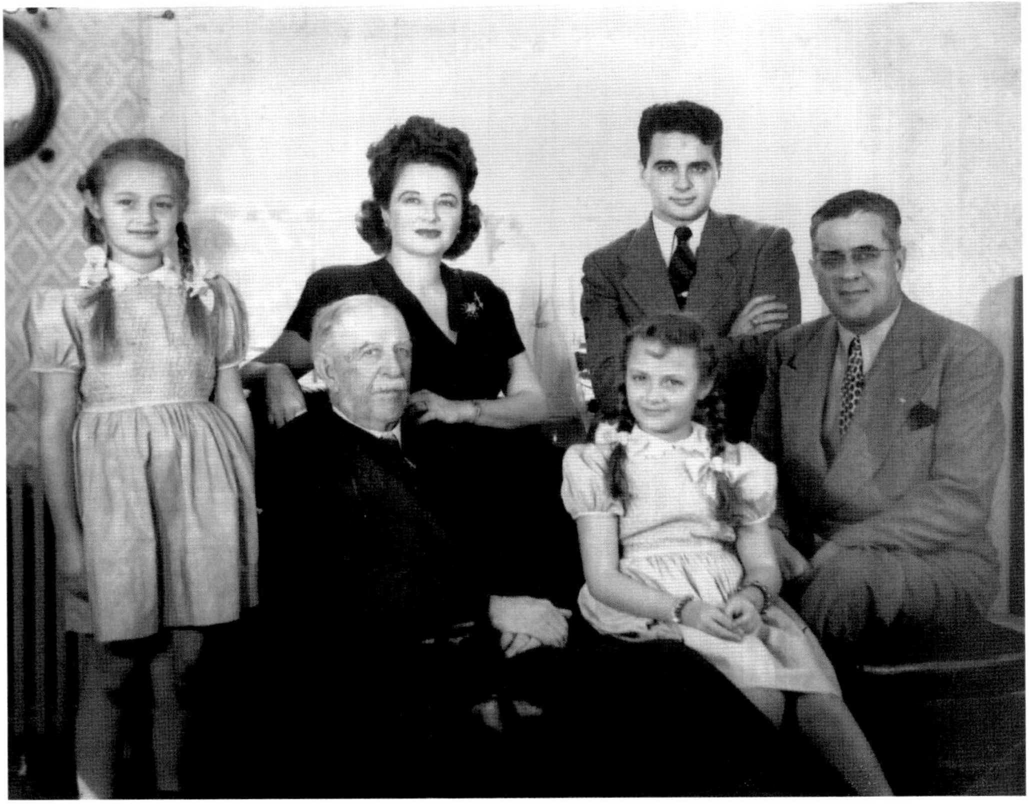

Nate Ellis and Family

Nathan Snow Ellis (1863–1947) was elected highway supervisor in 1902, serving at various times in that position until 1931. The planning board of Falmouth named Route 151, from Route 28 to Mashpee, in honor of Nathan S. Ellis after his death in 1948. Nathan Ellis Jr. (1890–1957) continued in his father's position for 30 years. Nathan Ellis III (1926–) also served as highway supervisor and is currently on the board of the Oak Grove Cemetery. Pictured here, from left to right, are Myra, Nathan Snow Ellis, Rebecca, Rubretta (seated), Nathan S. Ellis III, and Nathan S. Ellis, Jr. (Courtesy Nate Ellis.)

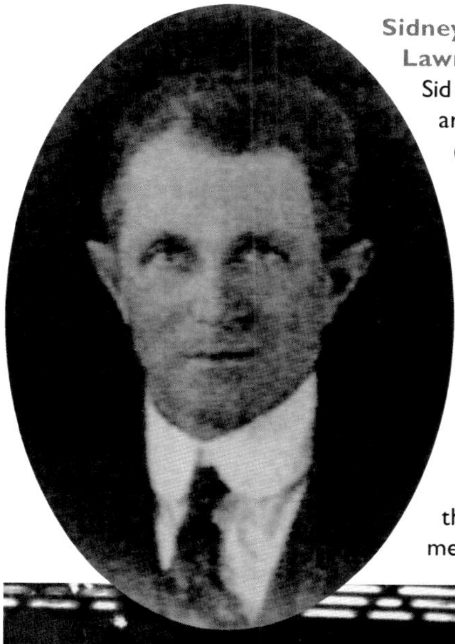

Sidney Warren Lawrence (1879–1965) and son Frederick V. Lawrence (1903–1991)

Sid Lawrence and family pose in the 1930 photograph below. Pictured are, from left to right, Fred V. Lawrence and Sidney Lawrence (standing), daughter Margaret, daughter Virginia, and Josephine, wife of Sidney. When Sidney died, a local editorial mourned: "Men like him don't come along anymore because the land that produced them has disappeared." But they were wrong, and the Lawrence dynasty has continued. Sidney worked for 40 years at his Woods Hole Ice Co. and later sold produce from his Harbor Hill Farm. He was elected as town highway surveyor and ran for public works commissioner at the age of 82. He also served 18 years on the town planning board. Frederick V. Lawrence Sr. owned a large civil engineering construction company on Gifford Street, Lawrence Lynch Inc. Fred Lawrence was involved with the chamber of commerce, the county commission, the Rotary Club, and served as a town meeting representative. (Courtesy Fred Lawrence Jr.)

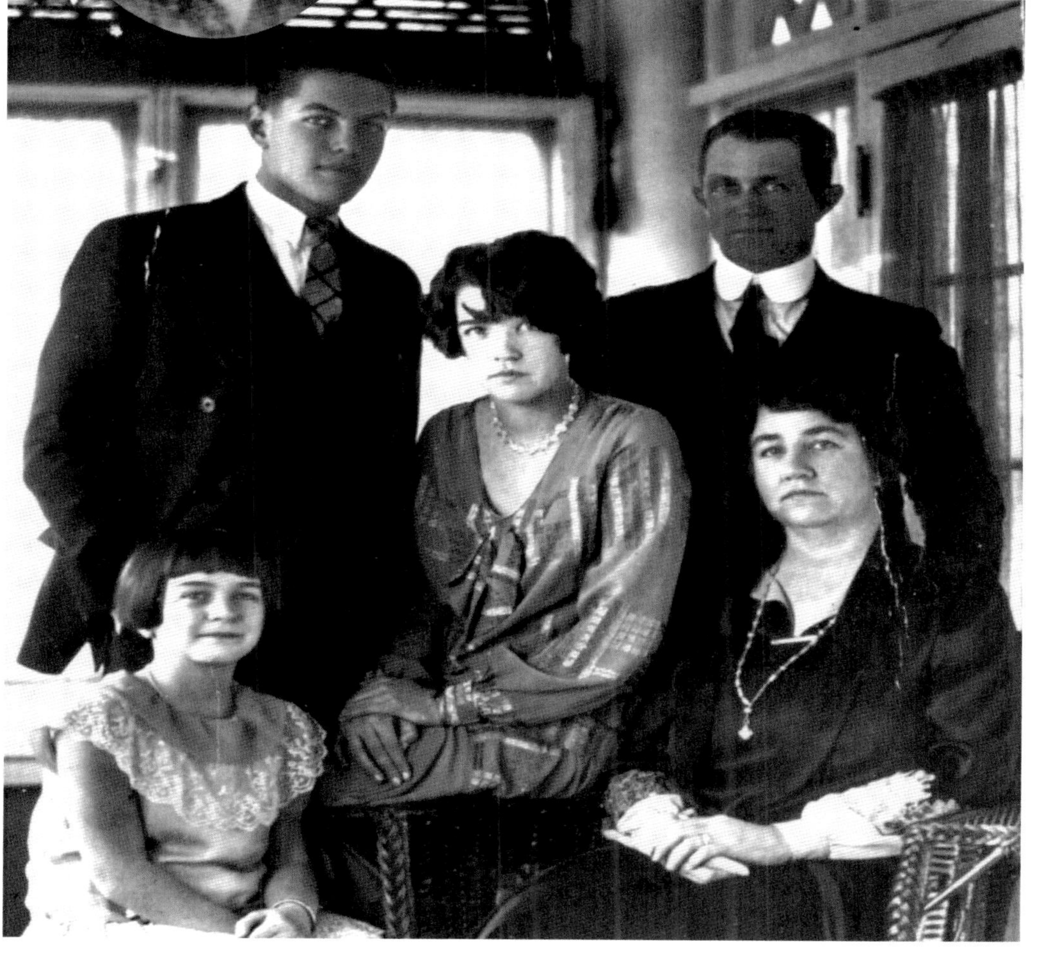

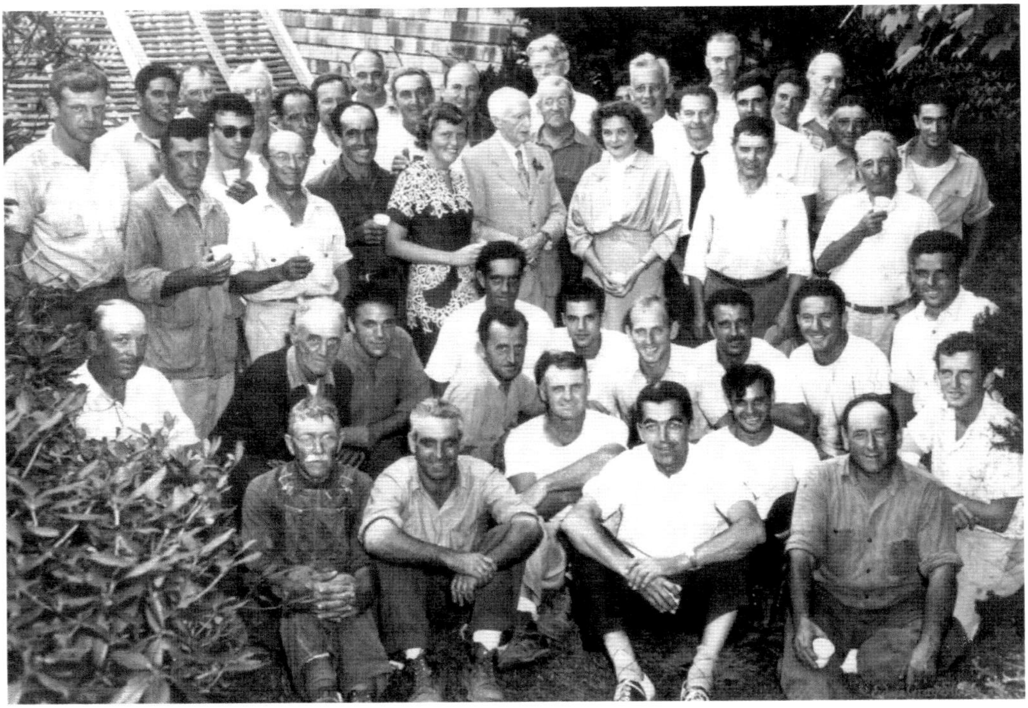

Henry Vincent Lawrence (1861–1953)
H.V. Lawrence will always be known for his greenhouses on Depot Avenue. As a nurseryman and florist, he designed some of the most important gardens on Cape Cod. His specialty was gardening by the sea, turning kettle holes into sunken gardens. He served on the first planning board of Falmouth and expressed his vision of Falmouth. He also was active in the chamber of commerce devising new ways to attract visitors. He was known for his intelligence and community spirit. Above, he is shown standing in the center of a gathering for his 90th birthday. Below is the H.V. Lawrence nursery that once stood on Depot Road.

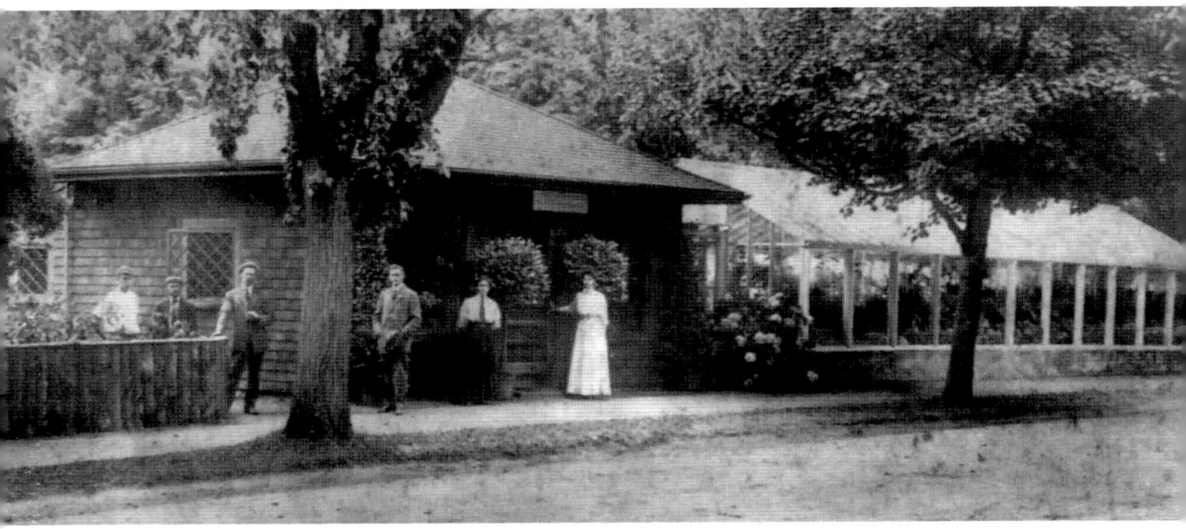

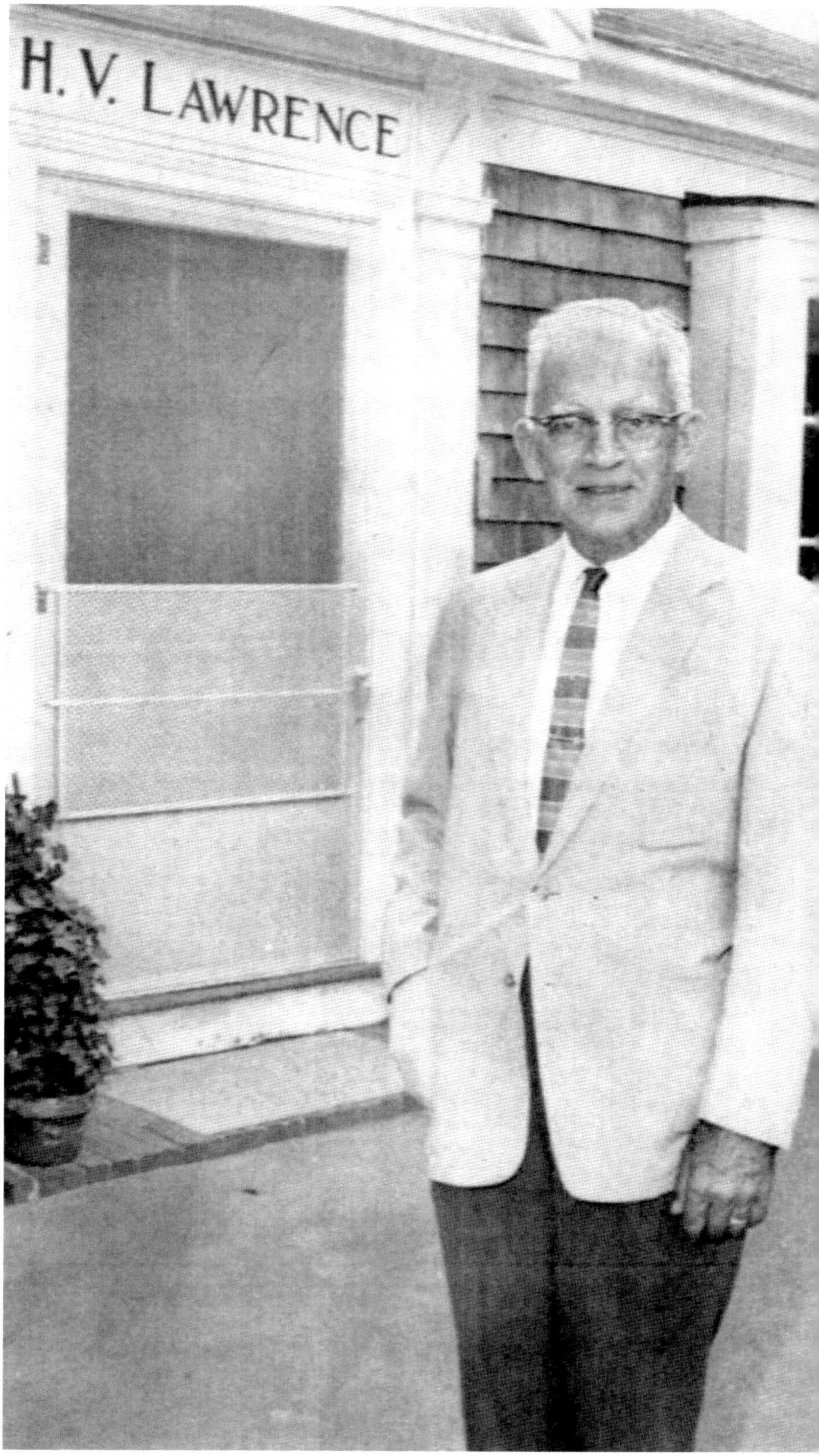

Milford R. Lawrence (1896–1971)
Milford Lawrence was honored as "a distinguished son of Falmouth" as he steppec down from 27 years as town moderator. His lineage was most impressive: he was the son of H.V. Lawrence, grandson of Capt. John Robinson Lawrence, and great-grandson of Solomon Lawrence, the whaling shipwright. He carried on his father's business, H.V. Lawrence Inc., with leadership roles in the Massachusetts Horticultural Society. He always maintained a lifelong interest in the civic affairs of Falmouth.

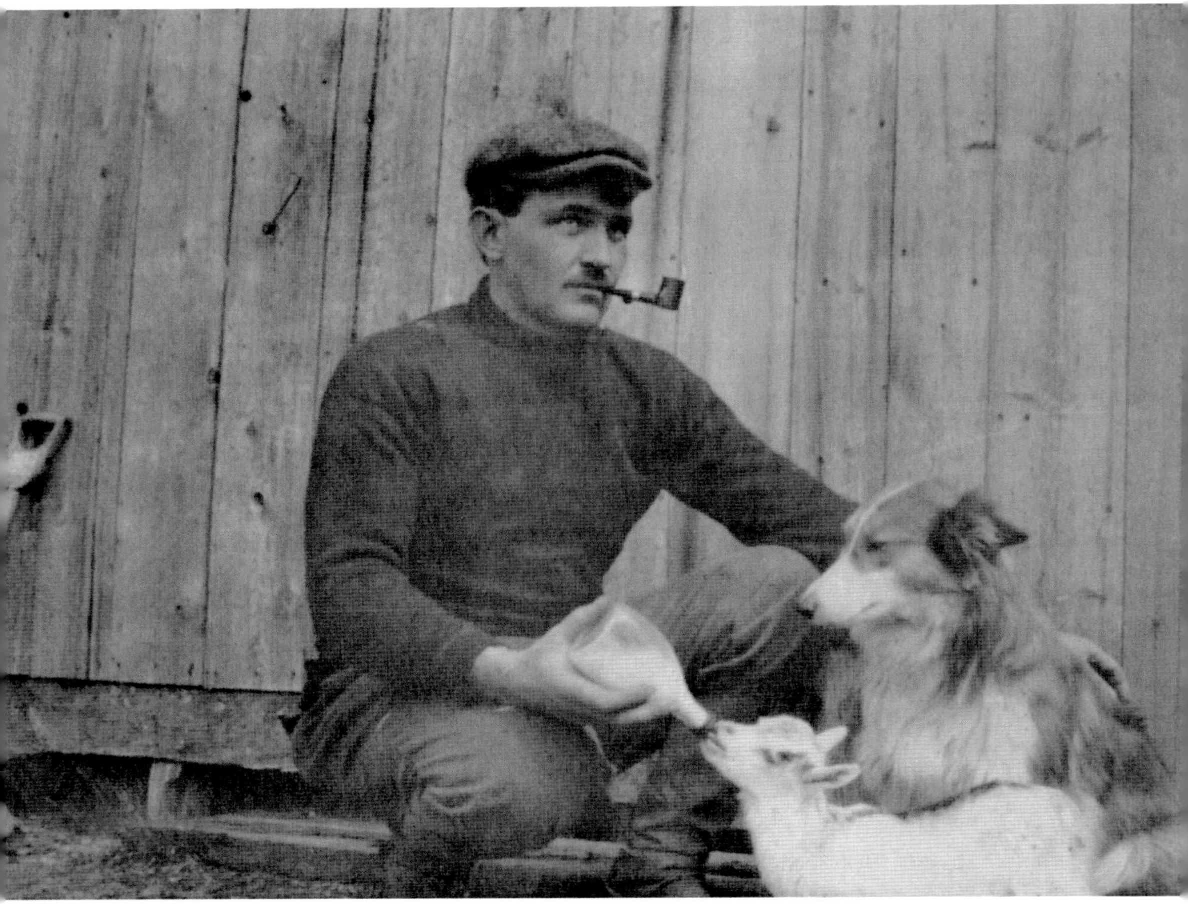

Allen Hatch (1886–1968)
Allen Hatch was one of the last Hatches to live in Hatchville. He was a farmer, carpenter, and handyman who remained close to the earth all of his life. He contributed recollections of his rural village to the *Book of Falmouth* and described his simple life in his ivy-covered cottage on Deep Pond. He was a direct descendant of Jonathan Hatch and benefited from the third purchase of the early proprietors that added the lovely village of Hatchville.

CHAPTER THREE

Mariners and Falmouth's Life by the Sea

Where gray captains, bronzed of neck / with a memory of the deck.

—Katharine Lee Bates, "The Falmouth Bell"

Science is really the practice of focused curiosity.

—Charles D. Hollister, *Book of Falmouth*

Falmouth has a mother lode of mariners, oceanographers, and persons who looked to the sea for their livelihoods and inspiration. This chapter includes just a few of this illustrious group. Sea captains, whaling wives, and oceanographers all breathed the same salt air and were fellow seekers of the sea.

It is not a stretch to compare these scientists to early mariners. Mary Sears and Cornelia Clapp were as daring and adventurous as Mary Chipman Lawrence and Bertha Boyce. It could be said that Arthur Redfield was as original as Capt. Silas Jones. The maritime trade produced outrageous tales and equally outrageous men and women. Capt. Nehemiah Baker and Capt. Edward B. Phinney showed the brutality of the ship trade. Perhaps with the exception of James Fisher, all exhibited extraordinary mariner skills and, above all, a sure instinct for survival.

Falmouth's people of the sea are the keystone to the nature of those drawn to live on coastal Cape Cod.

Silas Jones (1814–1898)

Silas Jones had a confident, commanding presence, fitting a man who had secured his reputation on the "bloody and harrowing" voyage of the *Awashonks* in 1835. He sailed as the third mate on this Falmouth-built ship, survived an attack by native aborigines off the Solomon Islands, secured the ship, and returned as de facto commanding officer as well as first-class hero. Proceeds from a sale of a native club that Silas Jones secured (perhaps from this voyage) went to build a new education center for the Falmouth Historical Society in 2012. It was a classic case of turning weapons into peaceful, educational uses.

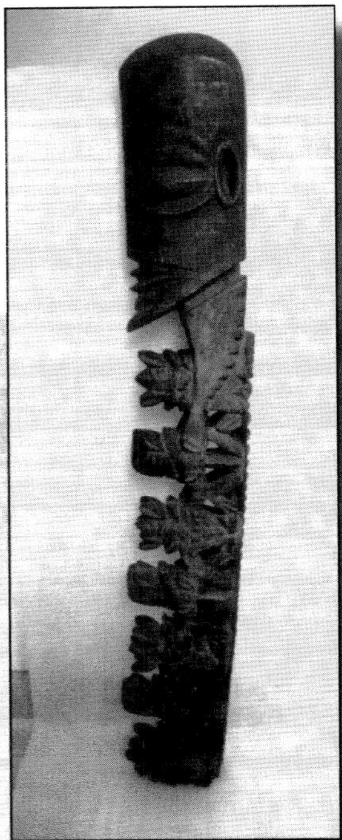

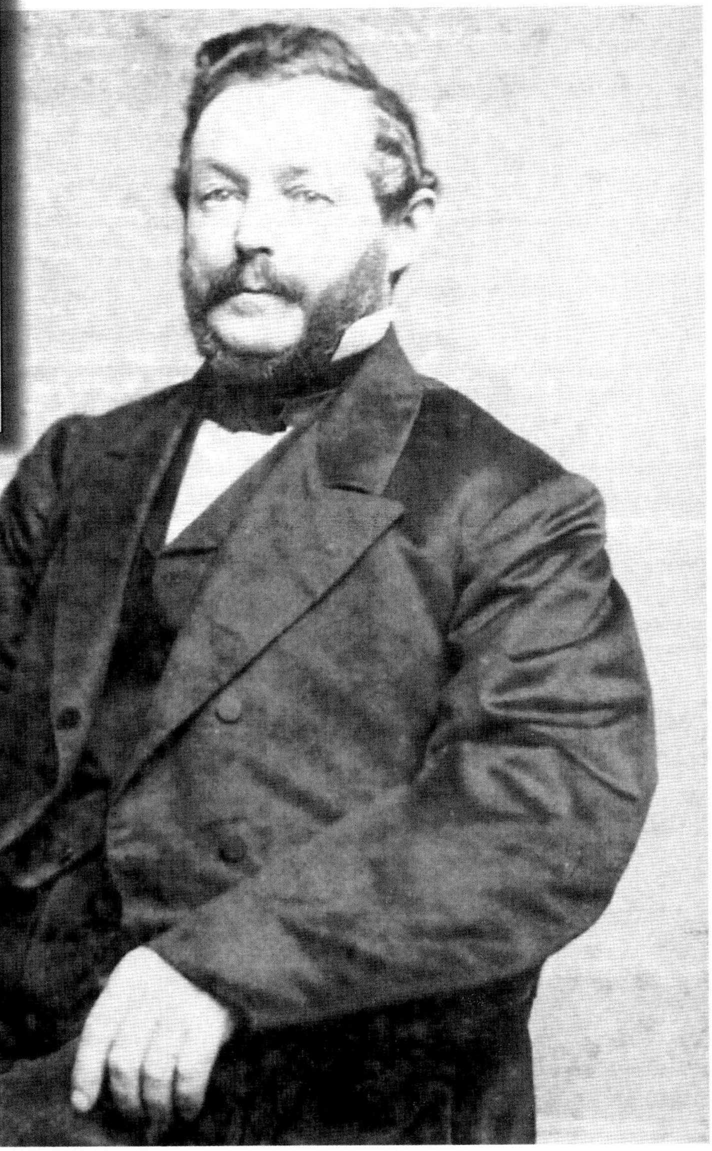

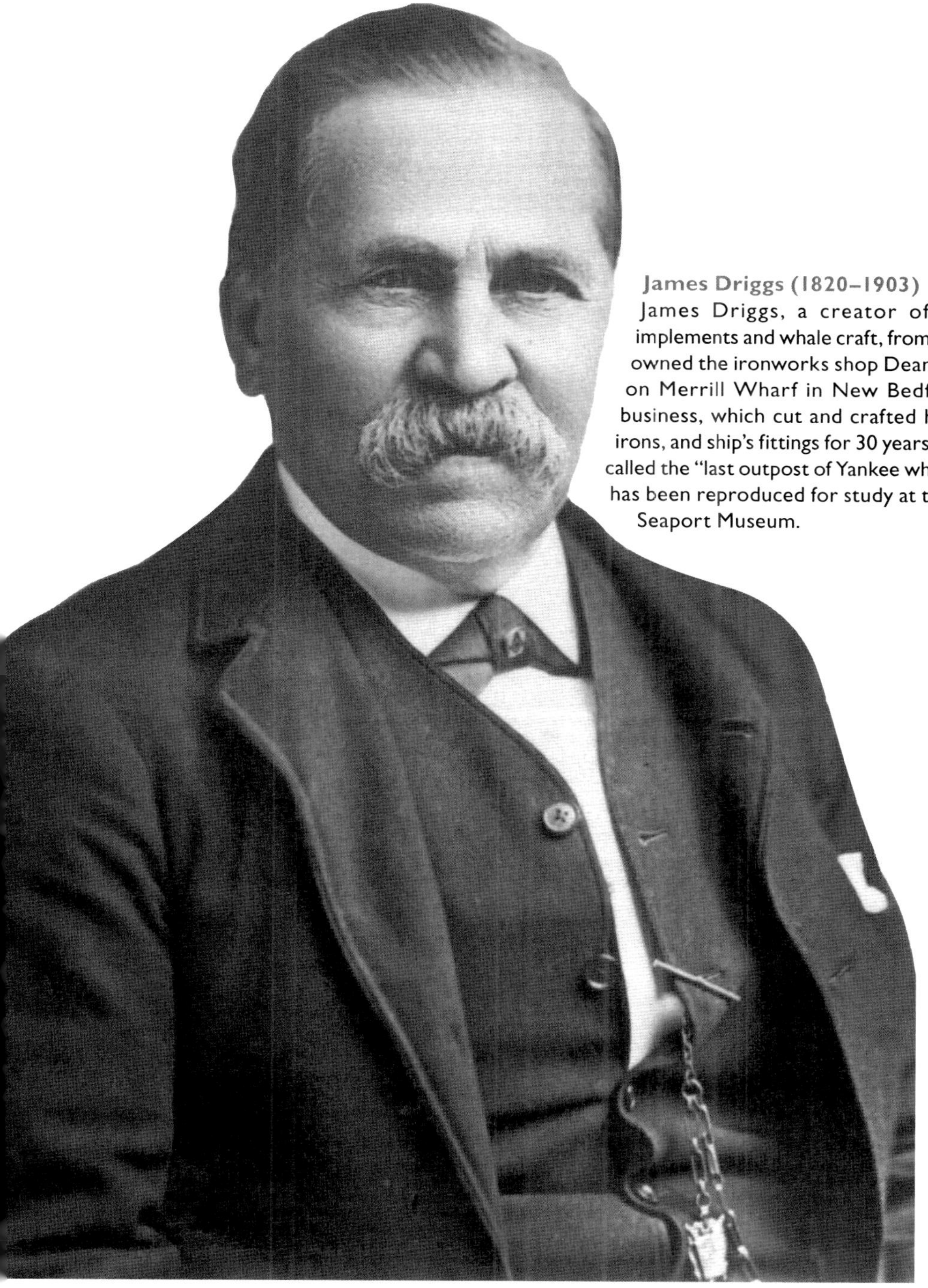

James Driggs (1820–1903)
James Driggs, a creator of whaling implements and whale craft, from Quissett, owned the ironworks shop Dean & Driggs on Merrill Wharf in New Bedford. The business, which cut and crafted harpoons, irons, and ship's fittings for 30 years, has been called the "last outpost of Yankee whaling" and has been reproduced for study at the Mystic Seaport Museum.

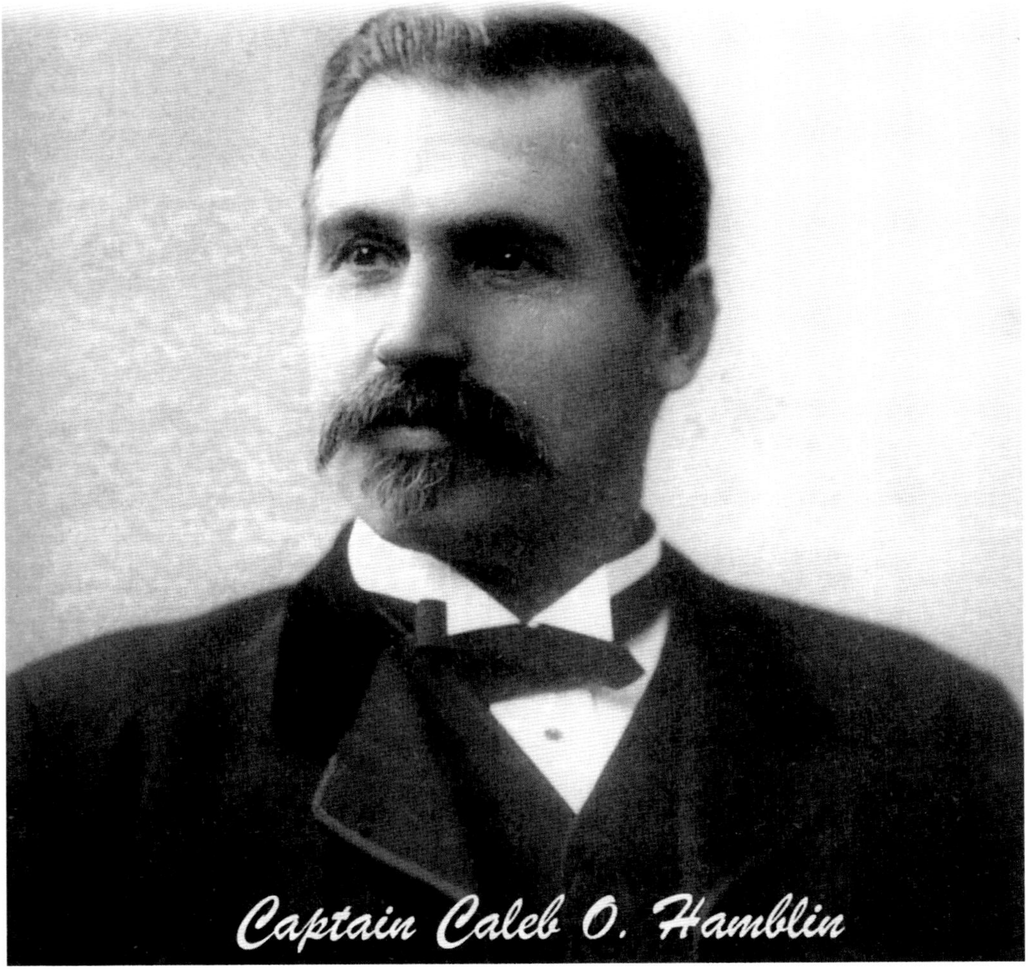

Capt. Caleb O. Hamblin (1835–1907)
Caleb Hamblin was a West Falmouth resident who had completed successful runs as commander of the whalers *Eliza Adams*, *Robert Edwards*, and *Henry Trowbridge*. This handsome, prosperous sea captain is noted for an incident that took place early on in his career when he was second mate on the *Congress*. Off the coast of Australia, Hamblin was poised with lance in hand when a whale struck the boat and sent him partially into its jaws. He was carried downward some 50 feet before the ship's line jerked him back on board the ship. This survivor's proud tale is often noted in Cape Cod and maritime histories.

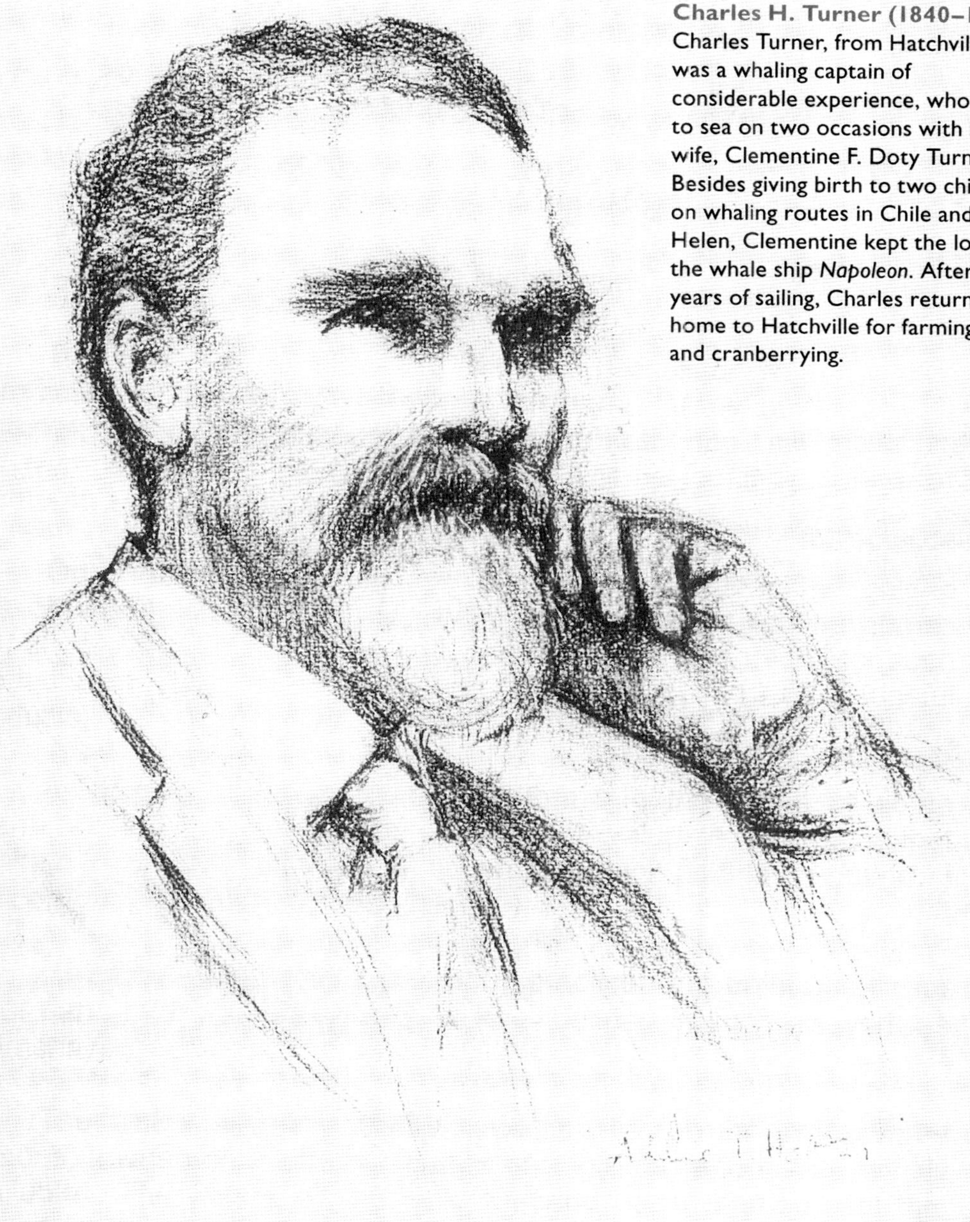

Charles H. Turner (1840–1914)
Charles Turner, from Hatchville, was a whaling captain of considerable experience, who went to sea on two occasions with his wife, Clementine F. Doty Turner. Besides giving birth to two children on whaling routes in Chile and St. Helen, Clementine kept the log for the whale ship *Napoleon*. After 28 years of sailing, Charles returned home to Hatchville for farming and cranberrying.

Captain Charles Henry Turner
by Adeline T. Holton

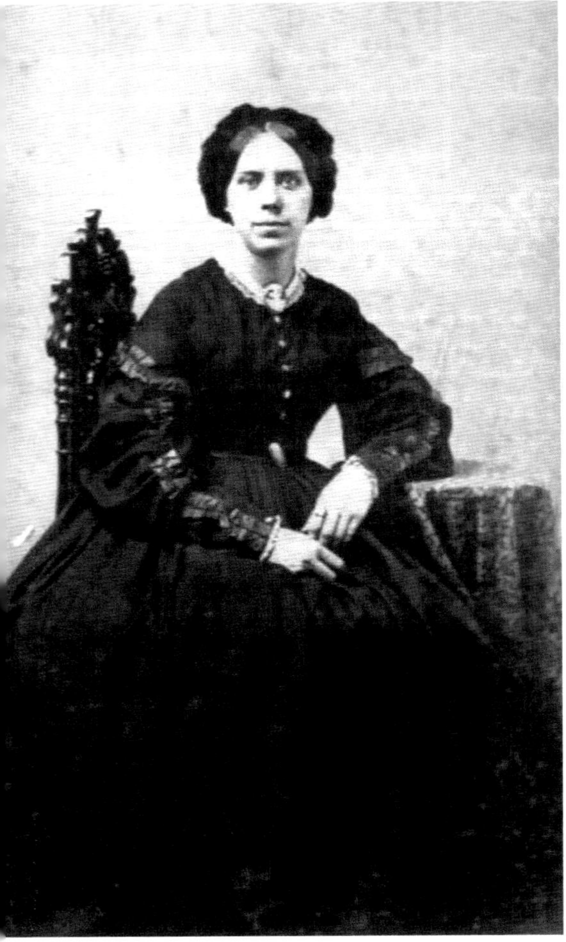

Mary Chipman Lawrence (1829–1906) and Capt. Samuel Lawrence (1854–1882)

Mary Chipman Lawrence was born in Sandwich, Massachusetts. She had the fortune to marry into an extraordinary mariner family when she married Capt. Samuel Lawrence. Her plain Yankee practicality and Calvinism are preserved in her journal, kept onboard the ship *Addison* (1856–1860), a whaling voyage on which she accompanied her husband, along with their six-year-old daughter, Minnie. She describes not only her separate kingdom aboard ship washing, sewing, and playing with Minnie but also the adventure and terror of the business of whaling. Mary represents perhaps the best of the class of individuals known as whaling wives. Capt. Samuel Lawrence was the undisputed master aboard the ship *Addison*.

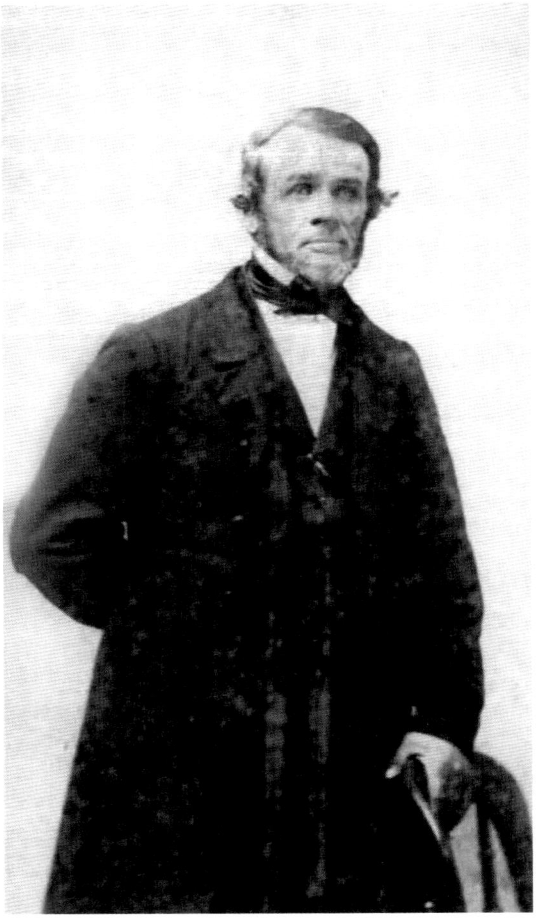

James H. Fisher (1838–1914)

James H. Fisher has been called the "unluckiest whaler." During his 11 recorded whaling voyages, he was captured by the Confederate cruiser *Alabama*, captured by the cruiser *Shenandoah*, and dismasted by gale winds while serving on another ship. As shipmaster of the bark *Oliver Crocker*, he abandoned ship with 31 others who were caught in the ice in the Arctic Ocean. On his final voyage as the captain of the ship *Lancer*, he left his post due to illness. He was a man of many hardships who suffered much for maritime glory. His family's dairy farm in Hatchville had a brief but more fortunate run.

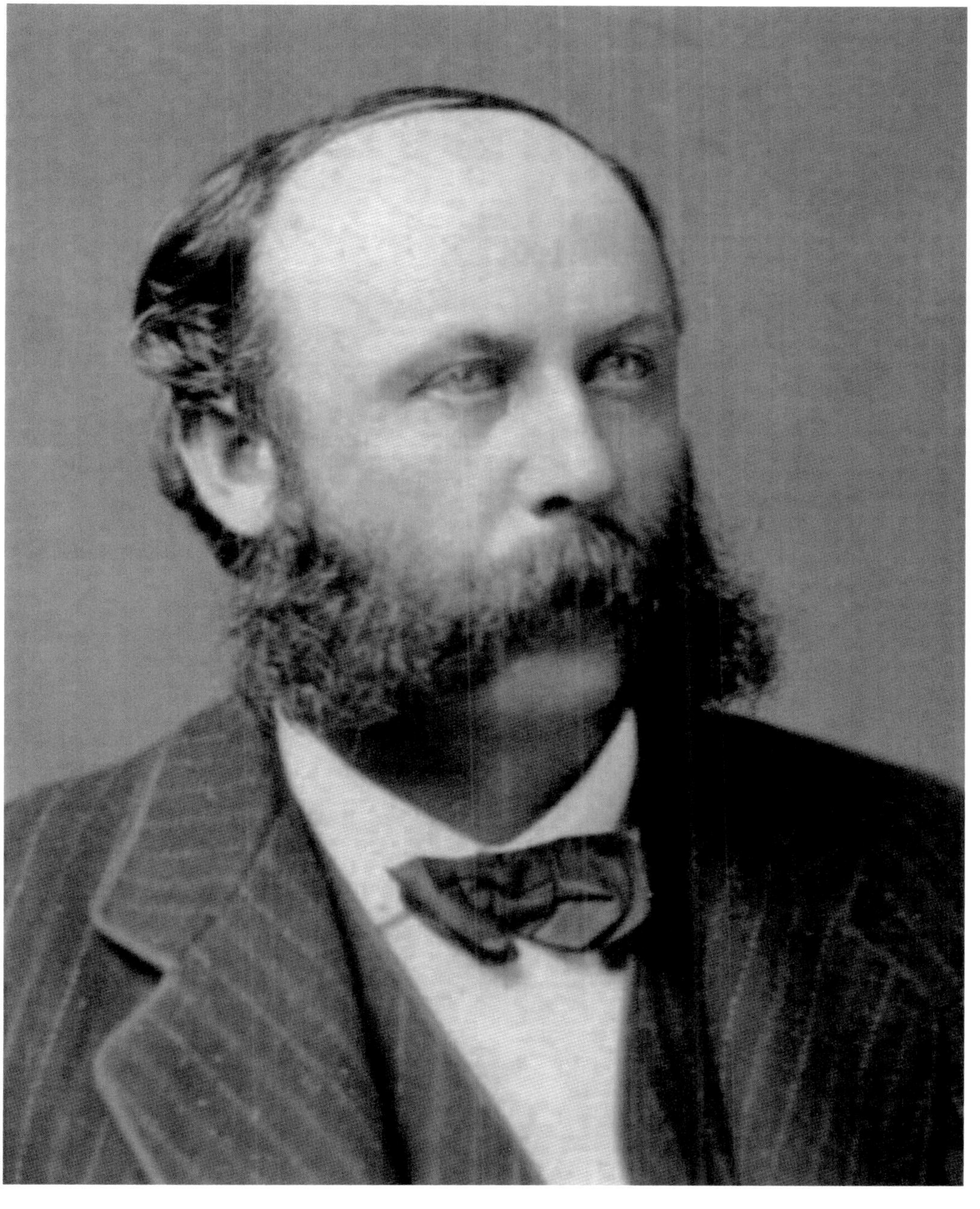

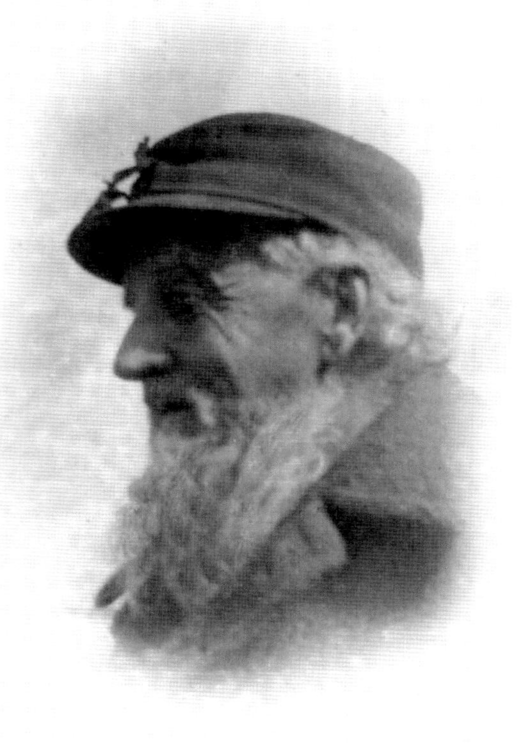

Capt. Edward B. Phinney (1825–1899)
Capt. Edward Phinney resided in the village of Waquoit and served his time on New Bedford whaling ships rising from boat steerer to captain. As master mariner, he sailed on the *Europa*, *Java*, and *Desdemona* from 1854 to 1869. After the glory of the seas, Captain Phinney returned to his Metoxit homestead to cranberry farming. His logbook, complete with brass knuckles and revolver, is held at the Falmouth Historical Society.

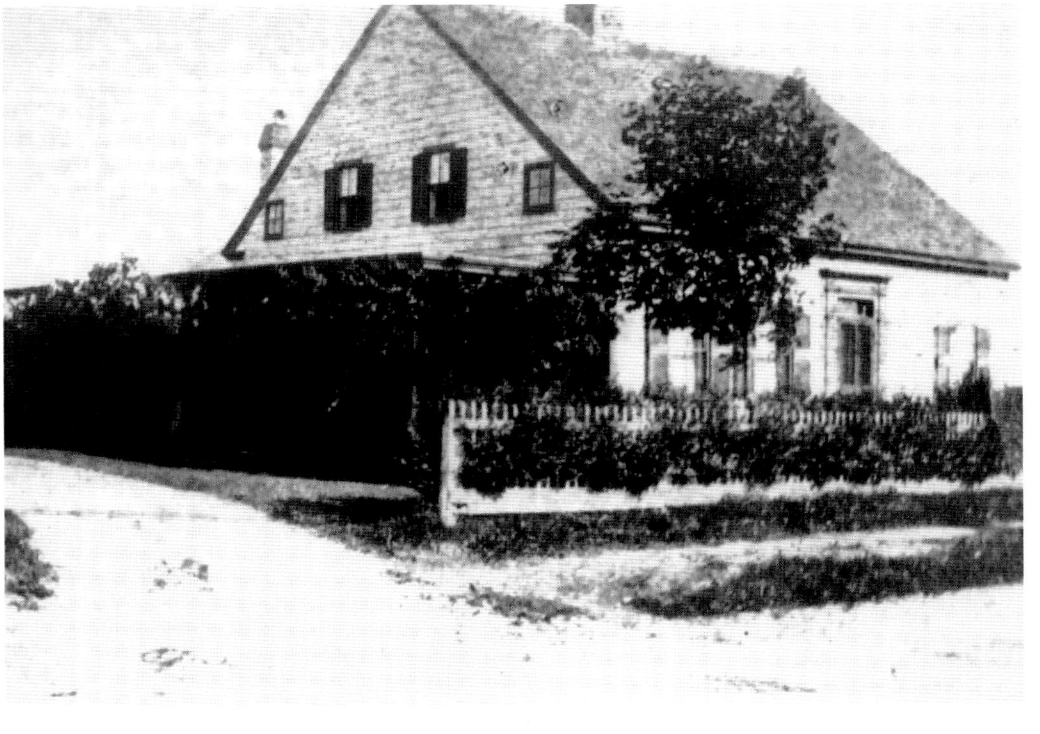

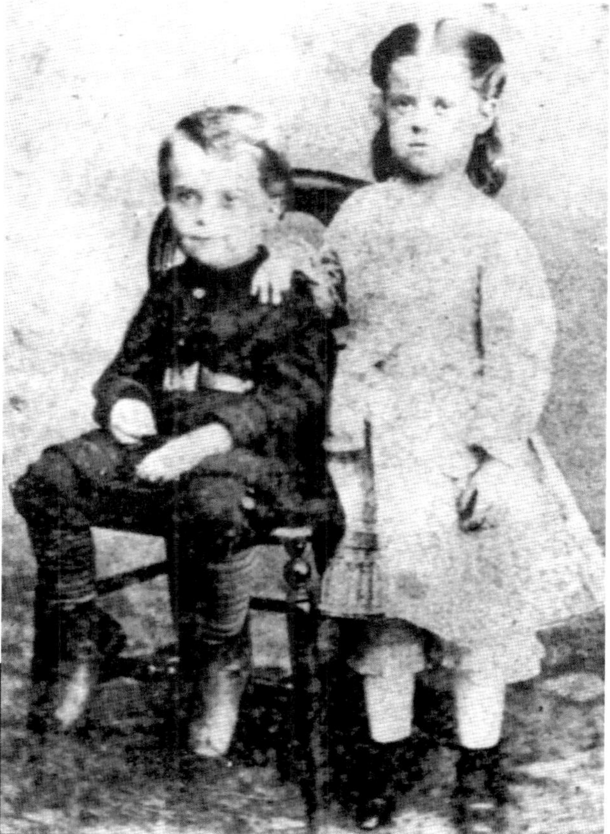

Bertha Boyce (1867–1968)
Bertha Boyce went to sea as a child with her father, Capt. John C. Hamblin, on the ship *Islander* in 1871. Her charming story was retold many times during her lifetime and finally written down when she was 96. She served many years as the children's librarian at the West Falmouth Library telling stories and sharing cookies. Many West Falmouth residents remember her sharing whaling artifacts from her old sea trunk and telling amazing tales of earlier days in Falmouth. A swift, or yarn winder, created by crewmembers on the *Islander* is displayed at the Falmouth Historical Society and was a gift from Bertha Boyce.

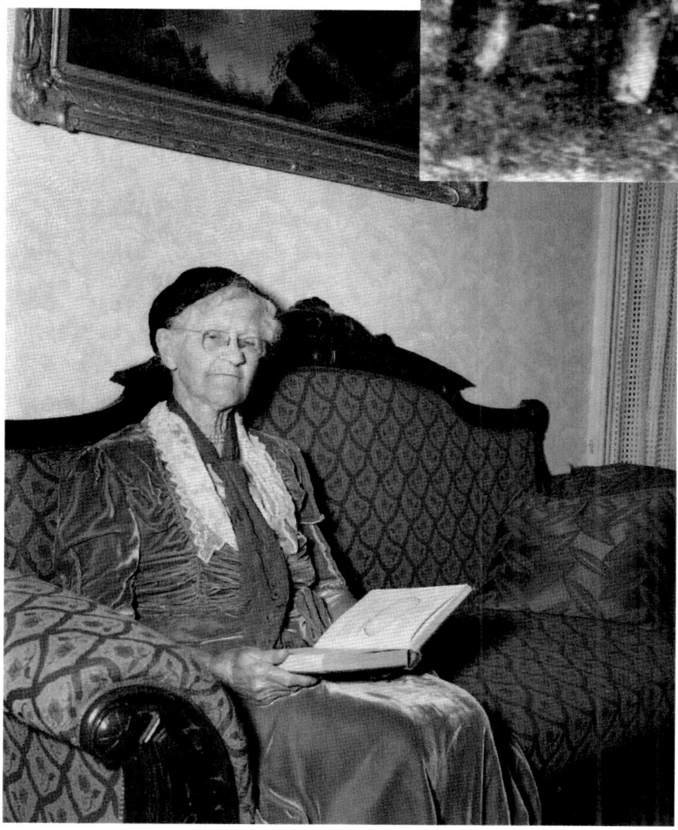

Capt. John Tobey (1807–1866)
Capt. John Tobey hailed from East Falmouth, but the sea was his second home. He commanded the ships *Japan* and *Edward Carey* and the *Uncas* and *Awashonks* of Woods Hole. During one voyage, a falling oil cask crushed his foot. Gangrene set in. With no land in sight, the captain amputated his own toes and recovered. Afterwards, he wore a shortened, custom-made shoe, which became a family heirloom. Tobey cultivated cranberries in his retirement and lived in a Greek Revival house that still stands on Route 28. Its attic yielded a trove of scrimshaw in 1968—relics of his storied whale-hunting career. Tobey is buried in the East Falmouth Methodist cemetery.

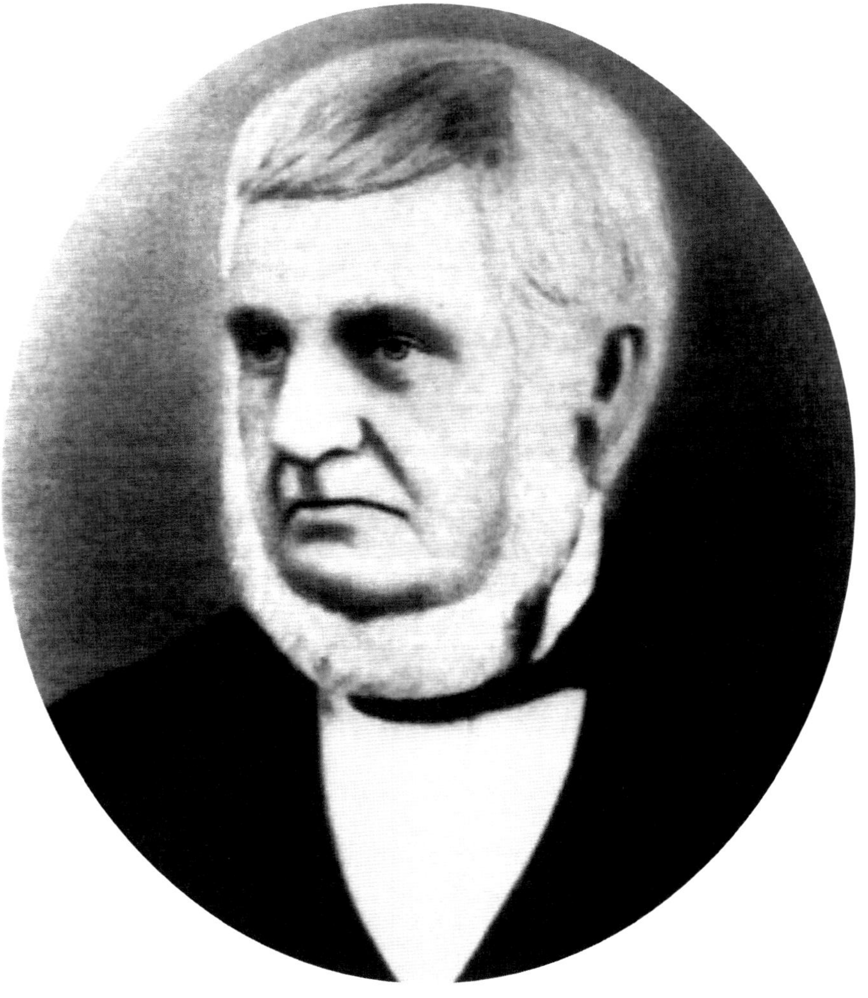

Capt. John Veeder (1859–1940))(OPPOSITE PAGE)
Capt. John Veeder was a descendant of the Cuttyhunk Veeder family of fishermen and lighthouse keepers. This Captain John was a Woods Hole transplant, working for the Marine Biological Laboratory (MBL) for 52 years as captain of a succession of research vessels. It was said that he never had an accident in 66 years of piloting, although he had seen his share of rough weather. In true Veeder style, he married the daughter of a lighthouse keeper. Captain Wheeler is shown at the helm of the wheelhouse.

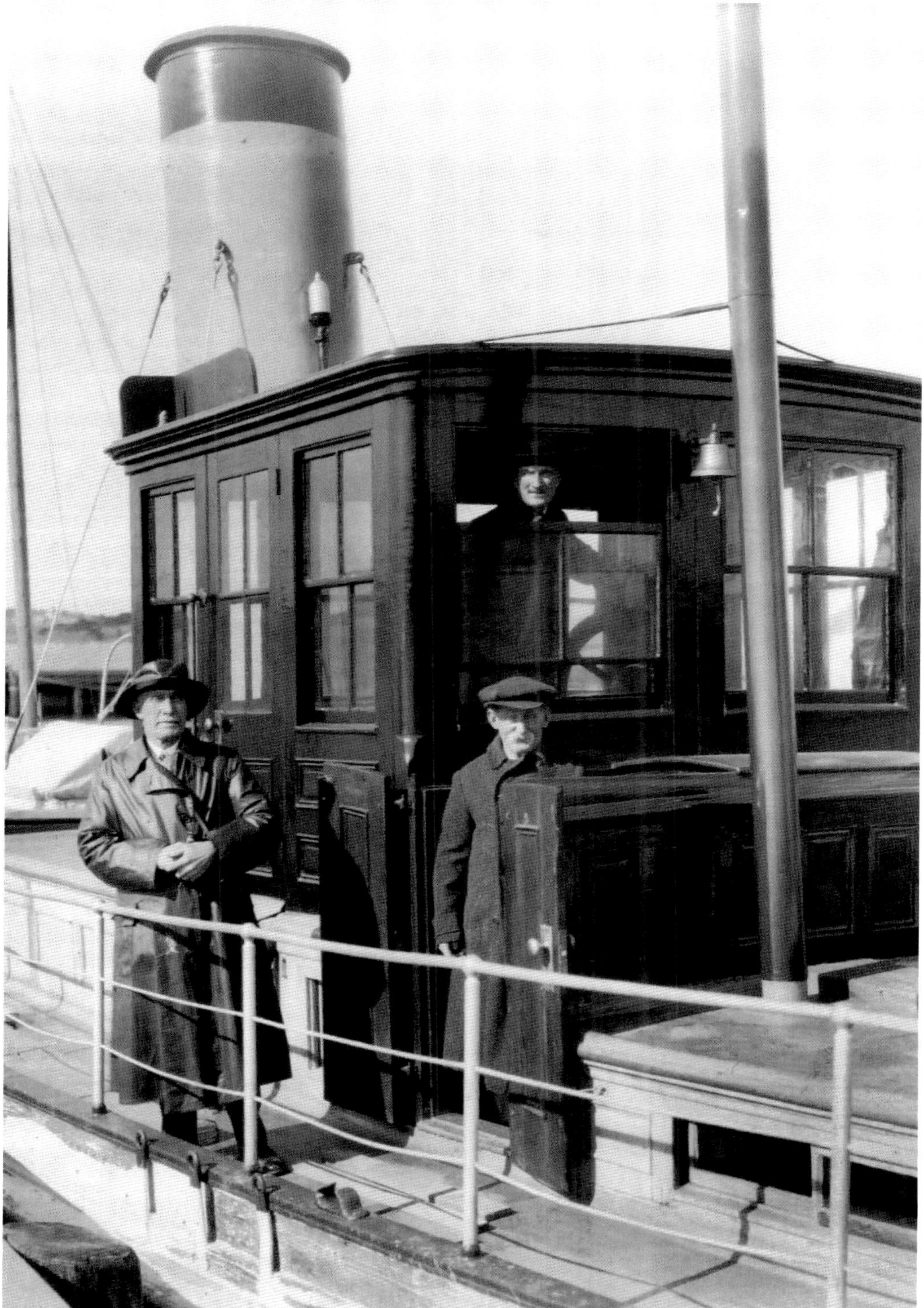

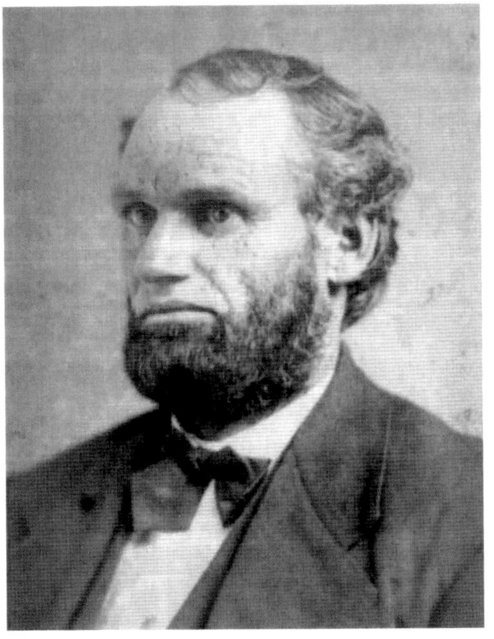

Capt. Nehemiah P. Baker of Teaticket (1823–1911)
Capt. Nehemiah P. Baker had considerable credentials as a sea captain, both as a whaler and merchant marine. He was master of the ship *General Pike* in 1850, followed by the *Nimrod*, the *William Gifford*, and the *Rainbow*. There are some accounts of a mutiny that he successful quelled by brute force, but his claim that he never lost a man on his voyages or encountered a serious accident stands.

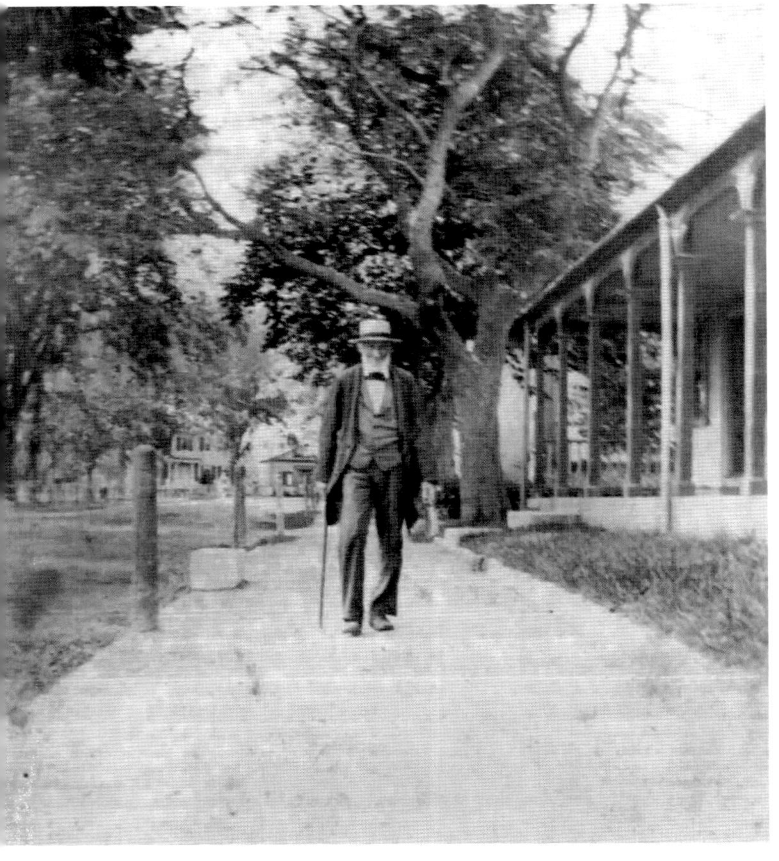

Henry F. Gifford (1818–1903)
Henry Gifford went to sea at the age of 12 with great excitement and anticipation. He was aboard the bark *Uncas*, a Swift ship, and sailed around Cape Horn in (1831–1835). But his optimism became tempered by the hardships of later voyages, including his experience as a boat steerer on the *William Penn* and as captain of the Fairhaven ship *Leonidas* (1849–1851). Henry left behind detailed narratives and accounts written in a wonderful style. He clearly expressed the high times and heartbreak of the seafaring life.

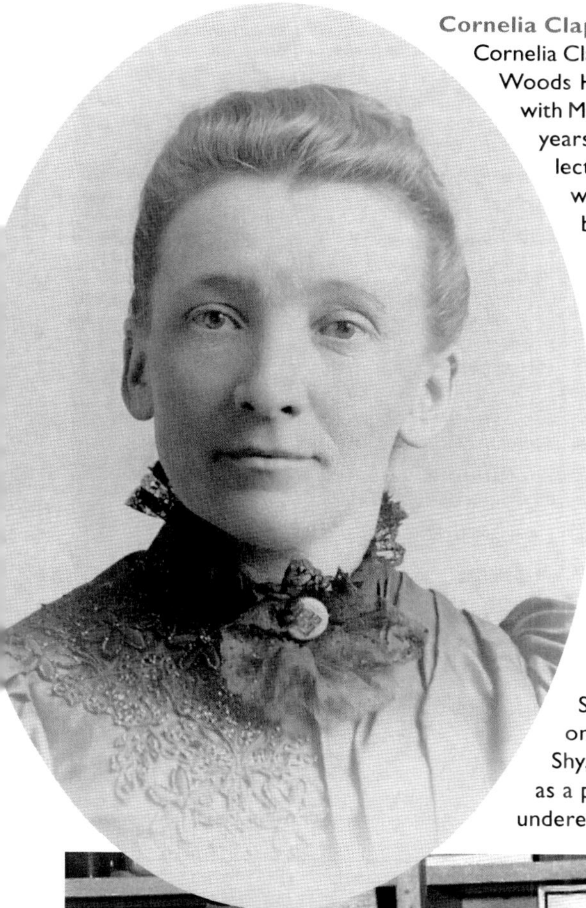

Cornelia Clapp (1849–1934)

Cornelia Clapp had two main interests: Mount Holyoke and the Woods Hole Marine Biological Laboratory. Her association with MBL began in 1888 in its inaugural year and lasted many years through her many roles, as student, investigator, lecturer, librarian, and finally trustee. Her philosophy was to keep MBL an independent association with both research and teaching. A Falmouth homeowner, she was a unique voice seeking science education for women in higher education. (Courtesy Mount Holyoke College Archives.)

Mary Sears (1905–1997)

Mary Sears was remarkable, not only because she managed to excel in oceanography at a time when women were not allowed on research vessels but also because she was a woman involved in naval intelligence during World War II. She was one of the first research assistants at the fledgling Woods Hole Oceanographic Institution, advancing to senior scientist in biology (1963–1970). A research vessel was named for her in 2007. What was truly remarkable about Mary Sears is that she served as a town meeting member for 35 years, as Falmouth School Committee member from 1952 to 1973, and on the board of the Children's School of Science. Shy, short, and prim, Mary Sears was once described as a powerful force of nature—one that was not to be underestimated. (Courtesy MBL/WHOI archives.)

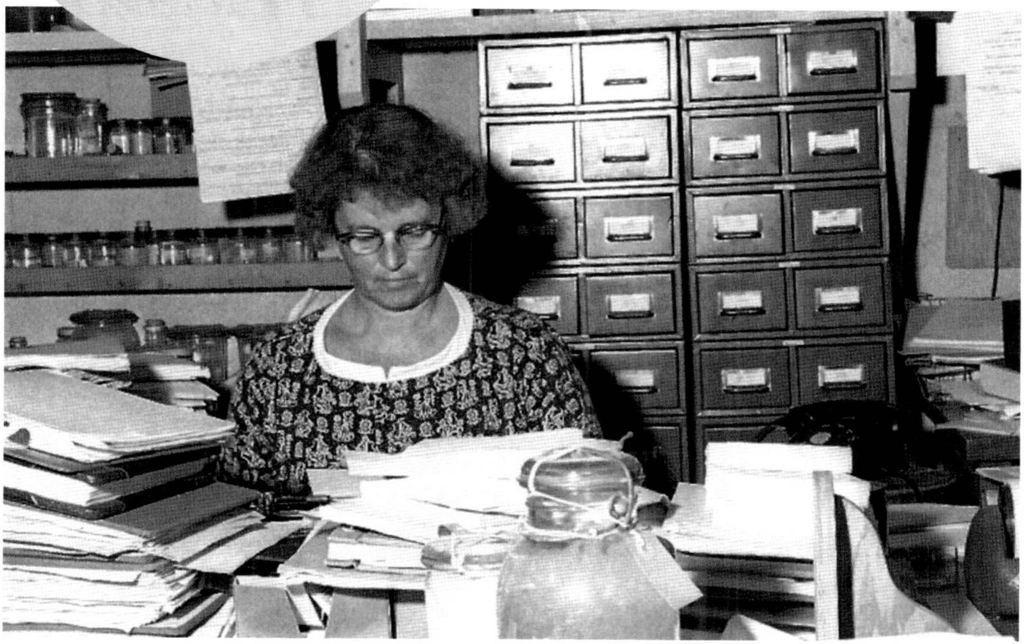

Alfred C. Redfield (1890–1983)

Alfred Redfield was a Harvard scientist, one of the first hired for the fledgling Woods Hole Oceanographic Institute (WHOI). He was a summer resident as early as 1898 and moved to Woods Hole in 1942. The achievements of this self-taught oceanographer, including the Redfield Index, were significant and numerous. This civilized and gracious man also made (if lesser known) contributions as a citizen of Falmouth. He was a town meeting member, president of the Woods Hole Public Library and Falmouth Chamber of Commerce, and served as the sixth president of the Falmouth Historical Society, leading the town in its tercentennial celebrations. Redfield Building still remains the heart of the WHOI campus. (Courtesy MBL/WHOI archives.)

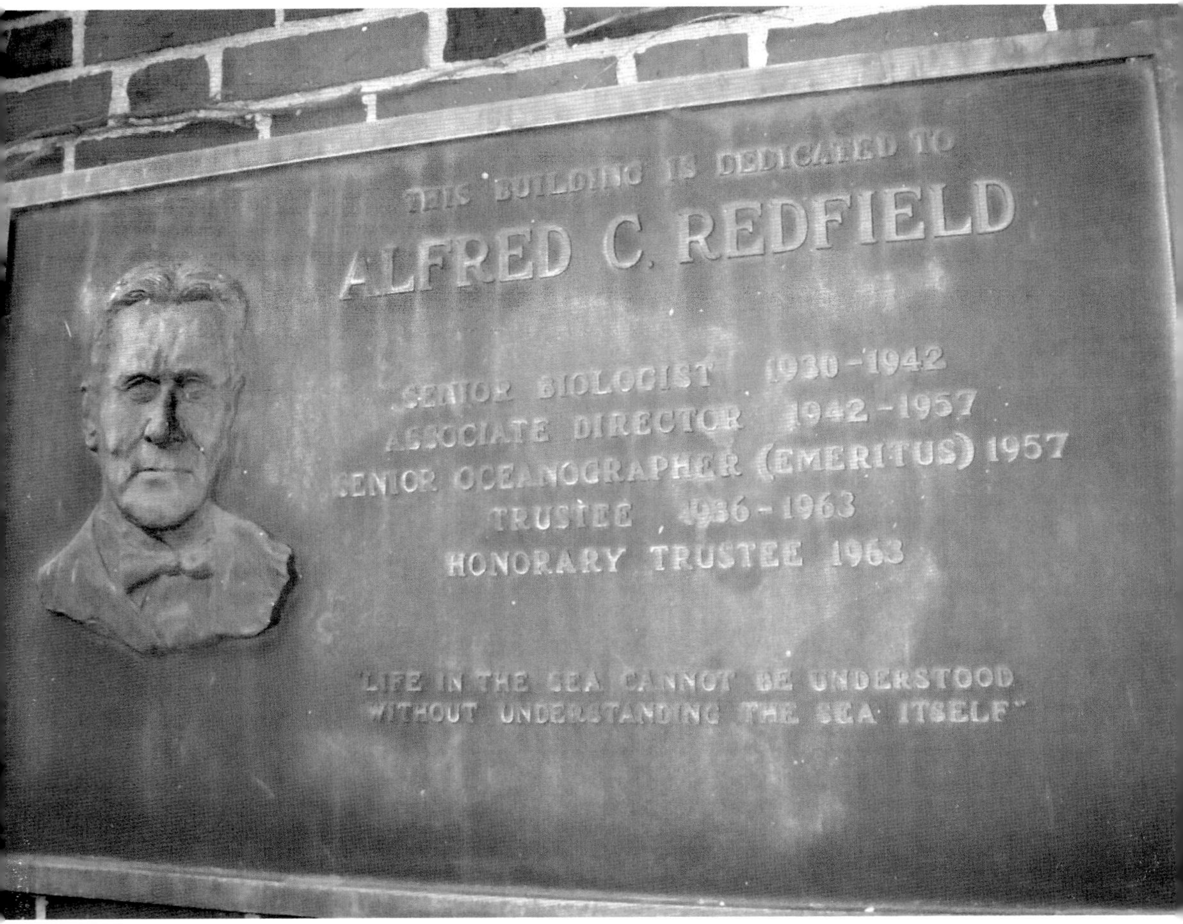

CHAPTER FOUR

Community Service

It is the kind of town that stands for democracy at its best.

—Theodate Geoffrey, *Suckanesset*

Service comes in all forms, with and without uniforms. It is a cornerstone of Falmouth that citizens organize in groups for the betterment of the town. This tradition began early with the sacrifices of the Civil War and the pride in returning servicemen in 1919 and again in 1945. The emotions of the Welcome Home Parade, Albert Hauser's march down Main Street on Veterans Day, and the little-known history of the Civil Air Patrol in Hatchville are included in this chapter. The grassroots beginnings of public health with the Falmouth Visiting Association and the beautification efforts of the Falmouth Garden Club also define community service.

The first fireman and police force of the 1930s are pictured in this chapter. The weekly antiwar vigil at the Falmouth Village Post Office and a costumed army of docents promoting the bicentennial at the Falmouth Historical Society round out this chapter. Community service is a watchword for Falmouth.

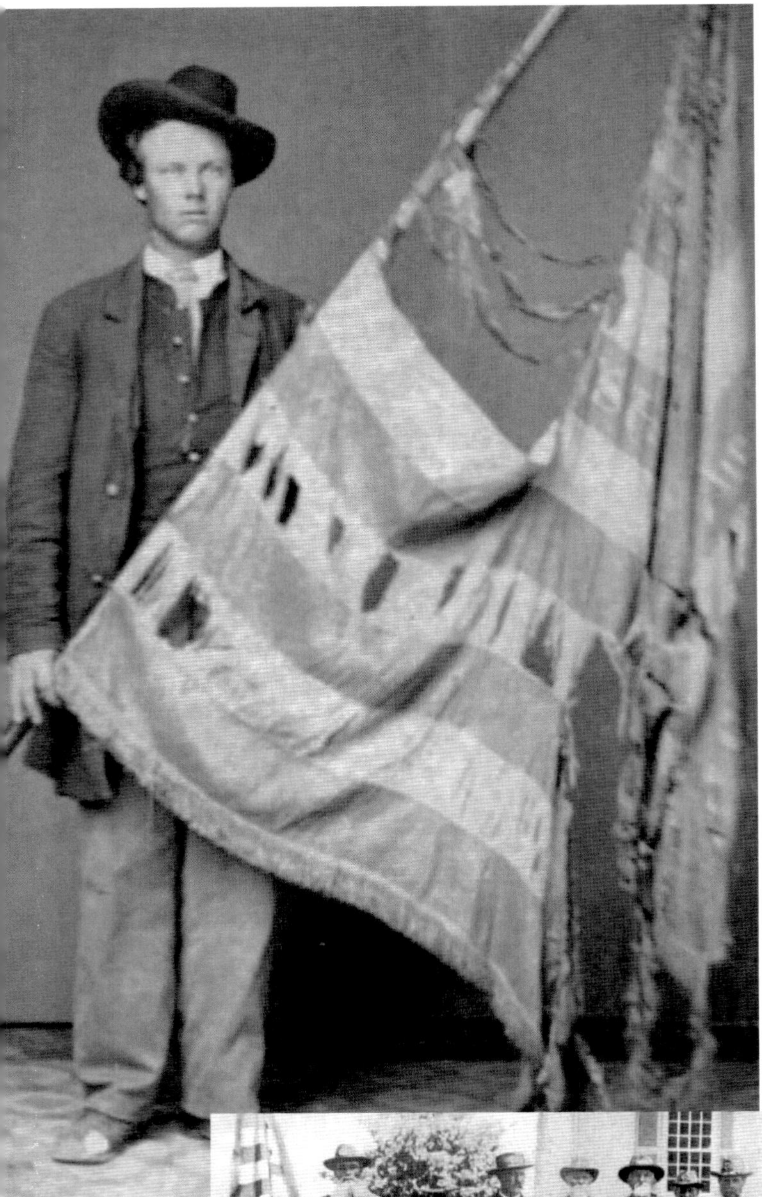

George Washington Swift (1819–1894)

Hailing from Waquoit Village, George Washington Swift was 19 when he enlisted into the 38th Regiment Massachusetts Volunteer Infantry, Company H. After fighting in the swamps of Louisiana, he joined General Sherman's army in the Shenandoah Valley. Later, as a corporal, he was captured and sent to the Confederate prisoner-of-war camp in Salisbury, North Carolina. He wrote of his ordeal in a pamphlet called "Experiences of a Falmouth Boy In a Rebel Prison." After the war, he became an active member of the Grand Army of the Republic (GAR) and ran a candy store on Main Street in Falmouth. Although he married, raised a family, and lived a long life, he never fully recovered from the posttraumatic stress caused by his wartime experiences. He is buried at the Oak Grove Cemetery. He is shown at left after his return home. Below, members of the B.F. Jones Post, Grand Army of the Republic stand in front of their headquarters building, now the Falmouth Chamber of Commerce.

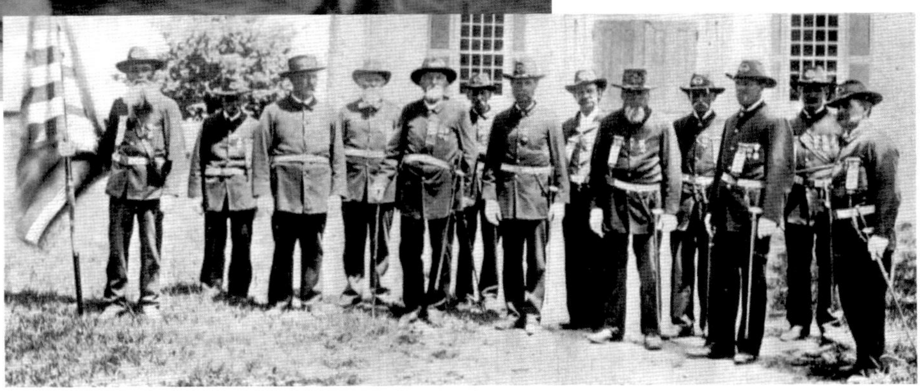

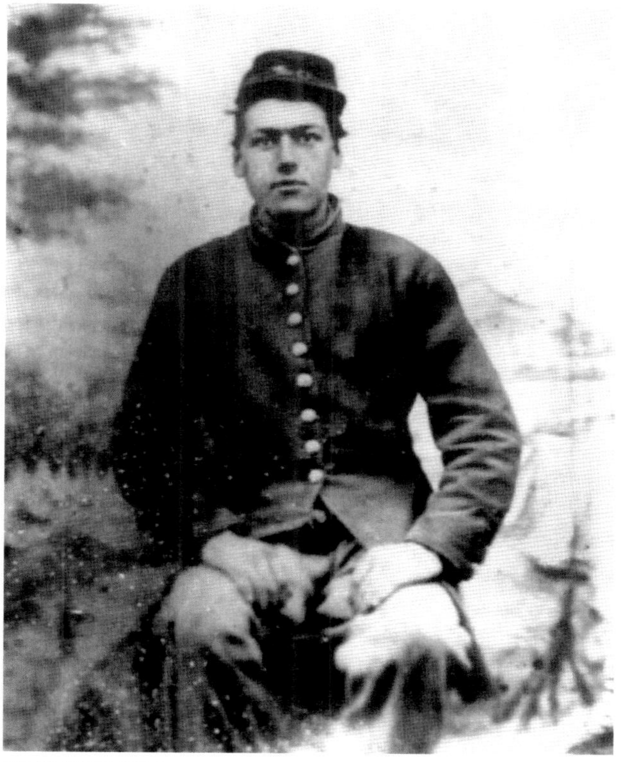

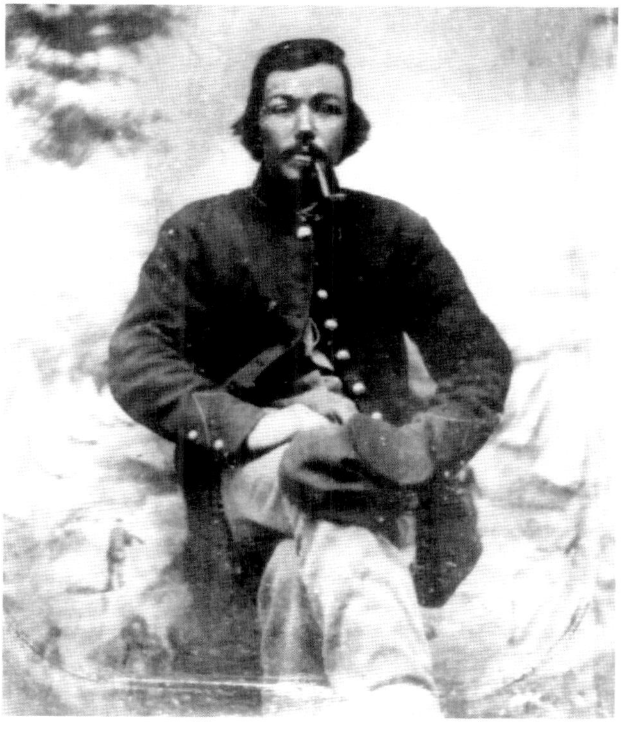

Alvin (1844–1864) and Rufus Fish (1841–1864)
Three sons of Eleazer Fish, of Hatchville, enlisted in the Union Army within months of each other, and none of them returned home. Both Alvin and Rufus became part of the same Company K, 33rd Massachusetts Infantry Regiment and endured some of the worst battles together. Older brother George had also enlisted. They were at Chancellorsville and the Battle of Gettysburg, surviving Pickett's Charge. As part of the Army of the Cumberland, their last stand was at the Battle of Resaca, Georgia, where 80 men in their unit lost their lives. This family's loss was one of Falmouth's most tragic stories of the Civil War. Shown are Alvin (top) and Rufus.

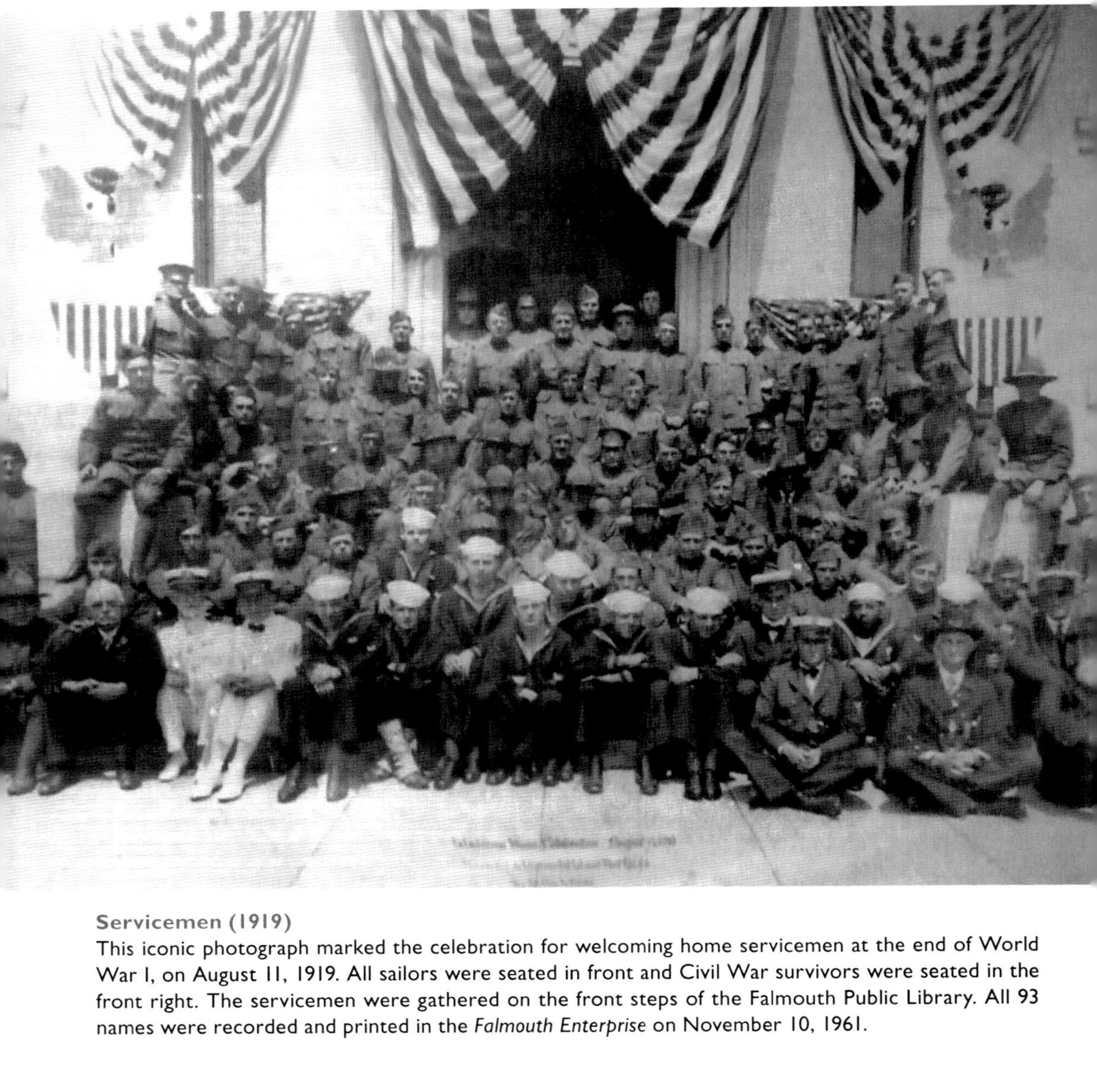

Servicemen (1919)
This iconic photograph marked the celebration for welcoming home servicemen at the end of World War I, on August 11, 1919. All sailors were seated in front and Civil War survivors were seated in the front right. The servicemen were gathered on the front steps of the Falmouth Public Library. All 93 names were recorded and printed in the *Falmouth Enterprise* on November 10, 1961.

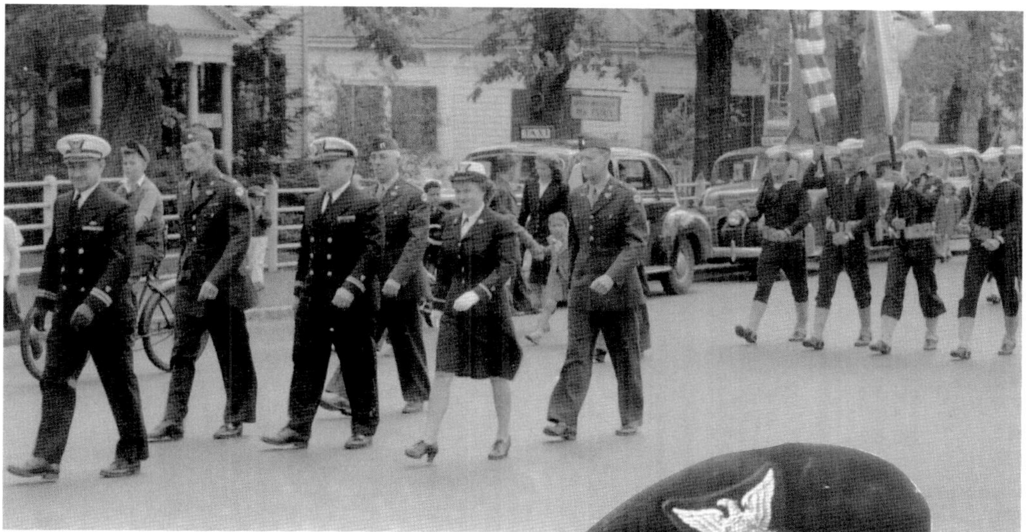

Albert H. Hauser (1918–2001)
Albert Hauser was a Coast Guard officer who lived on Lt. Hauser Lane off Gifford Street and was associated with the maritime trade for 53 years. He was group commander of the Woods Hole base and chief harbormaster for Falmouth. As commander at Woods Hole, he participated in the rescue of survivors on the *Andria Doria*. Through his skill in navigation and mapmaking, he redesigned the chart for Vineyard Sound and included a sandbar that he discovered. That island is now known as Hauser's Island. Above, he is shown in his Coast Guard uniform leading the Memorial Day parade down Main Street.

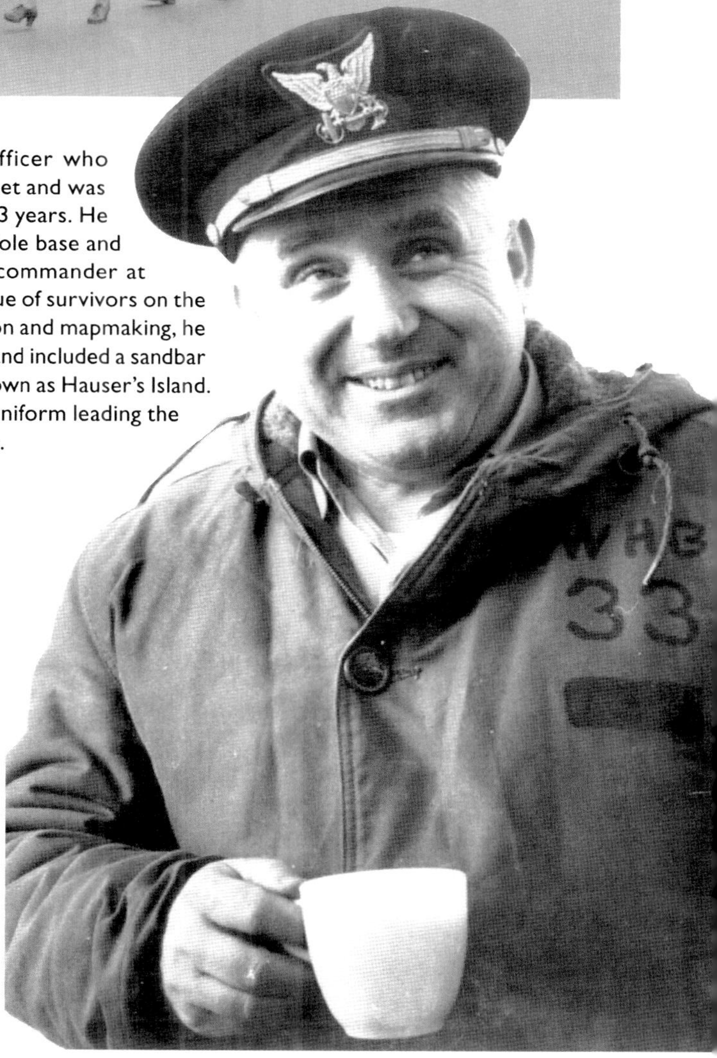

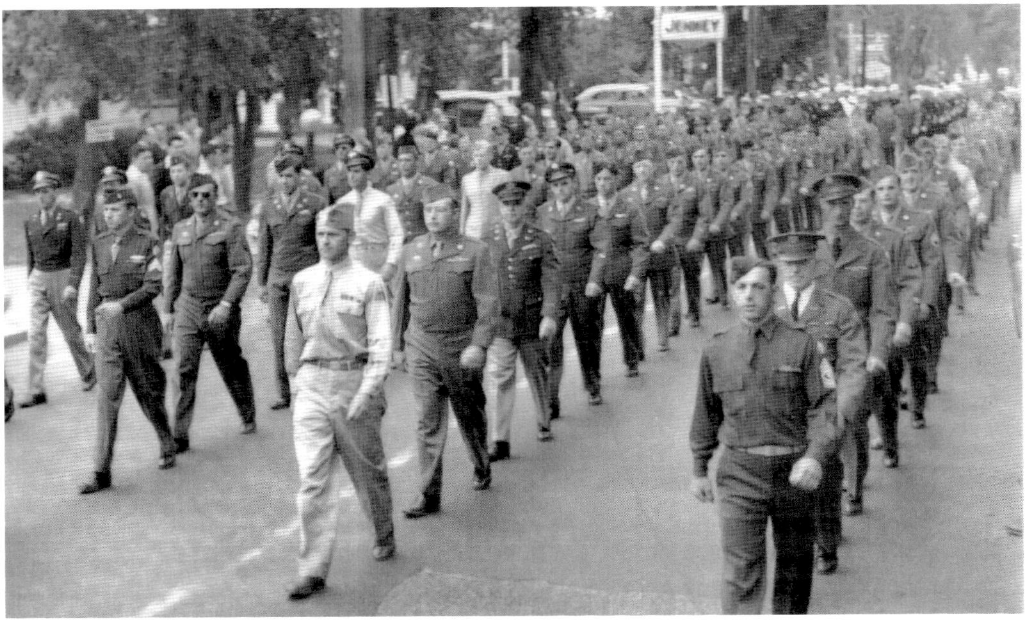

Welcome Home (1945)
The Welcome Home Parade for Falmouth veterans of World War II is shown here as they marched down Main Street toward the public library. Pride, joy, and gratitude are shown on the faces of each soldier as they pass in review. The special speaker at the ceremonies that day was Sen. Leverett Saltonstall.

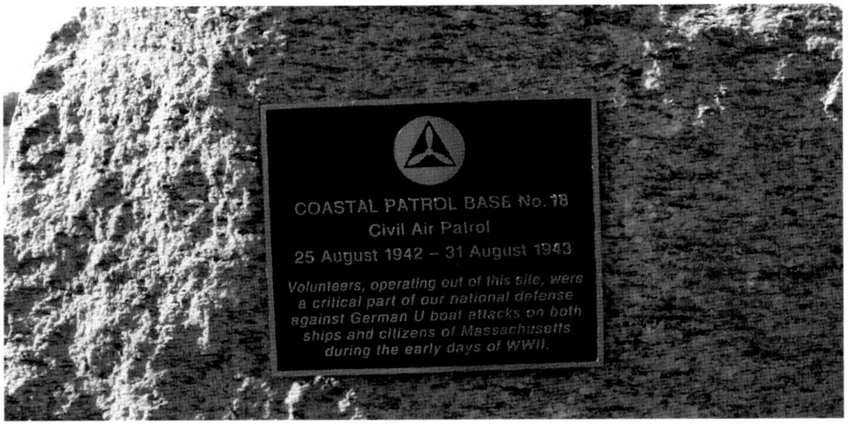

Civil Air Patrol (1942–1943)
The Cape Cod Civil Air Patrol (CAP) operated out of a grass field airport in Falmouth leased from the Coonamessett Ranch Co. This group of volunteer pilots patrolled the coast looking for German submarines and U-boats. Among the CAP were several women, including Falmouth resident Janet Hodgson Bosworth, who acted as radio operator and later earned her pilot's license. She also met her first husband there, fellow CAP pilot Frederick G. Hodgson. Sloat F. Hodgson, a West Falmouth native and a CAP mechanic, wrote about his experience with CAP, describing their uniforms and equipment as ragtag but their goals and achievements commendable. In 2011, the contributions of Cape Cod Civil Air Patrol were recognized with a memorial plaque placed on a rock near a field where the airport once stood. This memorial rock stands on a pathway at the Frances A. Crane Reservation.

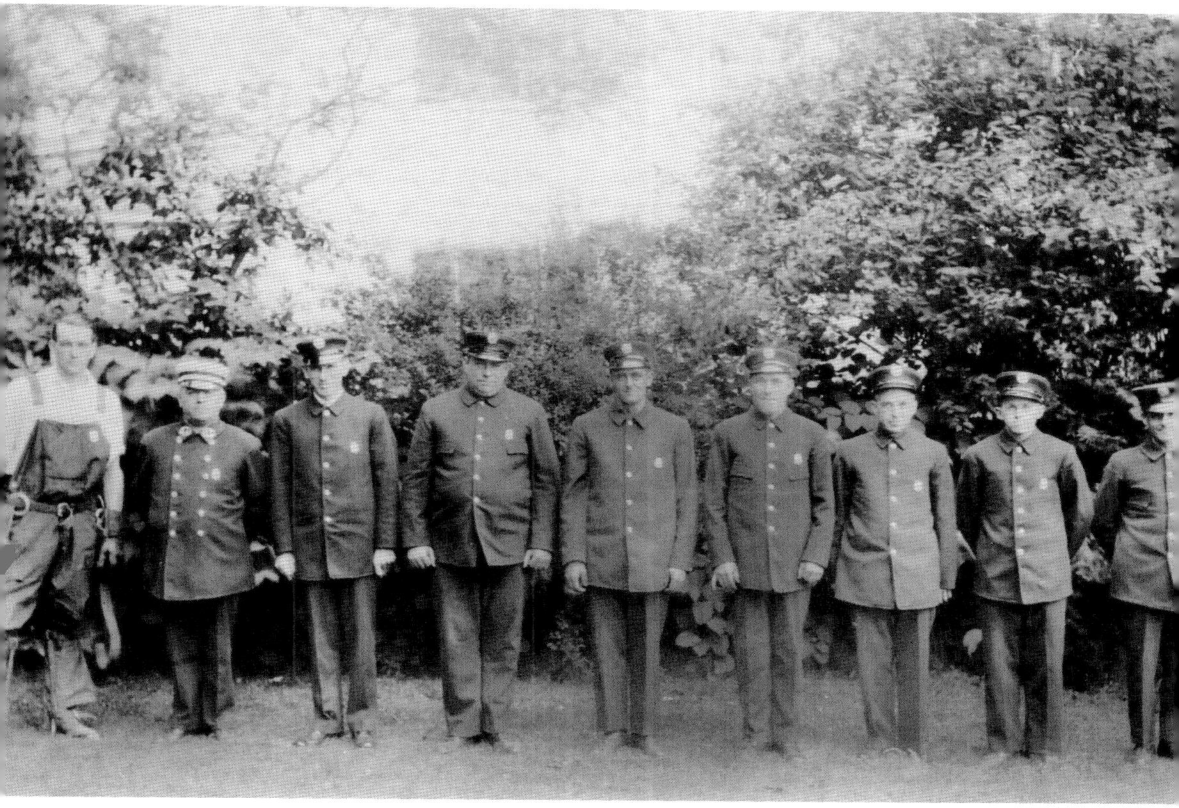

George A. Ferris (1896 –1985)
George Ferris was hired as the first permanent fireman in Falmouth. He added this title to his other jobs as school janitor, special policeman, and drawbridge operator. Here, he poses at the Falmouth station in 1921. He was deputy fire chief under Chief Ray D. Wells from 1948 to 1952. His most harrowing assignment was the three-day Beebe Woods fire in 1947. George Ferris is on a far left in this group photograph of the first firemen of Falmouth.

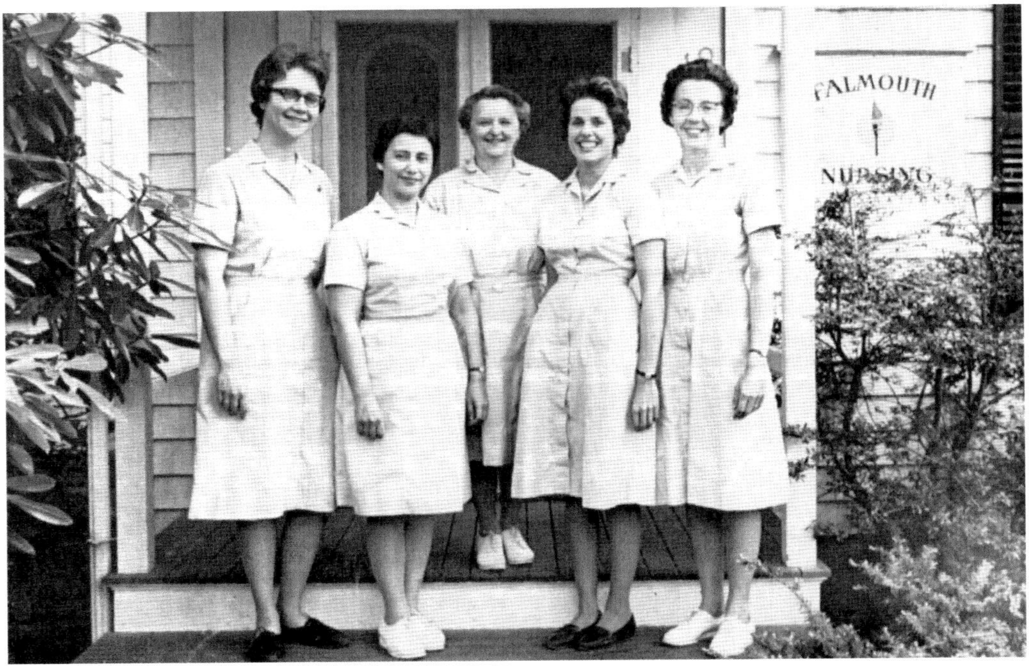

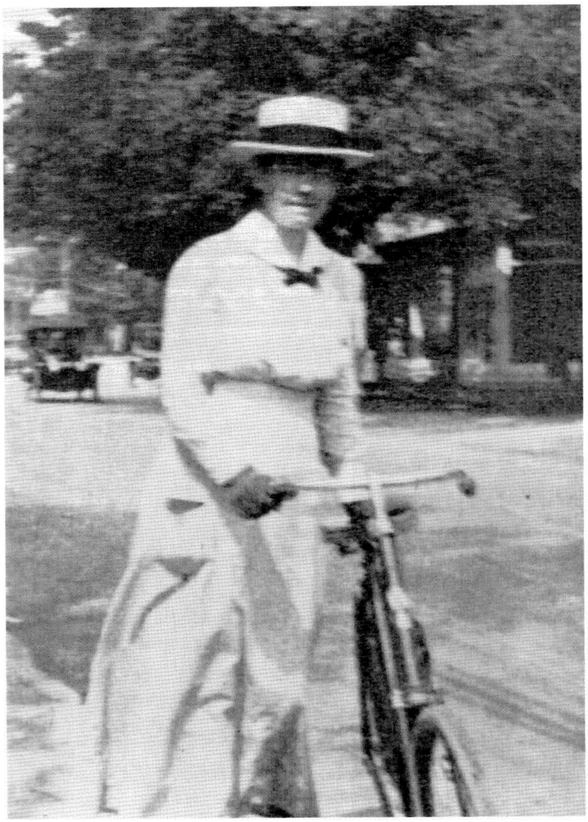

Marguerite (Rita) Thomas Kendall (1905–2001)

Rita Kendall once said, "It makes you feel good to pull your weight in the world." It was on April 30, 1972, that the town declared Rita Kendall Day with a parade and reception to honor all that she had done for Falmouth, including her 40-year career with the Falmouth Visiting Nurses. Rita expanded free health care for mothers, newborns, and young children in the 1950s. She increased nursing services in the schools and initiated preventative health programs for the elderly. The Visiting Nurse Association childcare center is now known as the Rita Kendall Building. Above, Rita stands in the middle of her fellow nurses at their Locust Street office. The first employee of the Falmouth Visiting Nurses Association in 1917 was Elizabeth A. Eliot-Smith who rode to her appointments in town by bicycle (left). From these beginnings, the Visiting Nurse Association of Cape Cod grew to 800 employees and now makes over 300,000 home visits annually.

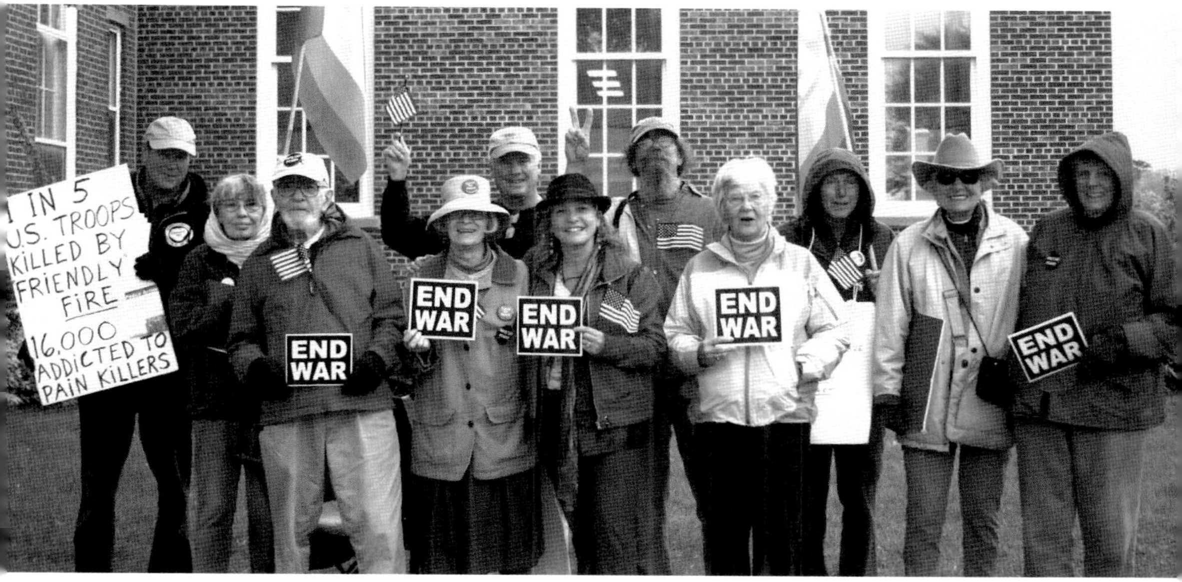

Falmouth Anti-War Vigil

The Falmouth Anti-War Vigil began in 1991 by Charles and Joyce Johnson as a response to Operation Desert Storm. This weekly stand against war had Quaker origins, but most of the participants are not Quakers. Originally held at the Village Green, this spirited, rain-or-shine gathering is held in front of the Falmouth Village Post Office. Charles Johnson stands third from the left with Joyce next to him. (Courtesy Paul Rifkin.)

Falmouth Garden Club (1931–)

The Falmouth Garden Club began with 12 women, under first president Rachel Swift, pledging to cultivate a love for and growing of flowers and gardens. In 1934, Frances Leatherbee became president, followed by Emily Wheeler. The club has a long history of community involvement, starting with the first planting of a Douglas fir at the Village School in 1931 and plantings at the entrance of Goodwill Park. Here, Falmouth Garden Club members gather at the home of Frances Leatherbee in 1934.

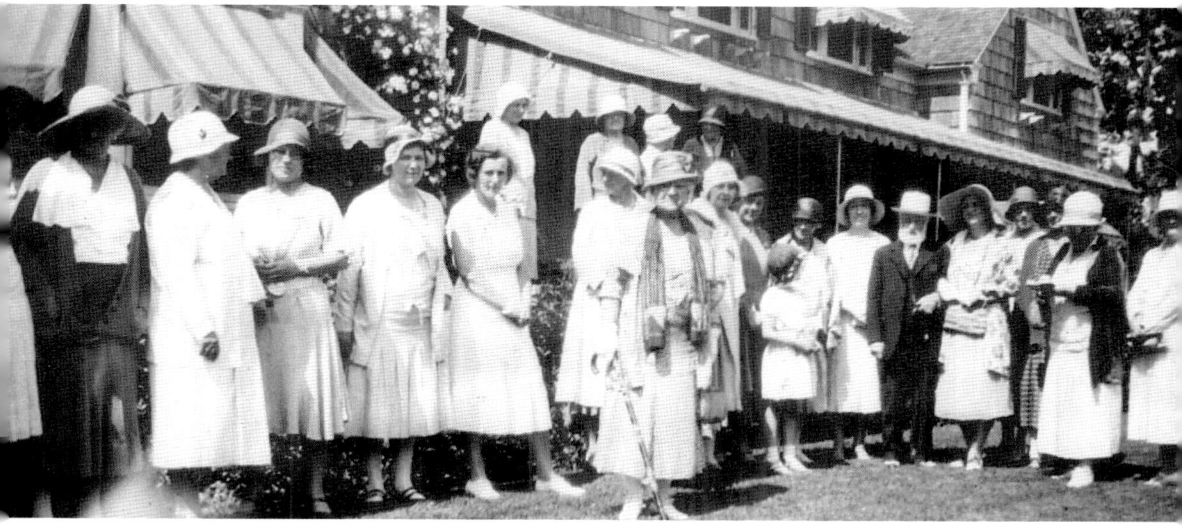

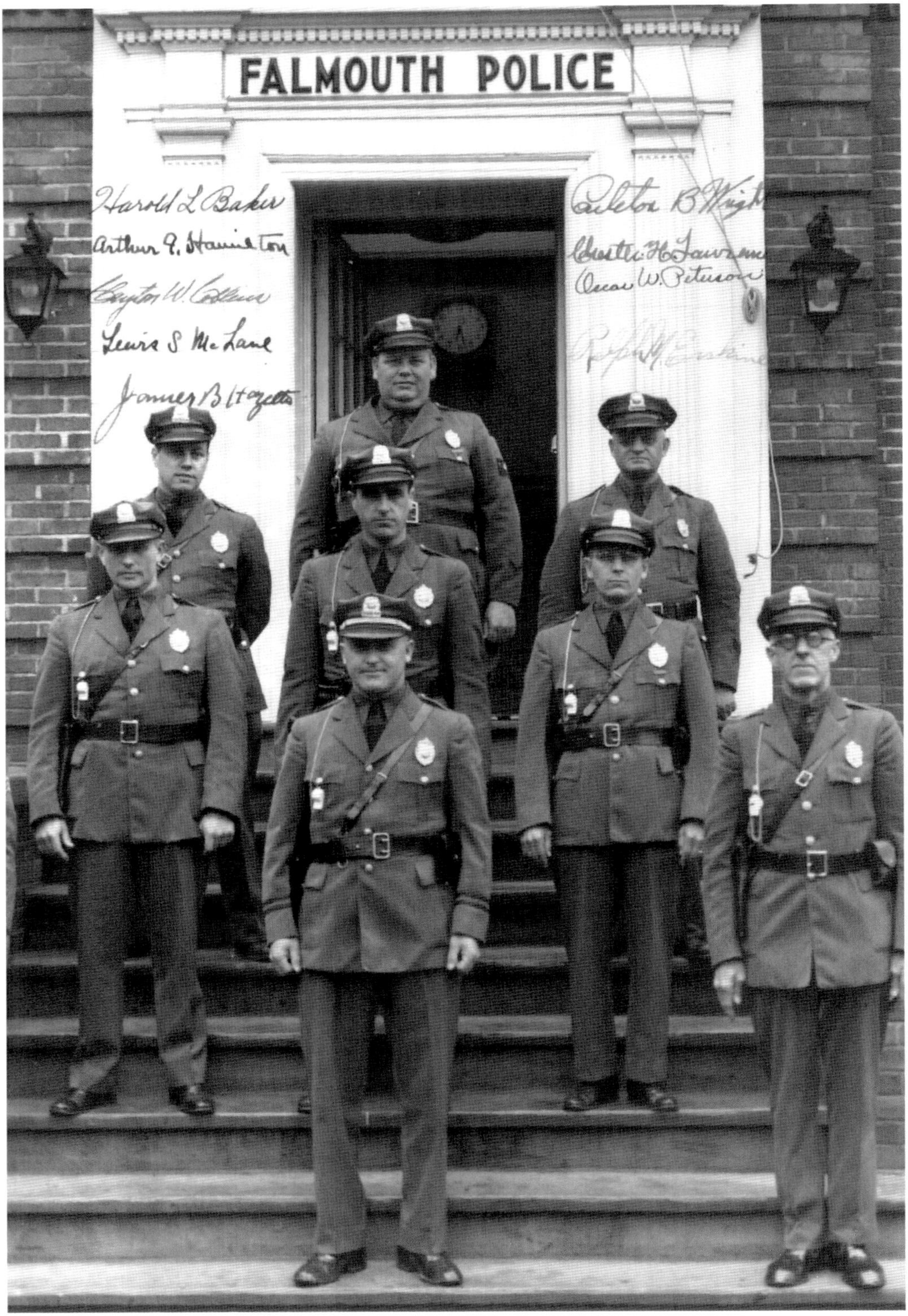
FALMOUTH POLICE
Harold L Baker
Lewis S McLane
Oscar W. Peterson

Massachusetts Guardsmen (1951)

Battery G of the Massachusetts Guard poses in front of the old town hall on May 4, 1951, preparing to leave for Camp Edwards. Some familiar local persons include Capt. William Covill (front) and Matt Souza (first row, third from left). Henry Hall, Bruce Espey, and Henry Behrens are identified on the verso as being part of this battalion.

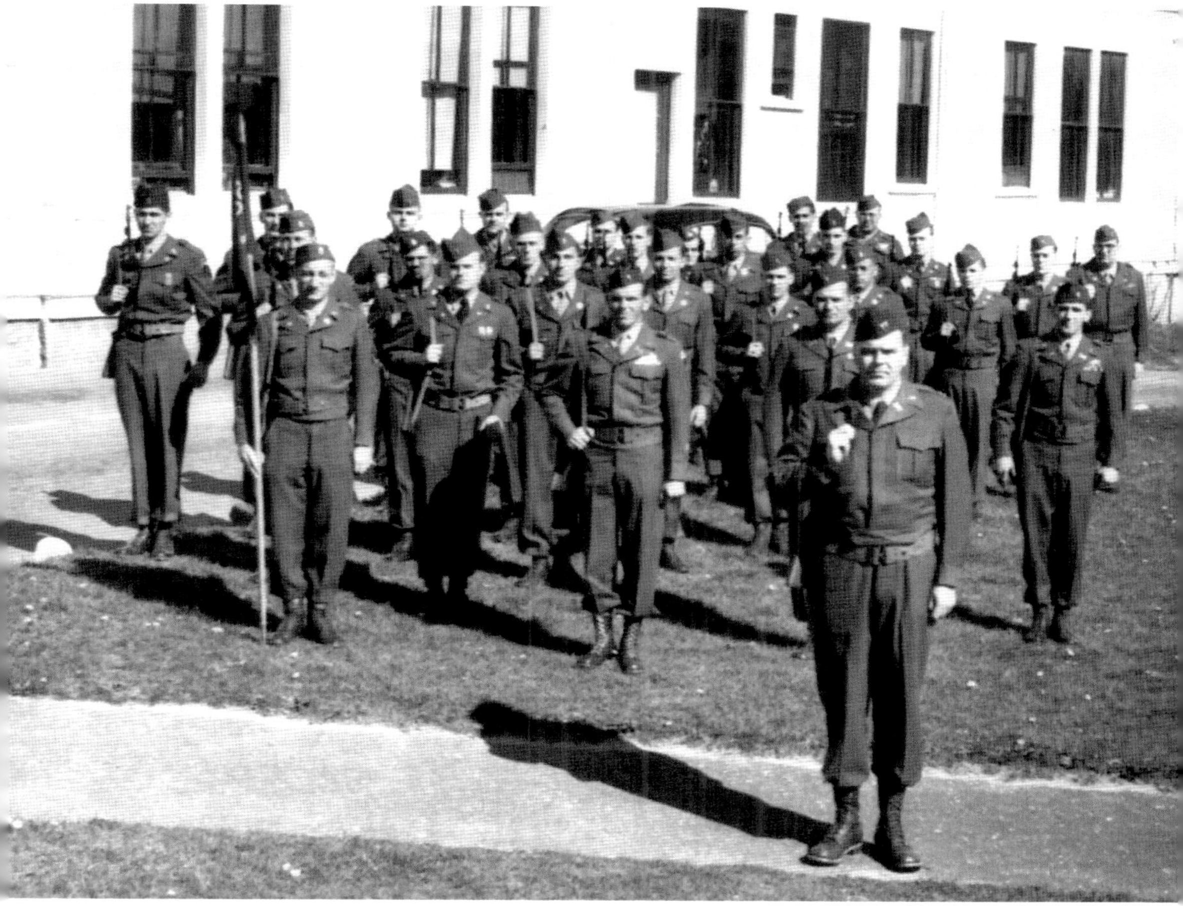

Policemen (1937) (OPPOSITE PAGE)

Falmouth policemen stand on the front steps of the old police station next to the old town hall in 1937. They are self-identified. Harold Baker and Arthur Hamilton lead the way.

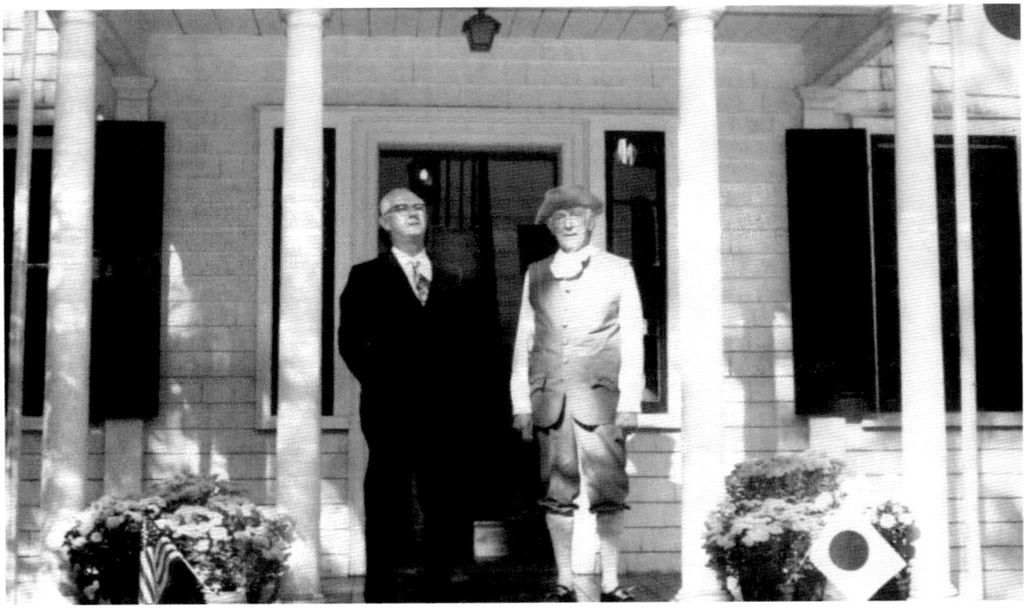

Dudley W. Hallett (1903–1990)

Dudley Hallett started coming to Falmouth as a summer resident of Old Silver Beach. He became involved with the Falmouth Historical Society in 1967 and served as president for 17 years. During his terms, the museum acquired the Conant House and the Katharine Lee Bates house and began educational programs for elementary children. He led the town's bicentennial committee in 1976. The barn at the Museum on the Green was named the Dudley W. Hallett Museum Barn. Clarence Anderson (left) stands next to Dudley Hallett on the porch of the Katharine Lee Bates house. Below, Dudley stands in front of the Conant House with costumed docents.

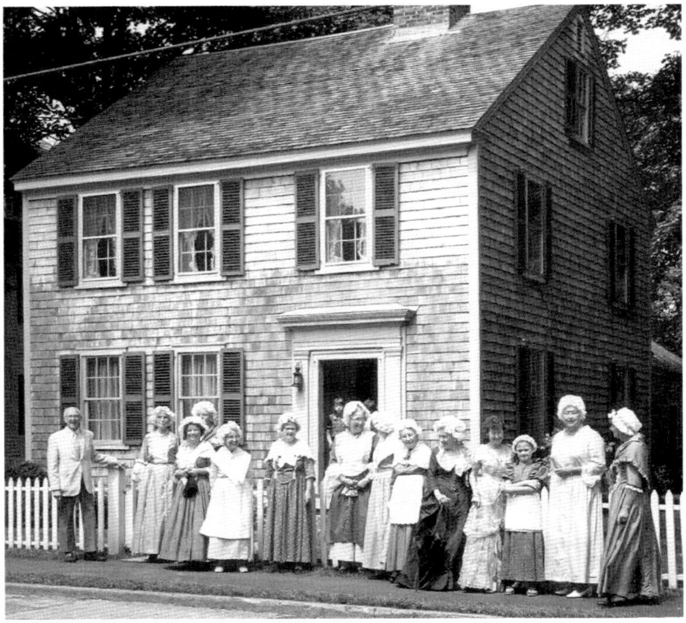

CHAPTER FIVE

Falmouth's Royalty

Mr. Fay drove me in his light buggy all over his woodlands and acres of rough pastureland . . . showing me many parts of interest and all the wonderful results of his planting of trees.

—Elizabeth Fay, *Book of Falmouth*

That the world was wonderful and wide we knew, / For we had watched the vanishing of sails.

—Katharine Lee Bates, "Falmouth"

Wealthy visitors to Falmouth brought new cultures, new resources, and progress to Falmouth. Their contributions were dazzling and helped create the cosmopolitan savvy that marks Falmouth. Their lives were played large with many extraordinary philanthropic acts from these visitors who loved Falmouth as if they were natives.

The first summer visitor was also one of the most influential, beginning with the arrival of the powerful Joseph Story Fay, followed closely with the entrance of the Beebe family and their extraordinary estate, long a curiosity to locals. Royalty also has a subset of meritocracy with individuals of achievement like M. Sylvia Donaldson, R. Louise McManus, and Rev. Henry Herbert Smythe. Emperor Hirohito's visit to Falmouth in 1975 caused a mild sensation and merited a place in this chapter. The Faxons tell a little-recalled story of the building of the Falmouth Hospital. All of these people marked their territory and changed not only the names of the land but the future directions for Falmouth.

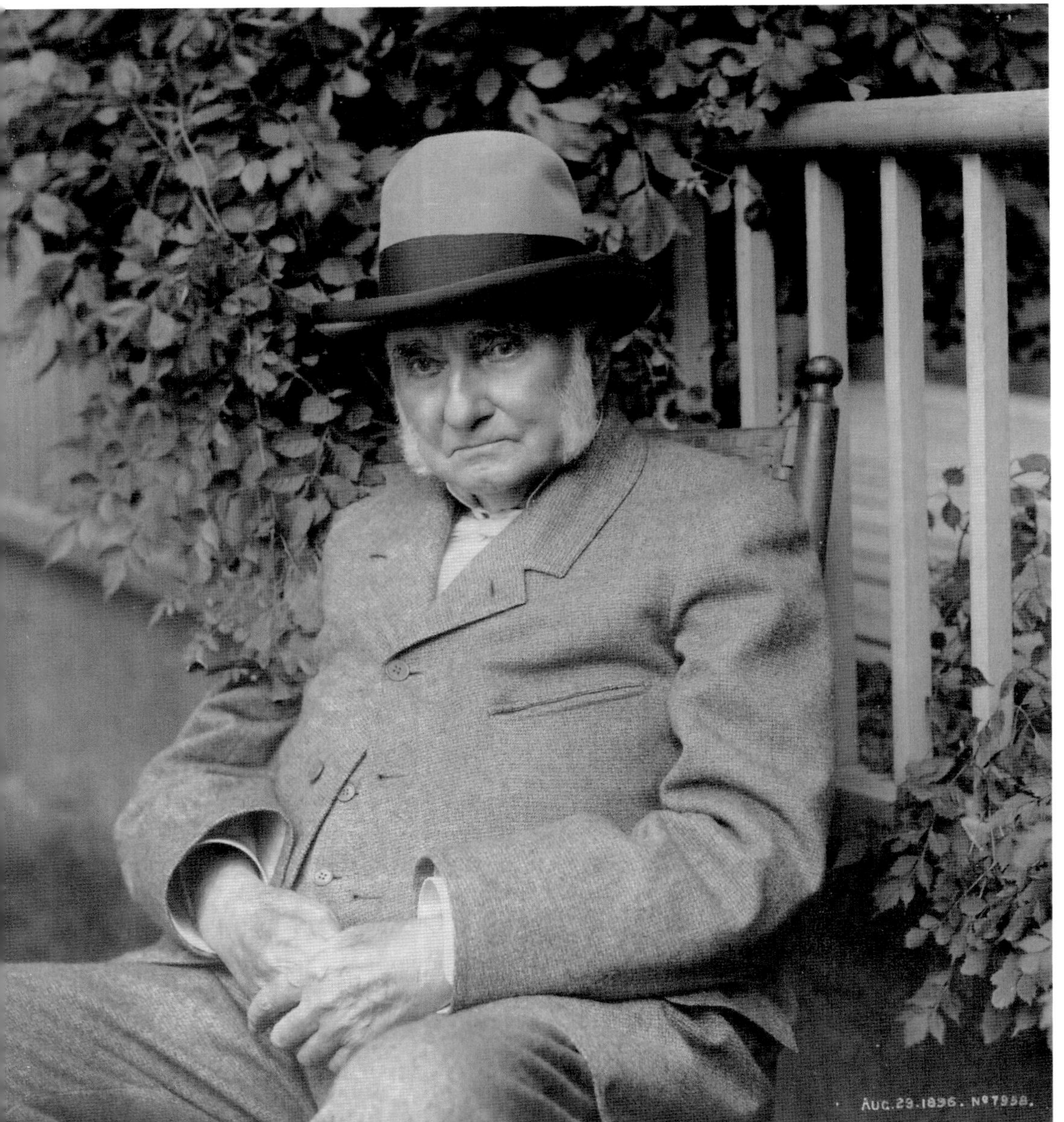

Joseph Story Fay (1812–1877)

Joseph Story Fay, pictured here at the age of 84, has been called "Falmouth's first summer resident." This wealthy cotton mills businessman settled near Little Harbor, Woods Hole, in 1850, and left his profound mark on this village. He built two churches, one school, and gifted a forested public park, Goodwill Park. He persuaded the Old Colony Railroad to extend its track to Falmouth and Woods Hole in 1872. His power was so complete that his theory that the Vikings had visited Falmouth, written in a pamphlet called "Track of the Norsemen," changed the name of the village from Woods Hole to the Viking spelling "Woods Holl" until after his death. (Photograph by Baldwin Coolidge, courtesy Woods Hole Historical Collections.)

Franklin Huntington Beebe (1853–1933)
Franklin H. Beebe represents the second generation of the Beebe family who lived in the prominent, Queen Anne–style Highfield estate. Franklin was the youngest of seven children of James Madison Beebe, one of the merchant princes of Boston and the greatest host ever to entertain in Falmouth. Franklin lived the cultivated, English-squire lifestyle, acquiring fine paintings and furnishings for Highfield. It was not until he was 73 that he became the sole trustee of his family fortune. He was known around town for his Pierce Arrow limousine and his keen interest in horticulture.

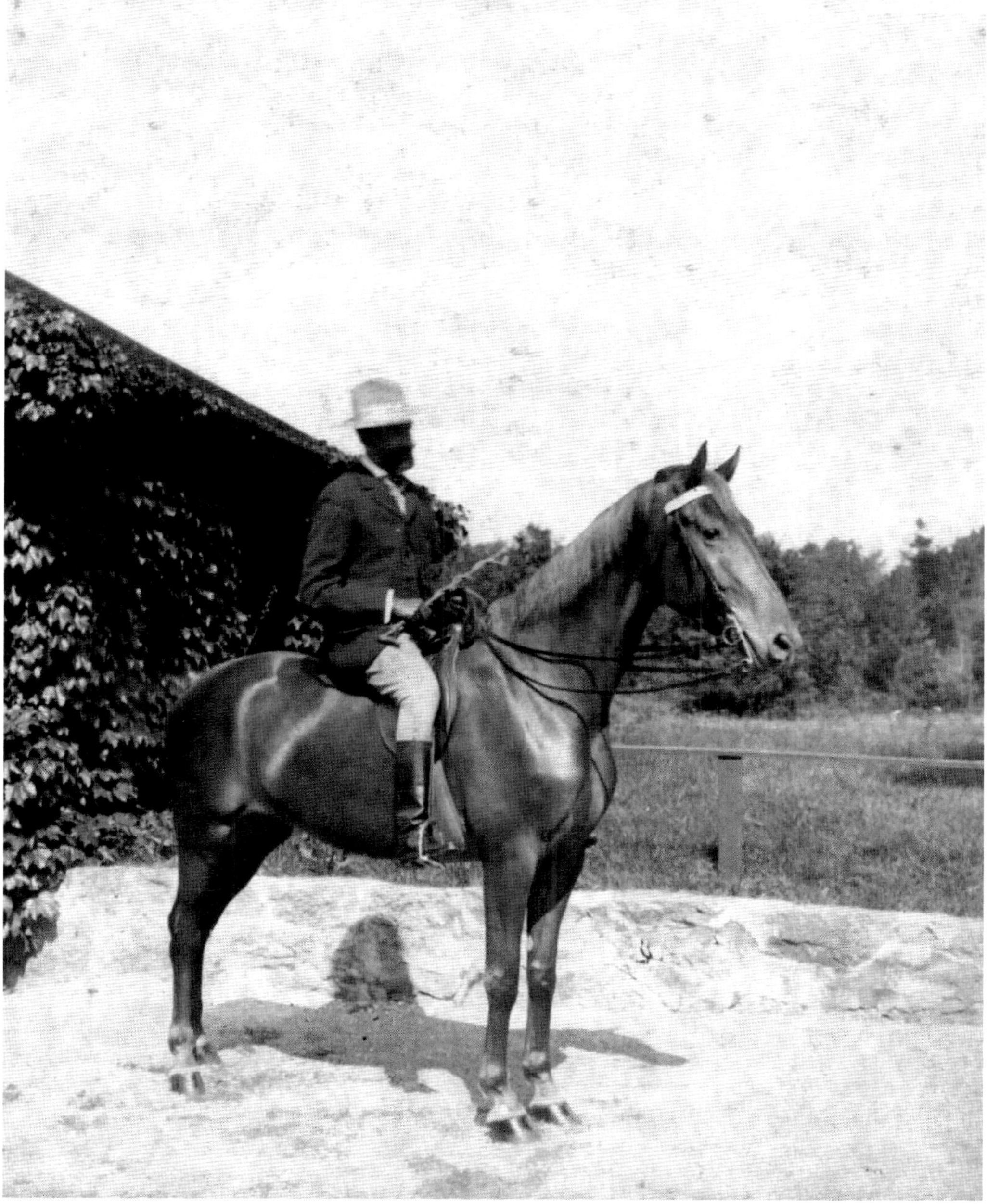

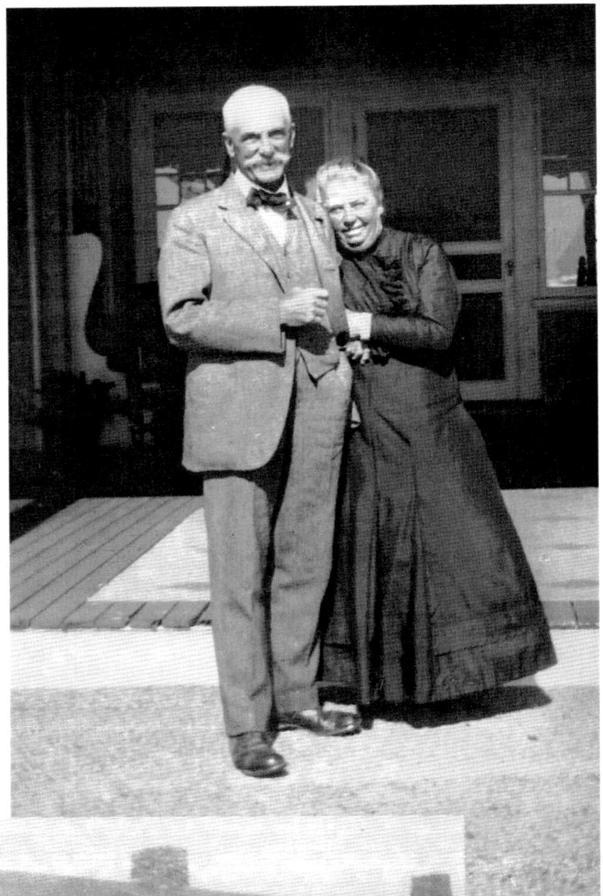

Edward N. Fenno (1845–1931)
Edward Fenno was one of the wealthy Boston visitors to Falmouth beginning in 1885 who changed the face and fortunes of the town. In 1887, he purchased 190 acres of land in Quissett to build his summer estate called "Makatiwik," now known as Fenno House. Edward and his wife spent quiet summers in Quissett with their two sons, Edward Jr. and H. Bradlee, and daughter Marian, playing on grass tennis courts and raising polo ponies. The estate was purchased in 1968 by the WHOI to become part of the Quissett campus. Ellen Marian Bradlee Fenno is pictured with Edward at right; below, she stands outside her lovely estate accompanied by her sons.

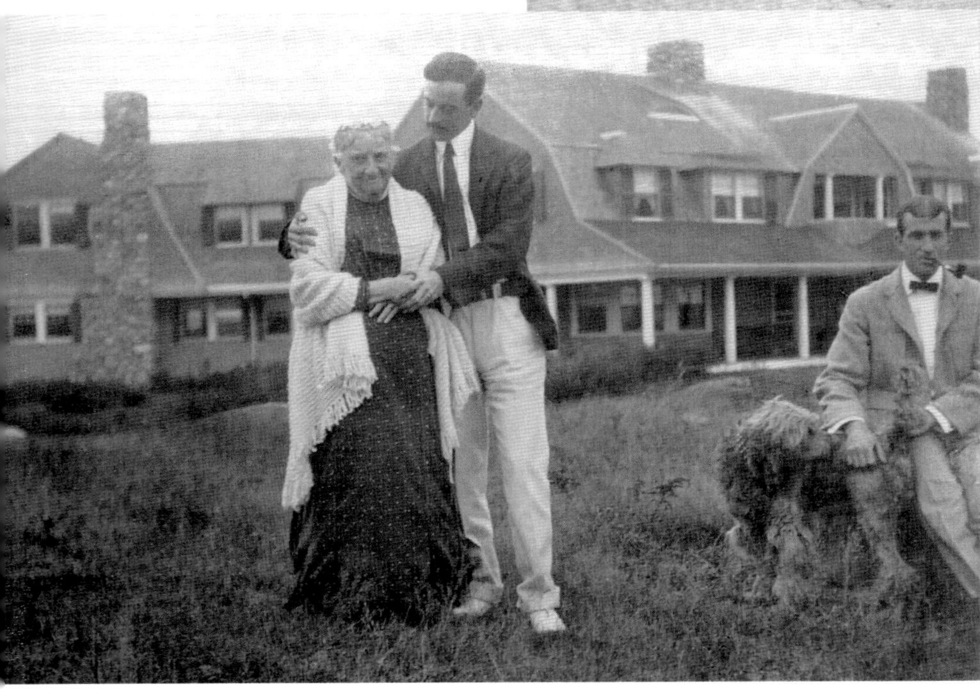

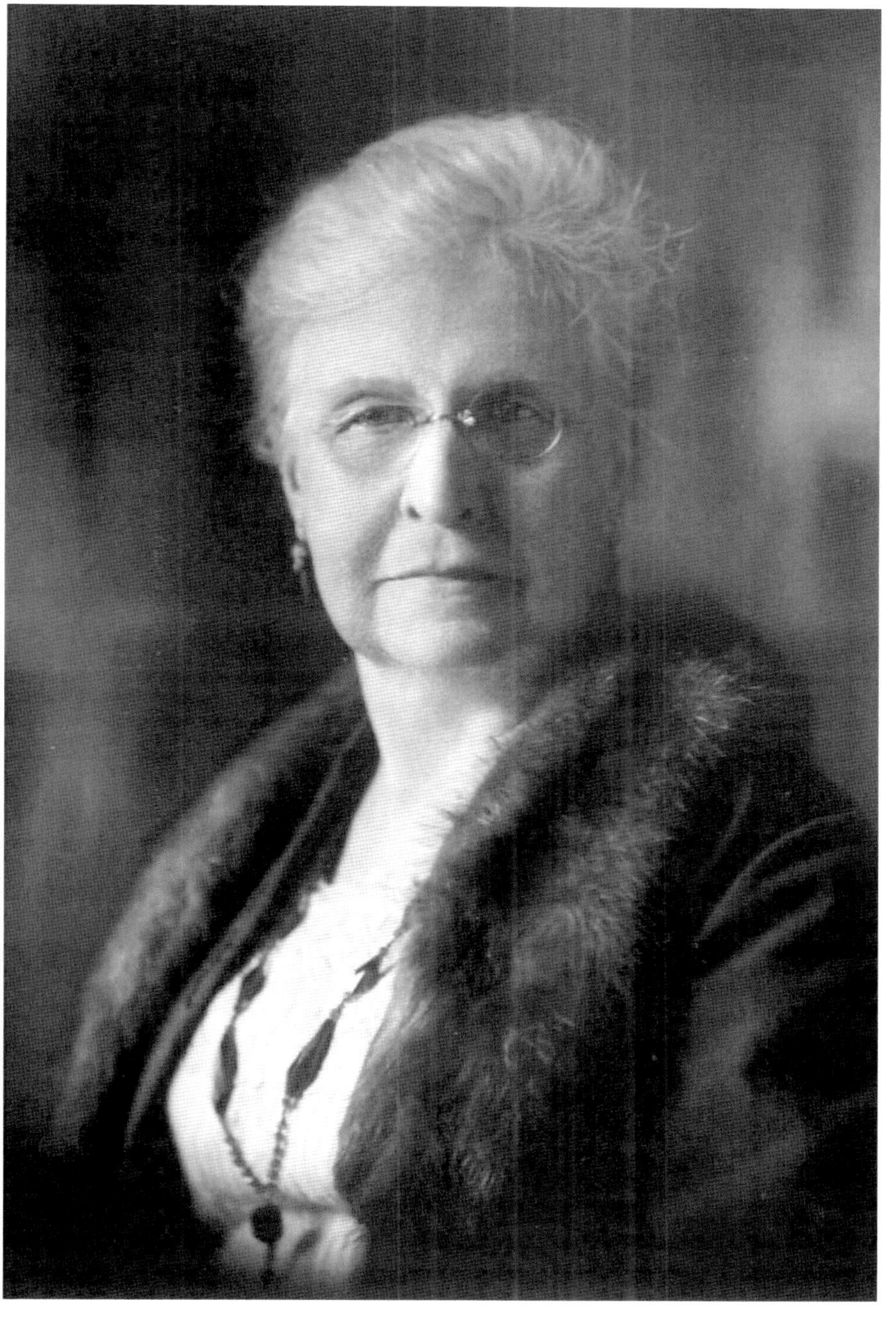

M. Sylvia Donaldson (1849–1937)
M. Sylvia Donaldson, a schoolteacher born in Falmouth, made her mark as the first woman elected to the Massachusetts House of Representatives. She was elected in 1923, only three years after women's suffrage, and wielded the gavel for one day, making her the first madam speaker of the state house in 1926. She died in 1937 at the age of 87 and is buried in the Oak Grove Cemetery next to her grandfather Dr. Hugh Donaldson. She left behind her writings and recollections of Falmouth in the historical society's archives.

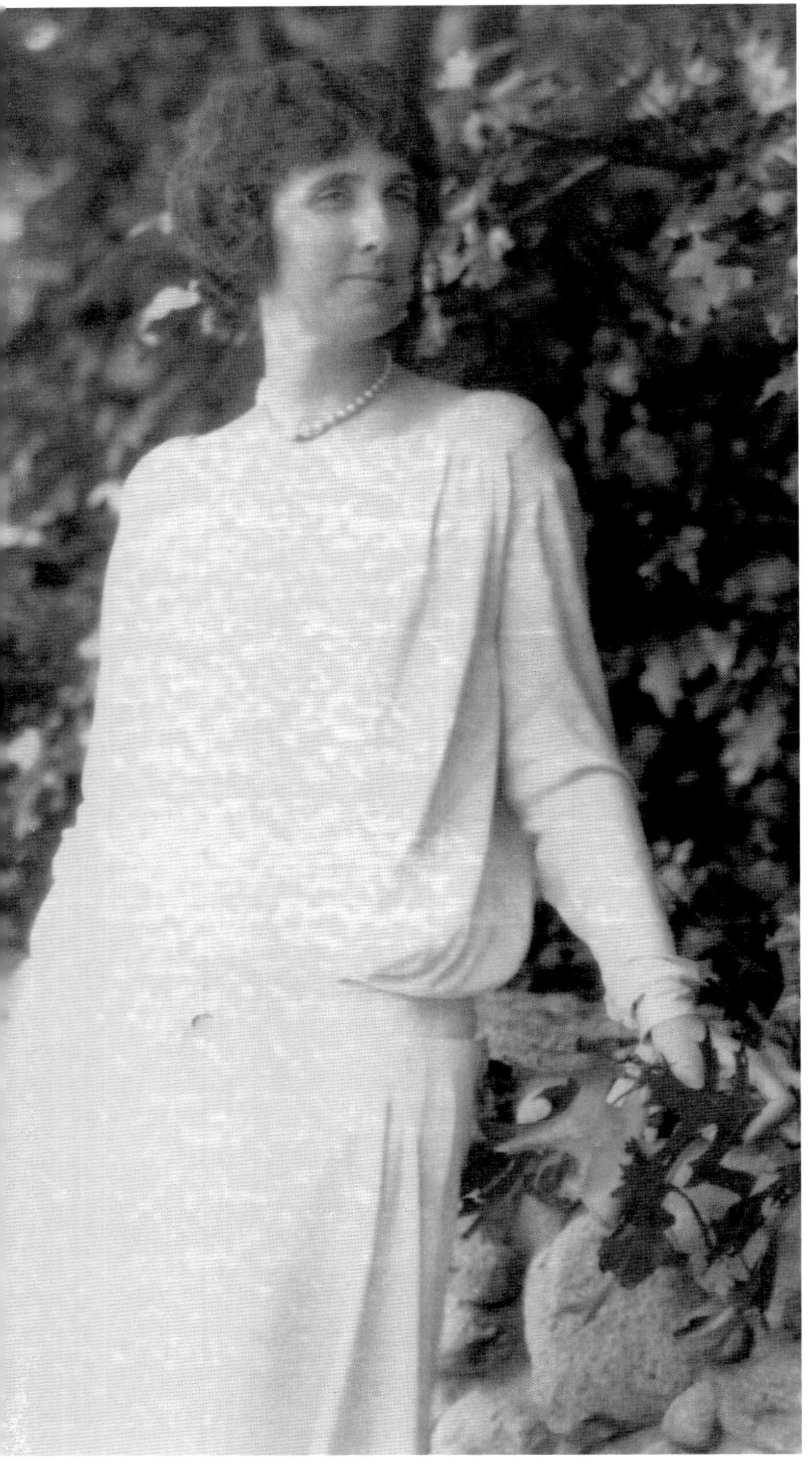

Frances Anita Crane (1900–1966)
Frances A. Crane, a socialite, lived in Woods Hole with her three sons. She is remembered today by the Wildlife Reserve in Hatchville that bears her name. After her untimely death by automobile accident, her sons requested that the family property sold to the state of Massachusetts as a reserve should retain her name. Her father, Charles R. Crane (1858–1939), was known internationally as a businessman, diplomat, philanthropist, and world traveler. Woodrow Wilson appointed him minister to China from 1920 to 1921, and by 1937, he had visited Russia 24 times. Crane summered on Jupiter Point in Woods Hole and in 1912. He commissioned the construction of the Airplane House overlooking Woods Hole Harbor, one of the most famous houses in Falmouth. Crane was the single largest benefactor of the Marine Biological Laboratory, Donating more than $1 million in money, land, and buildings from 1903 to 1937. He was president of the board of trustees and of the corporation of the MBL from 1904 to 1924, and on March 9, 1931, he was featured on the cover of *Time* magazine.

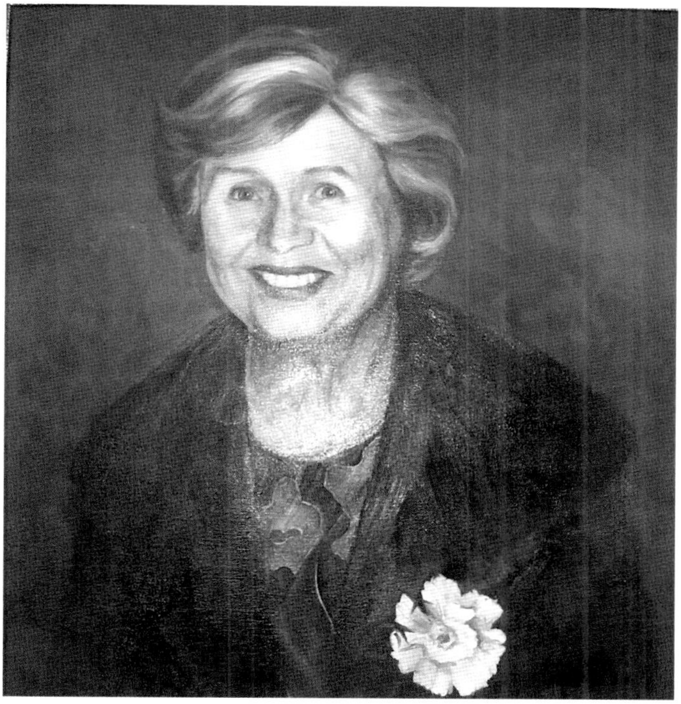

Constance B. Faxon (1918–1994)
Constance grew up in Fall River and came to Falmouth with her marriage to Raymond Faxon, noted financier. Constance had extensive hospital volunteer experience, first with the Blood Bank at Otis Air Force Base during World War II and later, chairing hospital boards including the Union Truesdale Hospital Building Board. In her will, she left $2.5 million to the planned ambulatory and outpatient wing to the Falmouth Hospital. Her husband, Raymond, also contributed to that fund. This facility is now known as the Faxon Center. Constance's portrait greets visitors at the front desk.

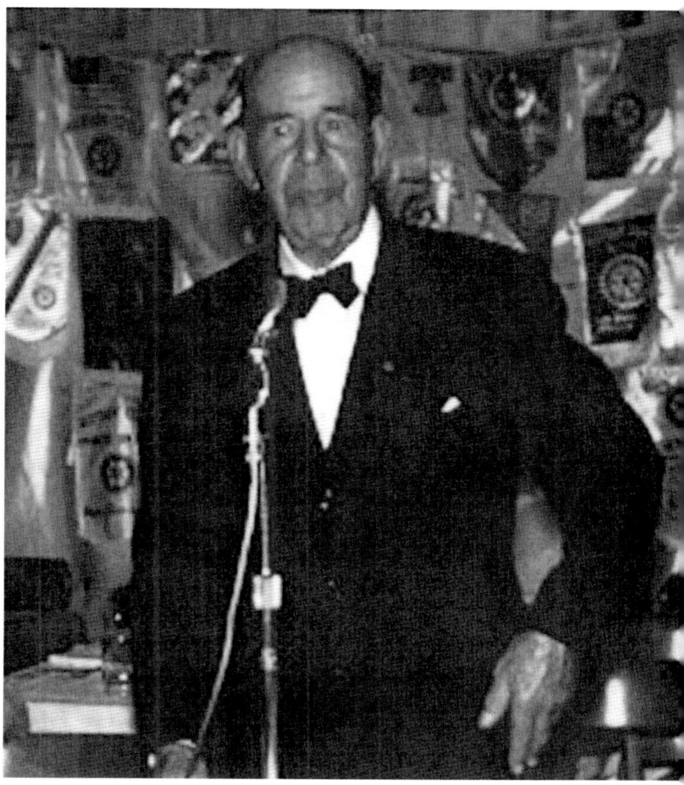

Dr. Nathaniel Wales Faxon (1880–1972)
Dr. Faxon was a summer resident of West Falmouth since his boyhood and became a year-round resident in 1953. This was also an important move for Falmouth. Just as a number of local physicians were organizing to build a hospital in Falmouth, the right man for the times was on the scene. Dr. Faxon had retired from an outstanding career as physician and hospital administrator. He was director of Massachusetts General Hospital for 14 years, was a Harvard Medical School graduate, and had expertise in the construction and design of medical facilities. He became an advisor and chairman of the Falmouth Hospital Committee in 1958. His expertise was instrumental in the construction of the Falmouth hospital building.

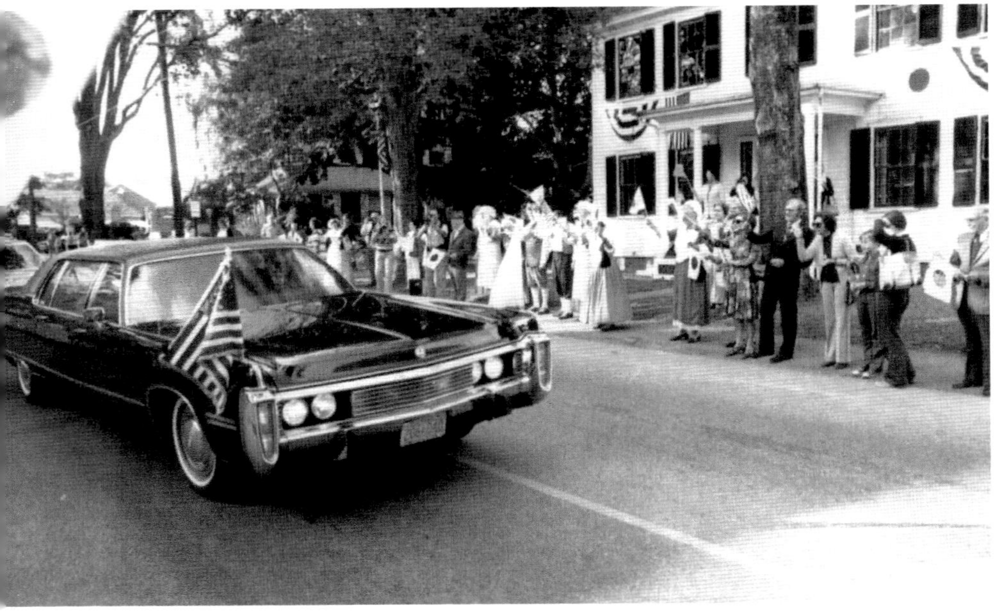

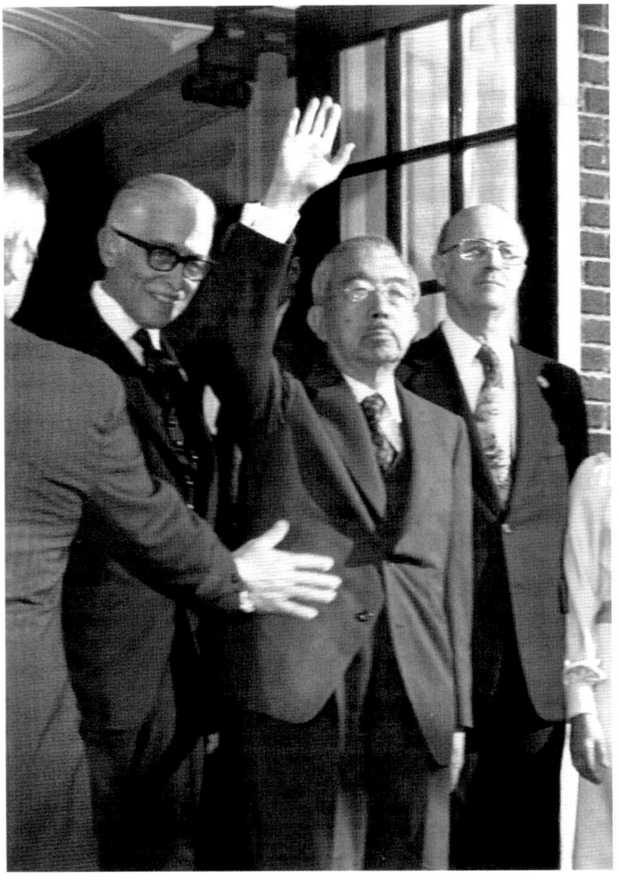

Emperor Hirohito (1901–1989) On October 4, 1975, at the request of several scientists from MBL and WHOI, Emperor Hirohito visited Falmouth and the village of Woods Hole. The emperor and his wife, Empress Nagako, came through town in a nine-car motorcade with stops at the Falmouth Artists' Guild and a slow drive by the Katharine Lee Bates house. With much media and secret service attention, the emperor was greeted by Paul M. Fye, director of the Woods Hole Oceanographic Institution from 1958 to 1977, before visiting with Dr. Howard Saunders and others. The emperor left a signed copy of his scientific paper for the MBL/WHOI library, and the empress left a Japanese doll at the Falmouth Artists' Guild. (Courtesy WHOI/MBL archives.)

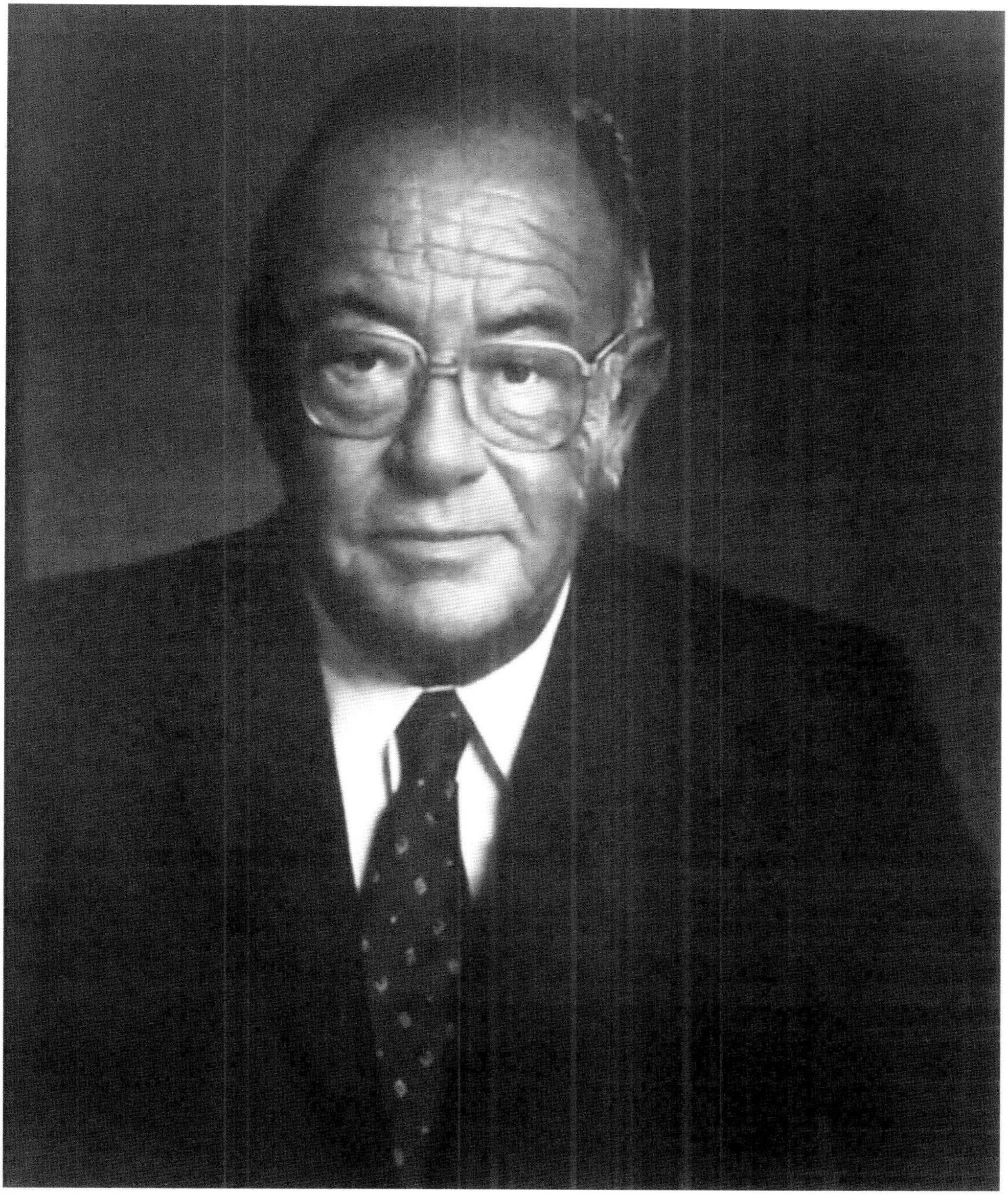

Josiah K. Lilly III (1916–1995)
As head of the Lilly Endowment Inc., Josiah Lilly's main business was philanthropy. He was a resident of West Falmouth since 1947, savoring all the pleasures of that village, including the West Falmouth Village Market. With his passing, many expressed the sentiment: "Mr. Lilly sure has done a lot for this town." He financially backed substantial projects that mattered to Falmouth, including the Falmouth Hospital, the JML Care Center, Falmouth Academy, the Visiting Nurses Association, Beebe Woods, the Cape Cod Conservatory, and the Ashumet Holly Reservation. He kept a low profile, preferring to remain anonymous when he could. His portrait at the Falmouth Hospital is probably the one exception and a reminder that Lilly loved Falmouth. (Courtesy T. Richard Miner Jr.)

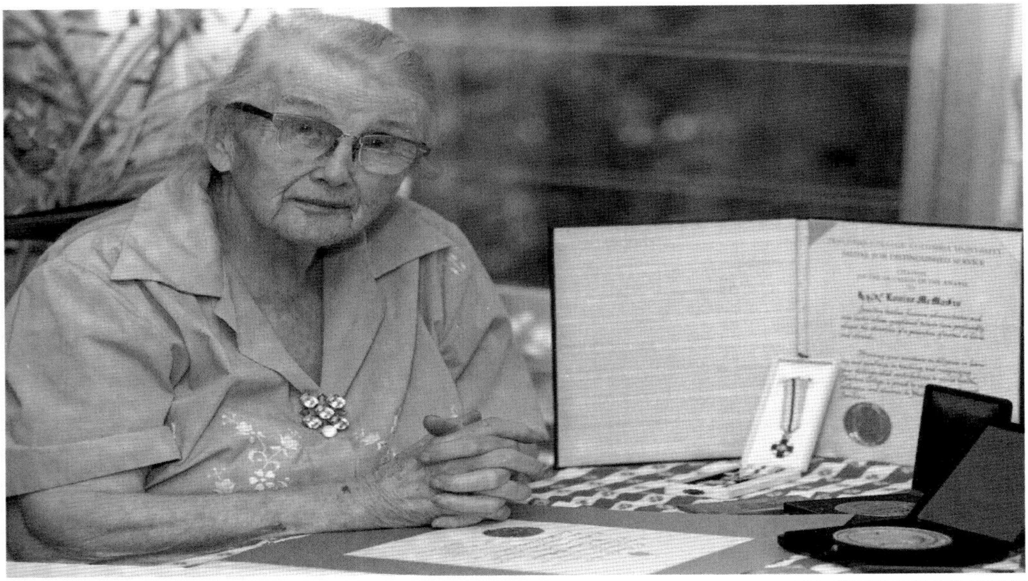

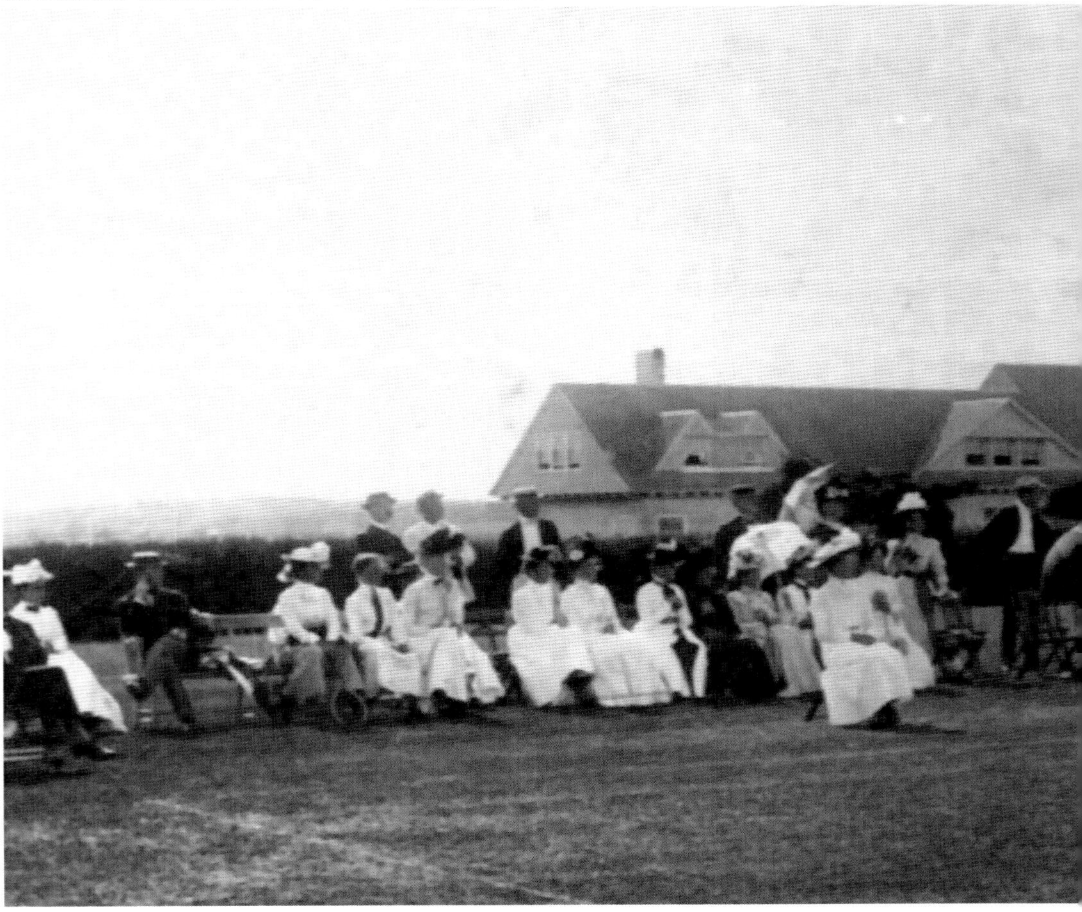

R. Louise McManus (1894–1993) (OPPOSITE PAGE)
Dr. McManus was a Sippewissett resident who made a lasting impact on nursing, locally and internationally. Her achievements were many: being the first nurse to earn a doctor of philosophy degree, promoting the creation of schools of nursing in colleges, establishing standardized testing for nursing licensure, and developing a patient's bill of rights. She was a birthright Quaker and followed her long family tradition at the West Falmouth Meeting House. After creating schools of nursing at Columbia University, Turkey, and elsewhere, she helped with the creation of the School of Nursing at Cape Cod Community College during her retirement. She was a recipient of the Florence Nightingale Medal and is listed in the National Women's Hall of Fame. (Courtesy Nickerson Archives, Cape Cod Community.)

Richard Olney (1835–1917)
Richard Olney lived in a formidable mansion on Mill Road in 1880. In 1895, he was named secretary of state under President Cleveland. Known as a stern, brusque character among locals, he was also known to play tennis into his 80s and hosted legendary tennis matches on his grass court. A creature of habit, he spent his summer vacations from 1880 to 1893 on Vineyard Sound in Falmouth. His mansion was damaged in the hurricanes of 1938 and was demolished in 1944. Shown here is a tennis match on the grass courts of the Olney's Mill road estate.

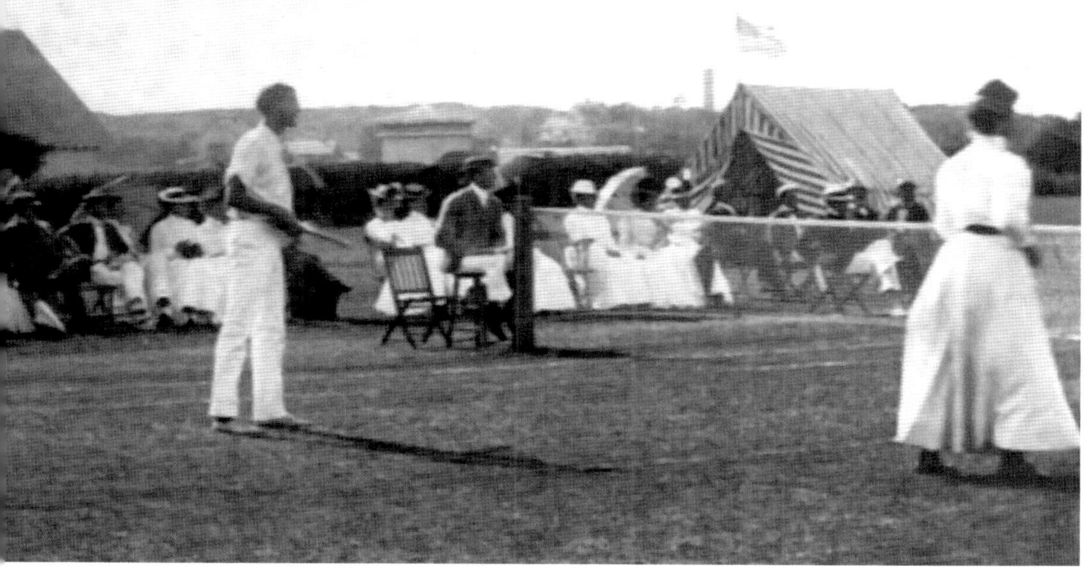

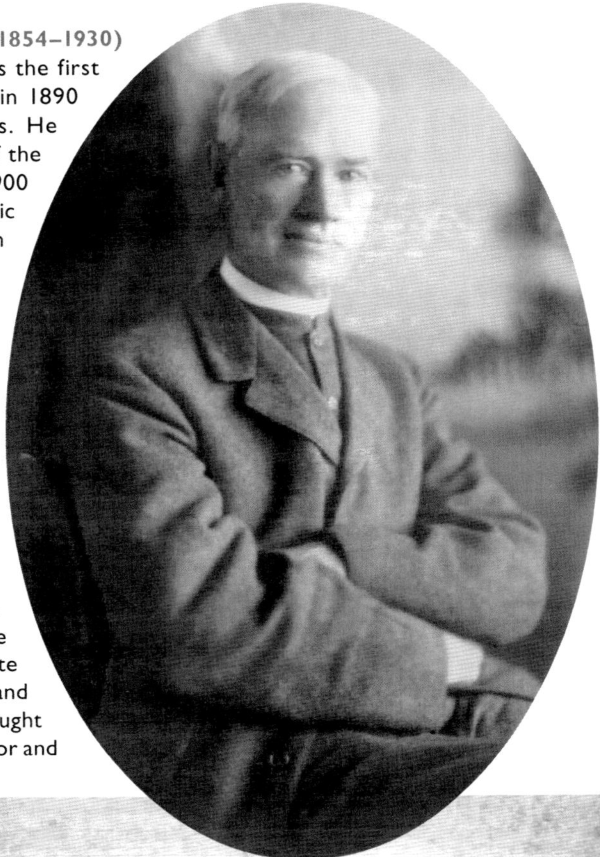

Rev. Henry Herbert Smythe (1854–1930)
Rev. Henry Herbert Smythe was the first rector of St. Barnabas Church in 1890 and served there for 32 years. He was influential in the founding of the Falmouth Historical Society in 1900 and the building of a separate public library, and he participated in commemorative events such as Old Home Week and the tercentenary of Gosnold Landing. A member of the Mayflower descendants, his extensive genealogical records for his church members and other Falmouth residents are still held at the Falmouth Historical Society. His name is still familiar in town due to the still extant and prestigious Smythe Scholarship offered to college-bound Falmouth students. He was left a widower in 1900 with two daughters. In the rare photograph below, Charlotte W. Smythe and daughters Evelyn and Helen, along with a friend, are taught the fine art of clamming by neighbor and friend Capt. Thomas Lawrence.

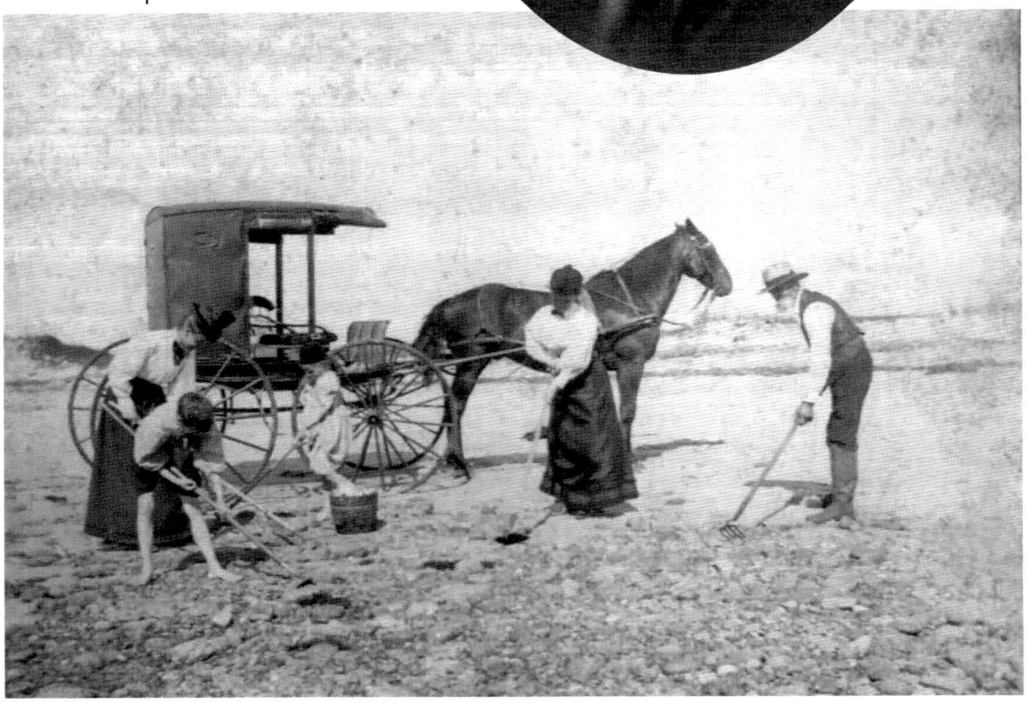

CHAPTER SIX

Movers and Doers

East Falmouth folk were farmers. We used to say that Woods Hole, and Falmouth village, have all the glory. But it was the Portuguese who built the town.

—Alene Soares, oral history

The following citizens tell many tales of hardships and many tales of family togetherness. They are craftsmen, laborers, and farmers who provided the basic services of the town. They are the families that stayed. As Alene Soares stated in her oral history (which is part of the Strawberry Collection at the Falmouth Historical Society), they are the ones who built this town.

The newcomers are the immigrants who came from Ireland, French Canada, Brava, the Azores, and Cape Verde. Some came with a craft but most came with a love of the land and a strong sense of independence. Joe Medeiros is a success story, along with Tony Andrews.

They are from a Falmouth where the strawberry and cranberry reigned and agriculture and tending the land were key to living well. Folks from this era took pride in the size of their families and acreage and the price of their crops. The Falmouth Festival of Strawberries was an experiment in green tourism, well ahead of its time, that created Strawberry Queens and Courts and many memories. Many in this chapter lived exceptionally long lives, survivors to the end.

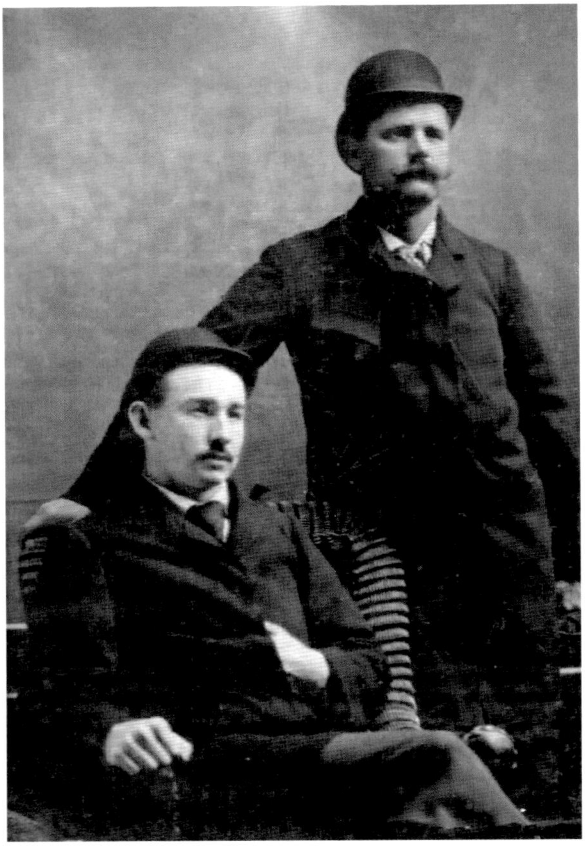

Edwin J. Donnelly (1870–1947)
Edwin Donnelly (seated) is shown with his brother Thomas as they arrived in Falmouth around 1890. The Donnellys represent one of the earliest Irish family migrations to Falmouth. A barber by trade, Edwin, known as "Pop," opened his first shop at the Hotel Falmouth on the corner of Shore and Main Streets. It was here he met his wife, Marie, a chambermaid from St. Pierre and Miquelon, a French Canadian island. A summer barbershop was set up in the Tower Hotel at Falmouth Heights for his summer customers as pictured in *Falmouth by the Sea*. Early Catholics in town walked to Woods Hole to attend St. Joseph Church, the only parish in Falmouth until St. Patrick's Church and St. Anthony's Church. Edwin Donnelly became chairman of the Democratic Party in town. This fledgling political party later became a force in town with republican rivalries under H.V. Lawrence.

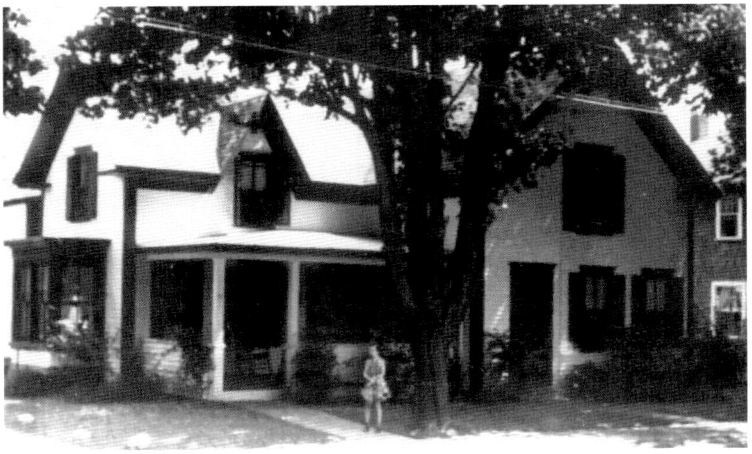

Alice Murphy (1929–)
Alice Murphy is the granddaughter of Edwin and Marie Donnelly. The family has lived at 30 Shore Street since 1900. Their house has been described as a shrine to the Donnellys. Alice's uncle Robert Donnelly lived at 36 Shore Street and worked as a linotype operator for the *Enterprise* newspaper. Alice Murphy is a true native of Falmouth. She either knows every detail of Falmouth's history or knows someone who knows the full story.

Joe Medeiros (1908–2000)

Joe Medeiros was one of the last Portuguese settlers living in Davisville. "Joe T." or "Vovo," as he was called, came to Falmouth when he was five years old from New Bedford. His father died at the age of 48, and Joe was forced to leave school in the ninth grade to support his family and work on the family farm. They grew mainly strawberries, along with turnips, corn, potatoes, grapes, and apples. He developed his carpentry skills and joined the government call for the construction of Camp Edwards. He formed a partnership with Antone Souza to create Medeiros and Souza and began building cape-style houses in Menauhant, Pirate's Cove, and elsewhere. He worked with Gunnar Peterson and Buckminster Fuller in creating the Dome restaurant. He retired at the age of 79. Joe participated in an oral history project in 2000 to explain the Falmouth of his times.

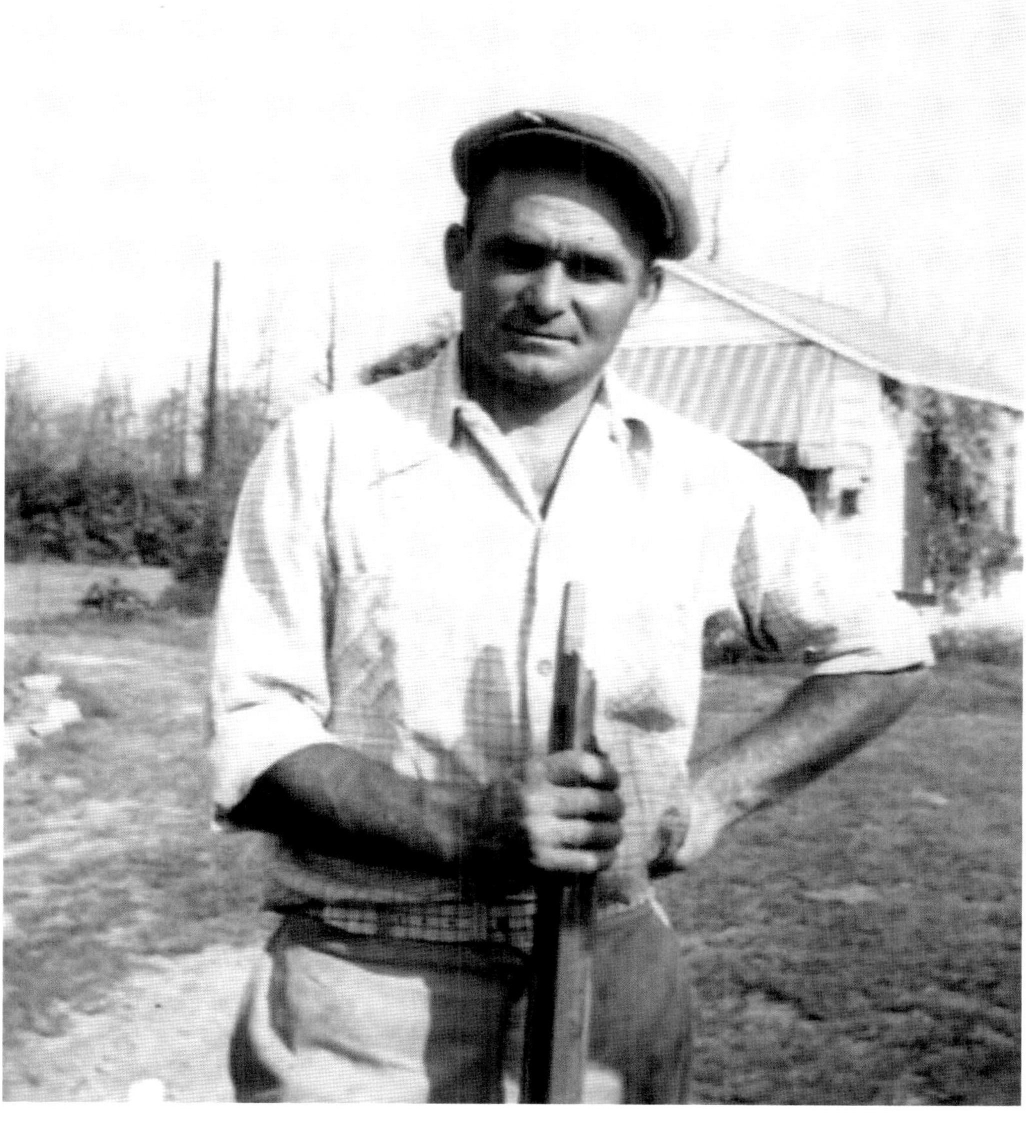

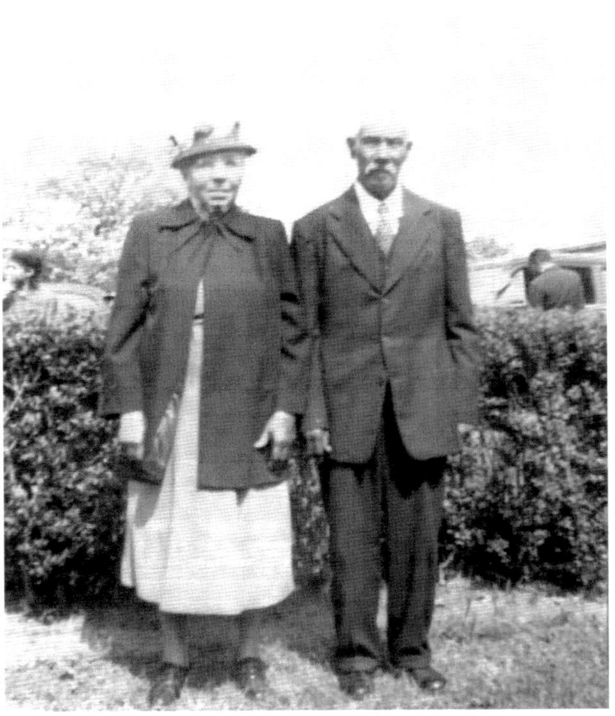

Manuel J. Roderick (1874–1965)
After a seafaring life, Manuel Roderick came to East Falmouth from Brava in 1900. He and his wife, Mary, preferred to make a living off the land, working the cranberry bogs and later the strawberry fields. He was able to buy a house in 1924 and farmed until he was 80. At their 74th wedding anniversary, the Rodericks were able to celebrate with their two children, five grandchildren, 12 great-grandchildren, and five great-great grandchildren.

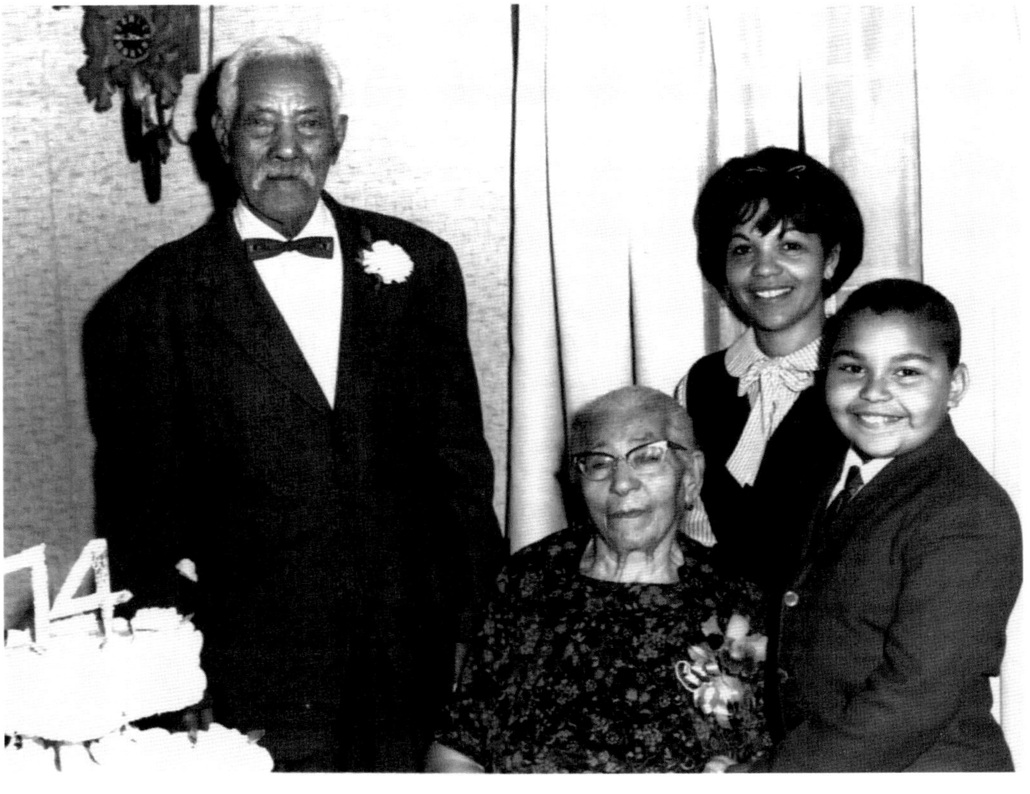

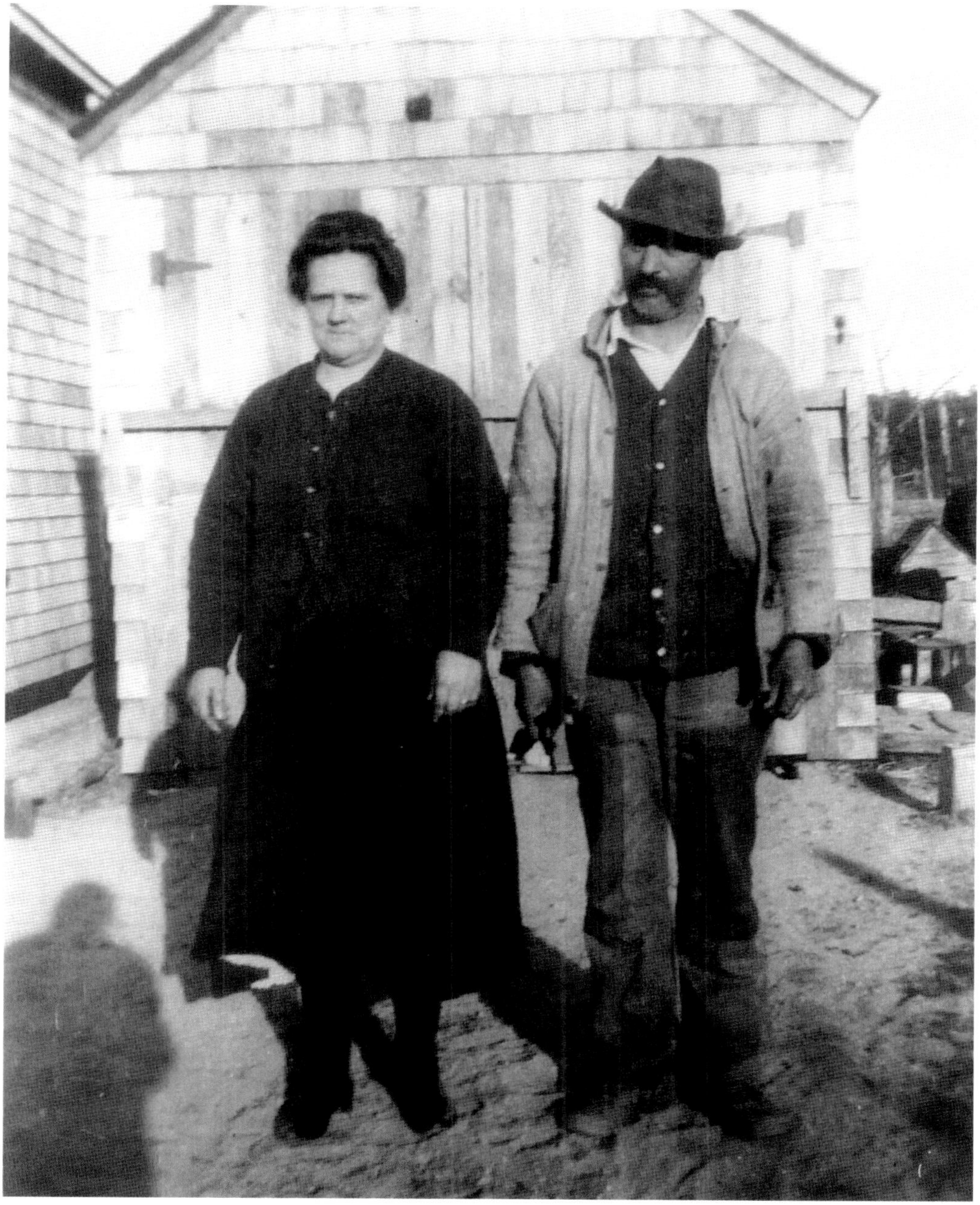

Manuel "Manny" Benevides (1883–1942)
Manuel and Mary Benevides had one of the largest strawberry farms—40 acres located on Davisville Road. He brought his family to Falmouth in 1910 and raised 12 children. Four died as babies, leaving three sons and five daughters to work the family farm. Arlene Soares, one of the last survivors of this family, remembered the hard work and the great pride of the East Falmouth Portuguese.

Tony Andrews (Antonio de Andrade, 1904–2008)
Tony Andrews emigrated from Fogo Island, Azores, starting his farm with a few acres in Falmouth in 1927. He once bragged that he could plant 5,000 strawberry plants in one day by hand. His 57-acre family farm became the first to have irrigation and became widely known as a "pick-your-own" operation. Andrews served on several state committees to encourage farming in the Falmouth area. He lived to celebrate his 100 birthday and to see the Tony Andrews Farm continue through his sons. Below is Tony Andrews as a young emigrant to Falmouth. At right, Tony and Marina Andrews were honored at the 2001 Heritage Awards.

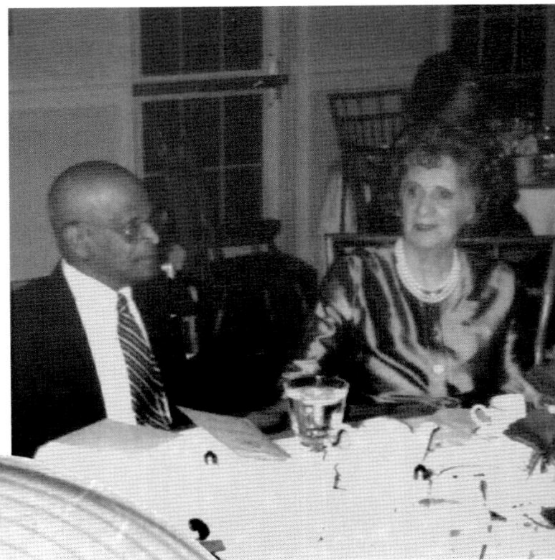

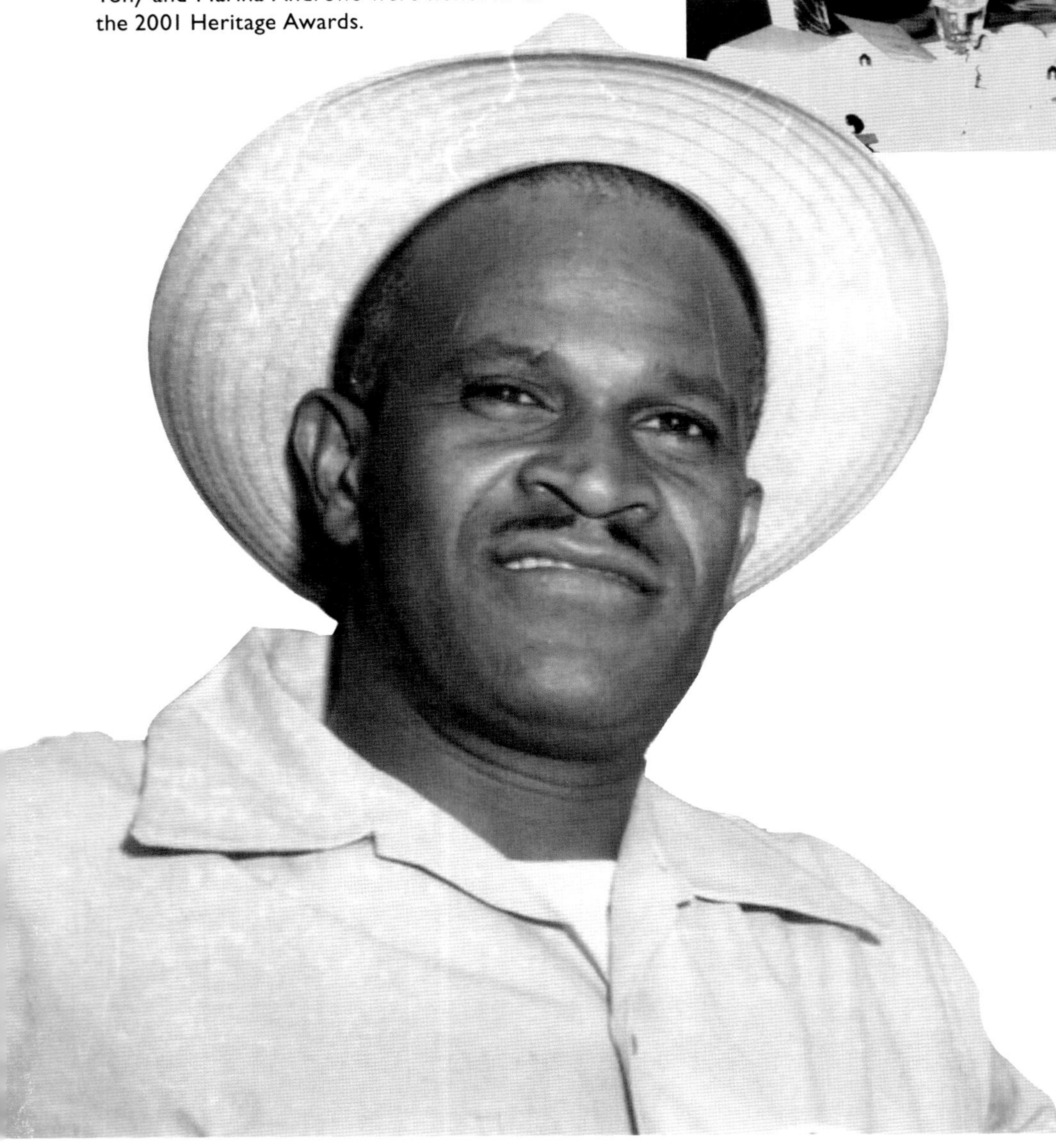

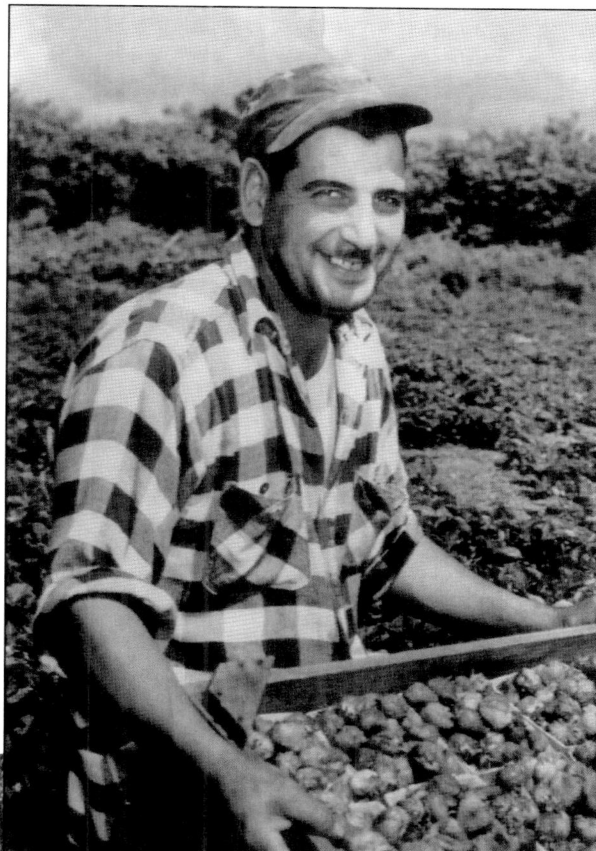

Albert Marks (1923–1985)
Albert Marks was one of several Teaticket growers to promote the first Strawberry Festival in 1951. He worked his own strawberry farm for several years until later working as a heavy equipment operator. His brother Edward L. Marks Jr., also of Teaticket fame, served on the Teaticket Civic Association and as town selectman. The former town poor house building was named the Edward L. Marks Jr. office building in his honor. Below is a publicity photograph showing the Marks Strawberry farm produce ready for market.

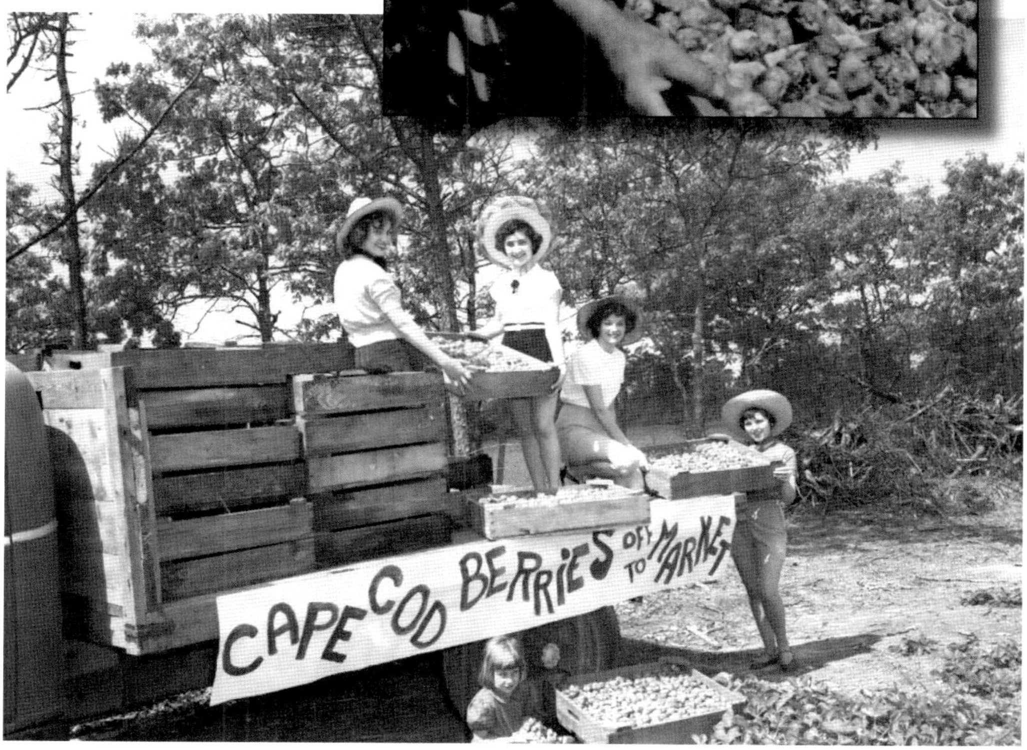

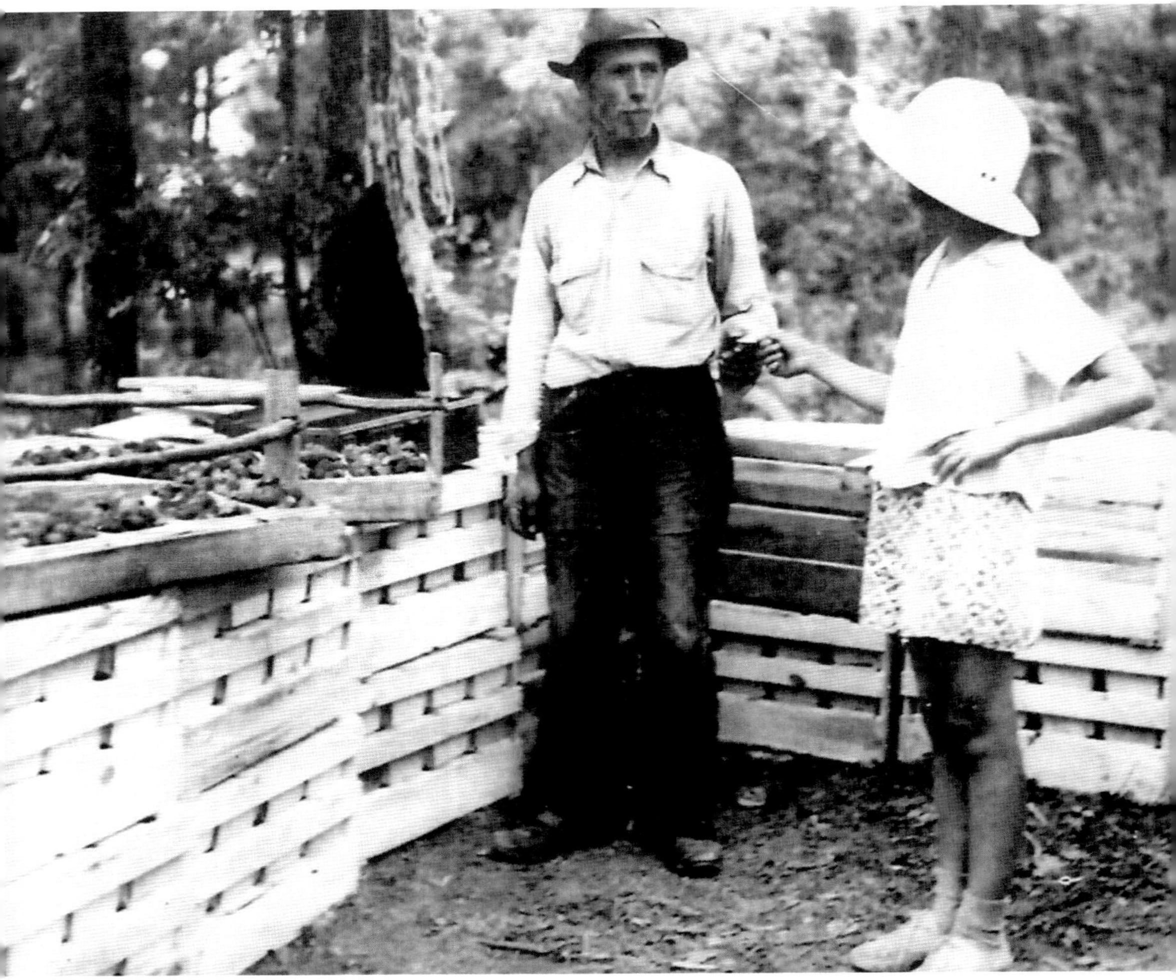

Manuel Emerald (1896–1956)
Manuel Emerald followed his brother John from the Azores to become one of the first settlers in East Falmouth. He bought his four-acre plot on Davisville Road in 1906 and called this home with his bride, Mary Estrella. They raised five daughters and three sons on this prosperous strawberry farm. The boss, as he was known, had a strong work ethic and was an important part of the agricultural dominance of Falmouth from the 1930s to 1950s. His homestead was purchased by the Town of Falmouth in 1995 and remains a shrine to this family and to this local industry.

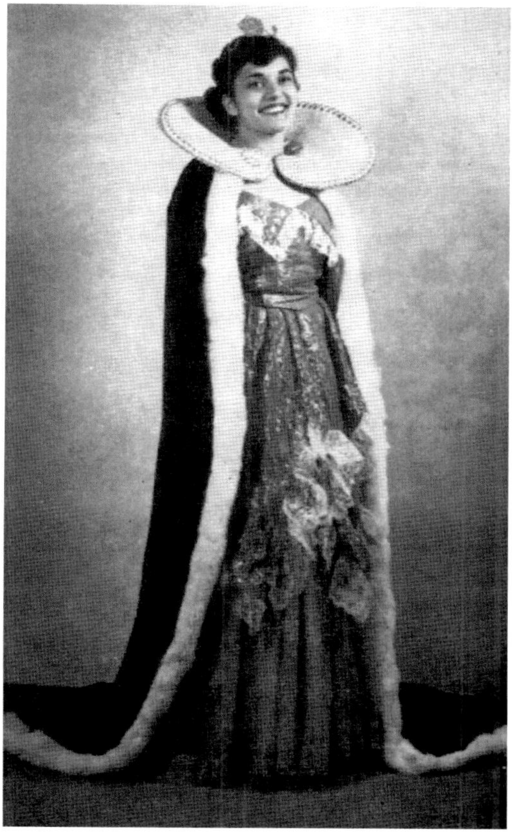

Cynthia Augusta Botelho

Cynthia Augusta Botelho was selected as the first Strawberry Queen in the 1951 Cape Cod Festival of Strawberries. This homegrown event featuring parades, strawberry picking, and a pie-eating contest was held to promote local farmers. The queen and her court were selected by virtue of the number of festival tickets that they sold. Cynthia always felt the honor was in part recognition of her father, Charles Augusta, who had organized the Strawberry Growers Association, and her grandfather Antone Augusta, one of the earliest strawberry growers in town.

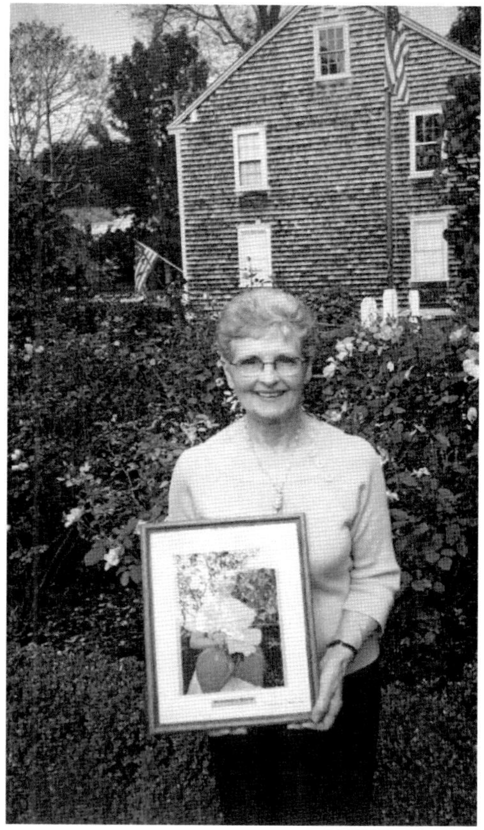

Margaret Medeiros Hunter

Margaret Hunter is shown with her prized portrait as Strawberry Queen of the Falmouth Festival of Strawberries on August 3, 1952. Her portrait, which made the cover of Boston's *Globe Magazine*, was a great source of pride for Margaret and her family.

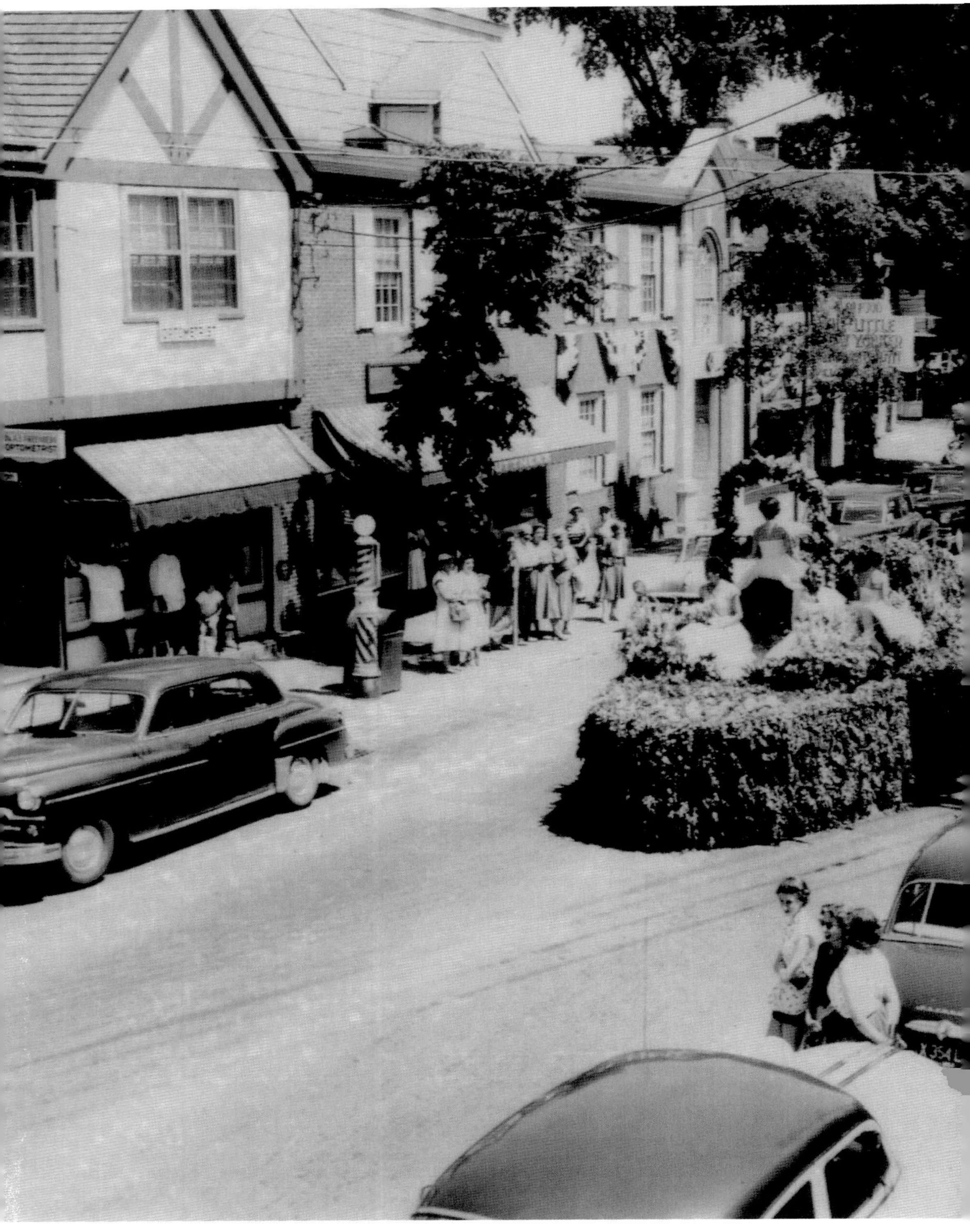
OPTOMETRIST
OPTOMETRIST

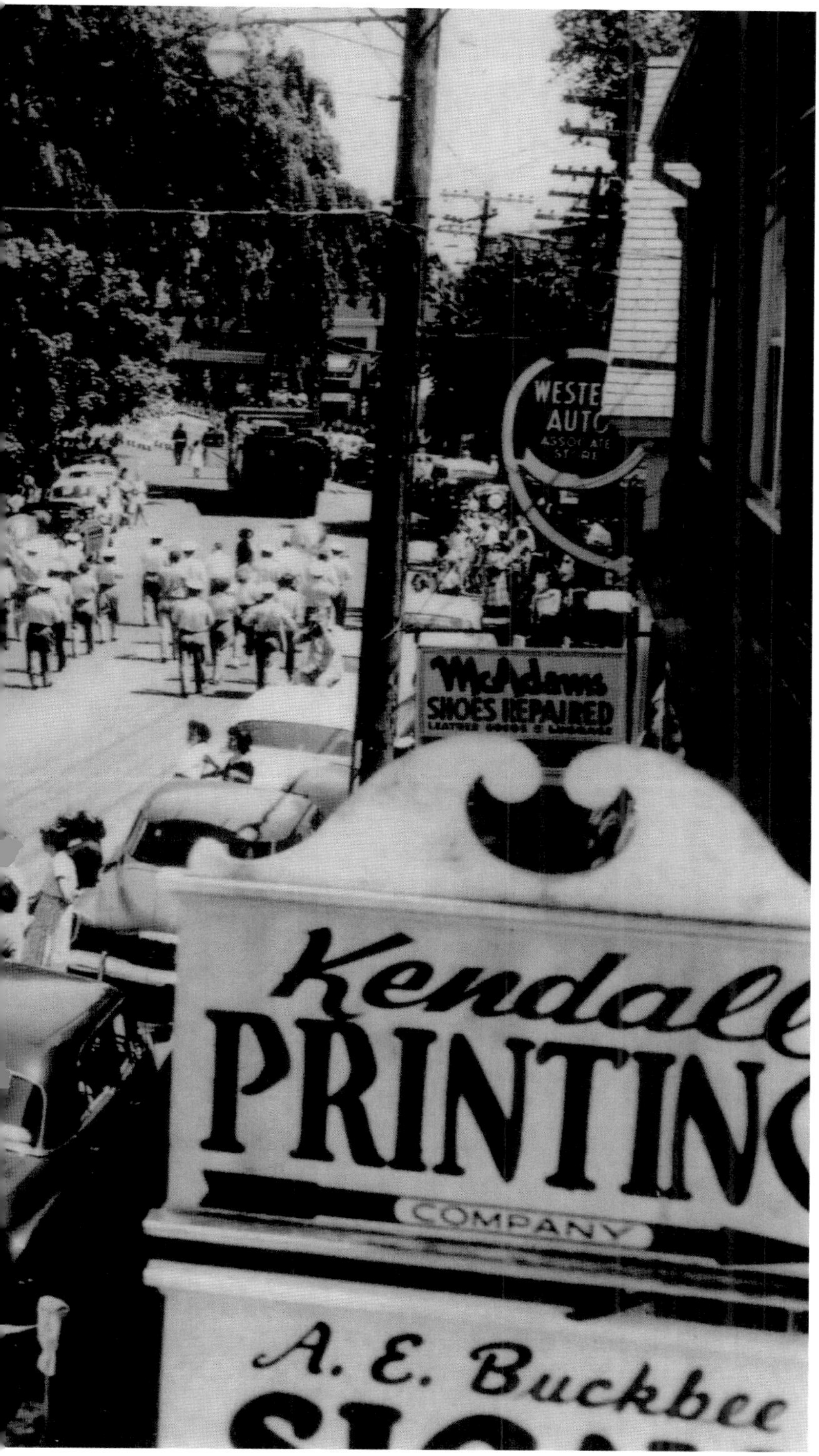

Cape Cod Festival of Strawberries
The Cape Cod Festival of Strawberries, later known as the Falmouth Festival of Strawberries, lasted from 1951 to 1955. It promoted tourism, but it was also hoped it might revive the strawberry industry in Falmouth. The festival was succeeded by the farmers markets and the St. Barnabas strawberry event every June.

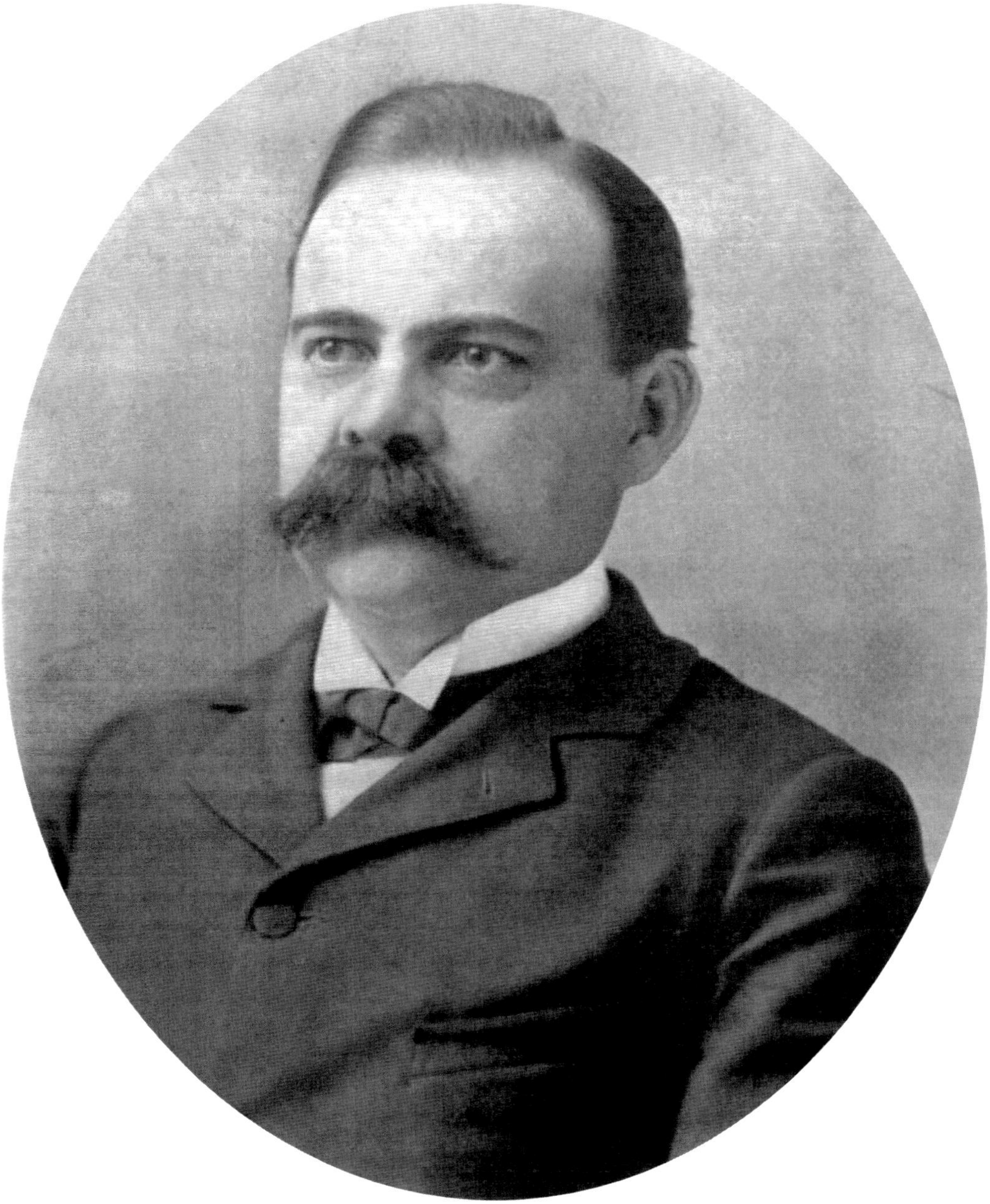

Rev. Charles Washburn (1860–1931)
As minister at the Congregational church, Rev. Charles Washburn was known for his religious influence but also for his civic achievements. He formed the first board of trade in Falmouth and published two pictorial books geared for the tourist trade: *Falmouth By the Sea* and *Residential Falmouth*. Once called a go-getting clergy, he envisioned Falmouth's future as a summer resort. His stay in Falmouth was from 1890 to 1898, but he understood the sea captain legacy of Falmouth and organized the creation of the Mariners Memorial on Locust Street. He saved souls, created the first public relations campaign for the seaside resort, and ushered in a new industry and a new wave of tourists.

CHAPTER SEVEN

Falmouth's Favorite Sons and Daughters

Like the white sails of the Sound, / Hast thou seen the years drift by?

—Katharine Lee Bates, "The Falmouth Bell"

Many of the following citizens have been honored with their own day, or have a school, street, park, or other piece of Falmouth named in their honor. Some are those who have touched lives of locals and heightened their vision and horizons.

These are the folk that are known by name or should be known by name and face. Not all of the these individuals are famous outside of Falmouth, but some of them, like Katharine Lee Bates and Rachel Carson, are world famous. These are people locals admire for their achievements, contributions, and success at being outstanding Falmouth citizens.

Honorees include a recreation director, a school principal, citizen activists, a school bus driver, a newspaper columnist, a graveyard preservationist, an environmentalist, a museum docent, and a restaurateur. Some in this chapter have earned the Heritage Award given annually by the Falmouth Historical Society, and all have earned an undeniable part in the history of Falmouth.

Katharine Lee Bates (1859–1929)
Katharine Lee Bates, poet and educator, became a celebrity in her own time as author of "America the Beautiful." Although she left Falmouth at the age of 11 and became a professor of English literature at Wellesley College for 39 years, she always remained mindful of Falmouth. Len Miele, a local author, described Falmouth Village as Katharine's playground. It can be said that along with writing an anthem for her country, Katharine wrote several anthems to her hometown. The following is an excerpt from "Falmouth:" "Lovely it lies within the rose of dawn / That village of my childhood by the sea, / A score of miles from railroads, that to me / Were marvelous as dragon-haunts agone." The following is an excerpt from "The Falmouth Bell:" "Never were there a friendlier folk / Than Falmouth by the sea, / Neighbor-households that invoke Pride of sailor-pedigree."

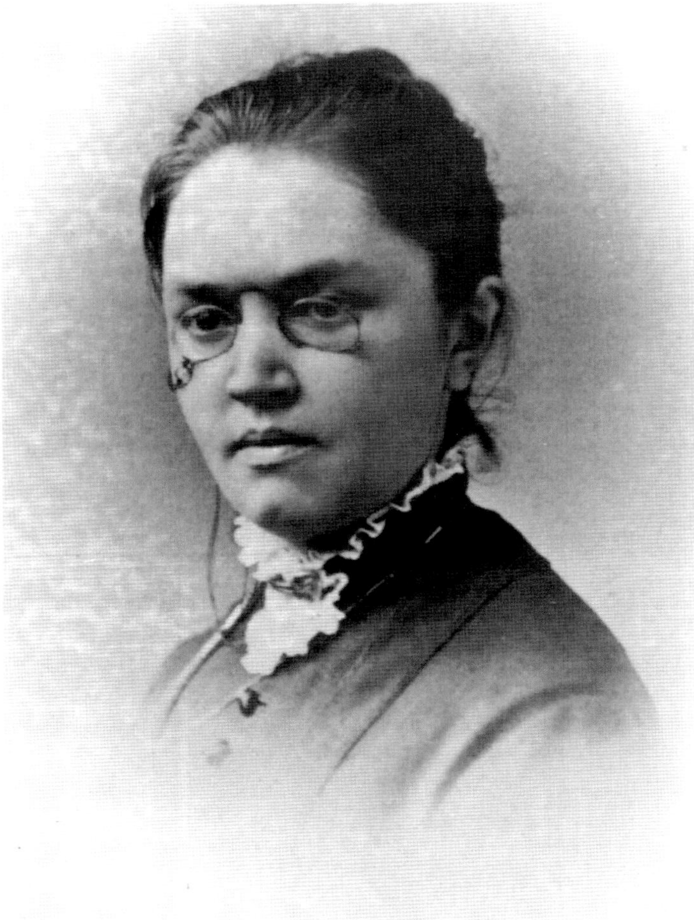

Rachel Carson (1907–1964) (OPPOSITE PAGE)
Rachel Carson is pictured in Woods Hole in 1951. In the background is the Woods Hole dock where Sam Cahoon's Fish Market once stood. This world-renowned scientist became a summer visitor and researcher in 1929 with continued visits until 1962. To mark the 50th anniversary of the publication of *Silent Spring*, a statue of Rachel is slated for Waterfront Park in Woods Hole. (Photograph by Edwin Gray, courtesy Connecticut College.)

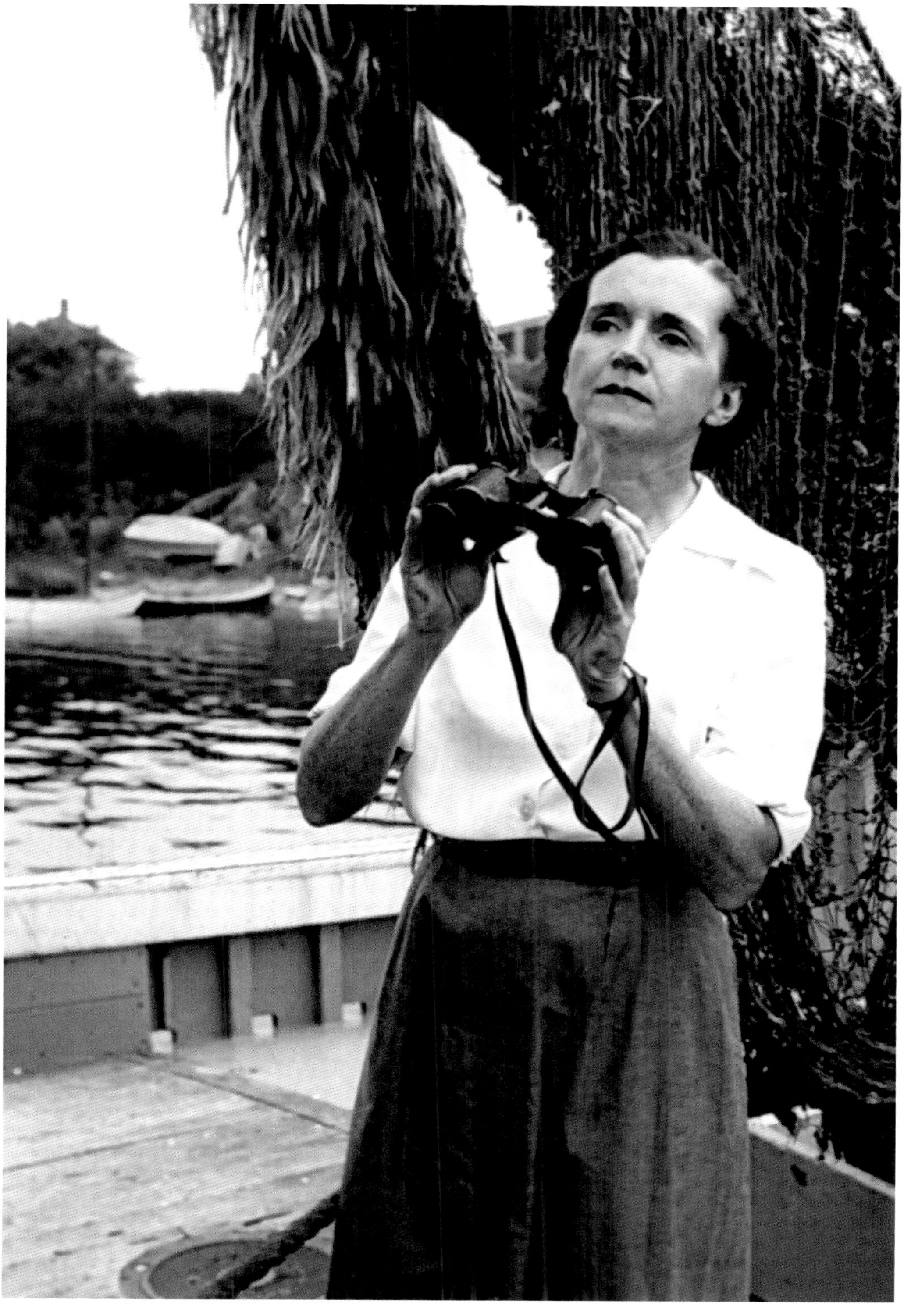

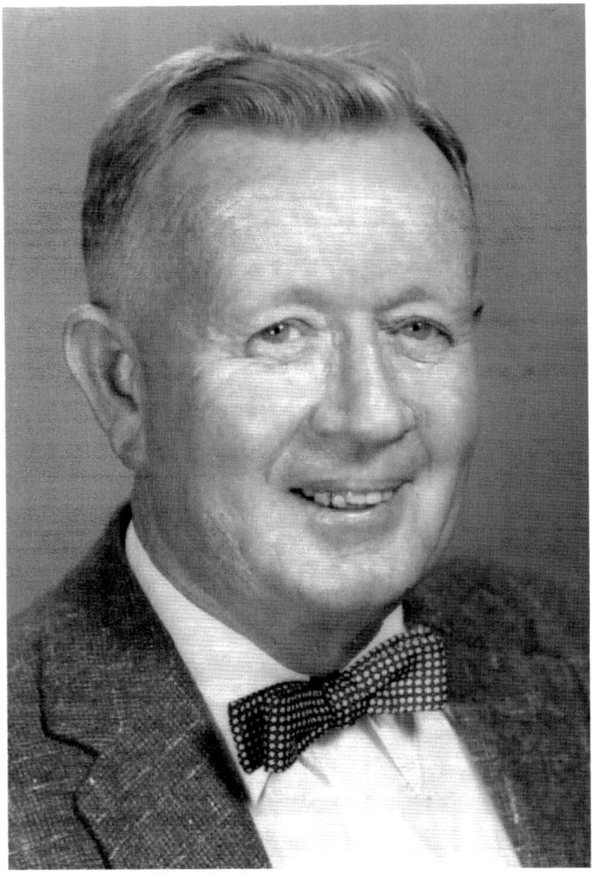

Augustus "Gus" T. Canty (1903–1982)

Gus Canty was a Bates College graduate and youth worker who first came to Falmouth to work with the USO at Camp Edwards. He started as recreation director in Falmouth in 1947 and never looked back. It was on May 3, 1964, when Falmouth celebrated Gus Canty Appreciation Day, that he knew how much he was appreciated. The local newspaper featured the headline "1,000 Honor Beloved 'Rec' Director Gus Canty." There was a parade, a field day program at Fuller Field, speakers, proclamations, and even a flyover. He was called "an institution in himself" and it was said, "Falmouth residents from every walk of life—old and young alike—today poured out their hearts to this beloved Irishman from East Boston." Below, Gus Canty stands behind the microphone on Gus Canty Day with Marina Andrews at the far right. (Courtesy Tom Canty.)

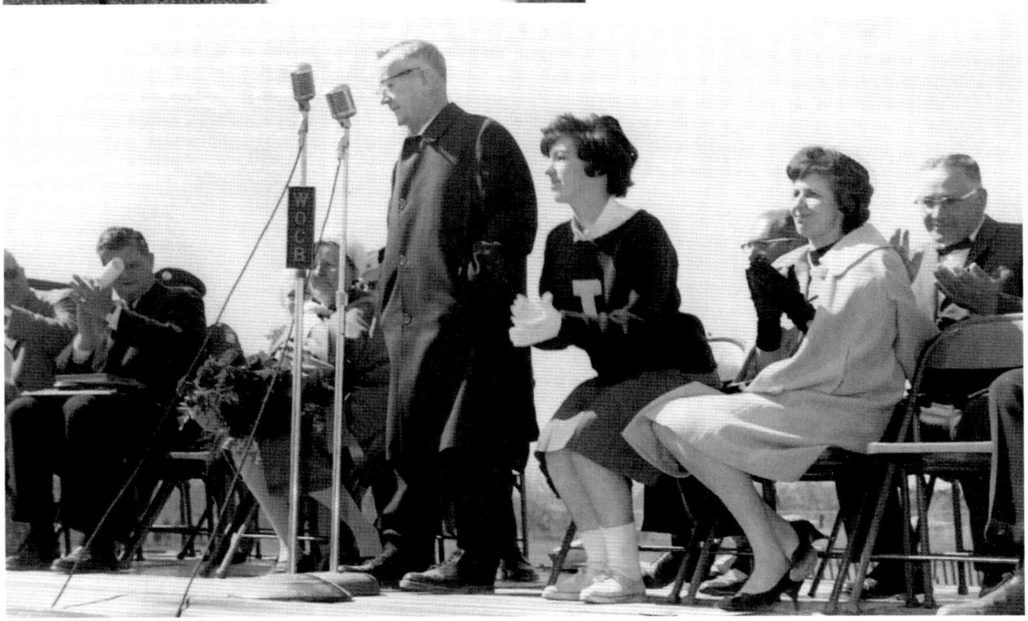

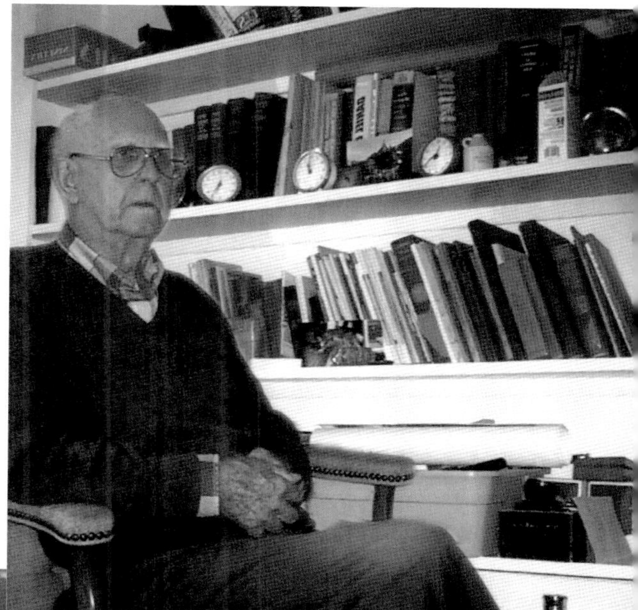

Clarence Anderson (1912–2004)

Clarence Anderson, "Falmouth's true historian," grew up on Elm Road at the 1659 house site of town founder Jonathan Hatch. He was voted an honorary Hatch by the Hatch Family Association for his devoted research on Jonathan and Moses Hatch and their early settlement in Falmouth. He was a jack-of-all-trades: he worked on his family farm, cut ice at Oyster Pond, was a carpenter and the owner of a television repair shop, and he worked in electronics for WHOI. The son of a stonecutter, he left oral histories on the significance of stone walls in Falmouth and could speak firsthand on the ice-cutting industry. He saw Falmouth through the transition from farming to tourism and recorded stories and observations on every detail of the land and its history.

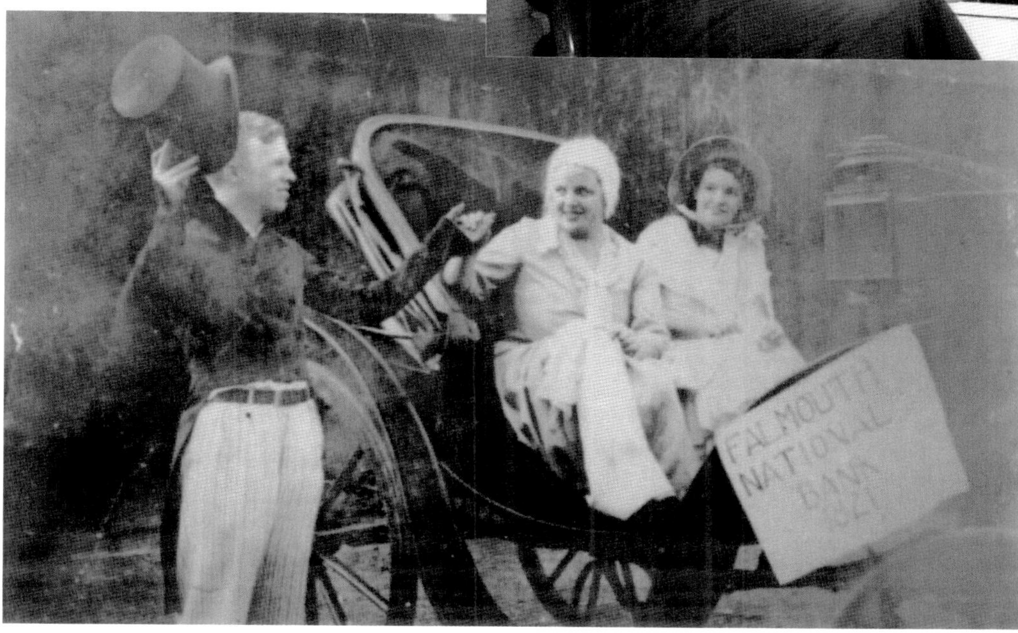

Arnold Dyer (1906–1996)

Arnold Dyer was a businessman and local historian who grew up in Falmouth right along with the town. He arrived in Falmouth in 1912 and attended Village School, Lawrence High School, and the Massachusetts Agricultural College. He worked for his father's business, Falmouth Coal Co., since 1919 and later became its chief owner. He served two terms as president of the Falmouth Historical Society, leading its 90th anniversary. He wrote the publication *Hotels and Inns of Falmouth* and updated *Residential Falmouth*. He was sought after as a lecturer on Falmouth history and still gave talks when he was losing his sight and was half deaf. From his humble beginnings, he served on every important board in town and was a force in town activities. Here, Dyer (with top hat) shows the Falmouth National Bank's award-winning surrey in a 1930s parade with Eleanor Conant Yeager (left) and Katharine M. Barry.

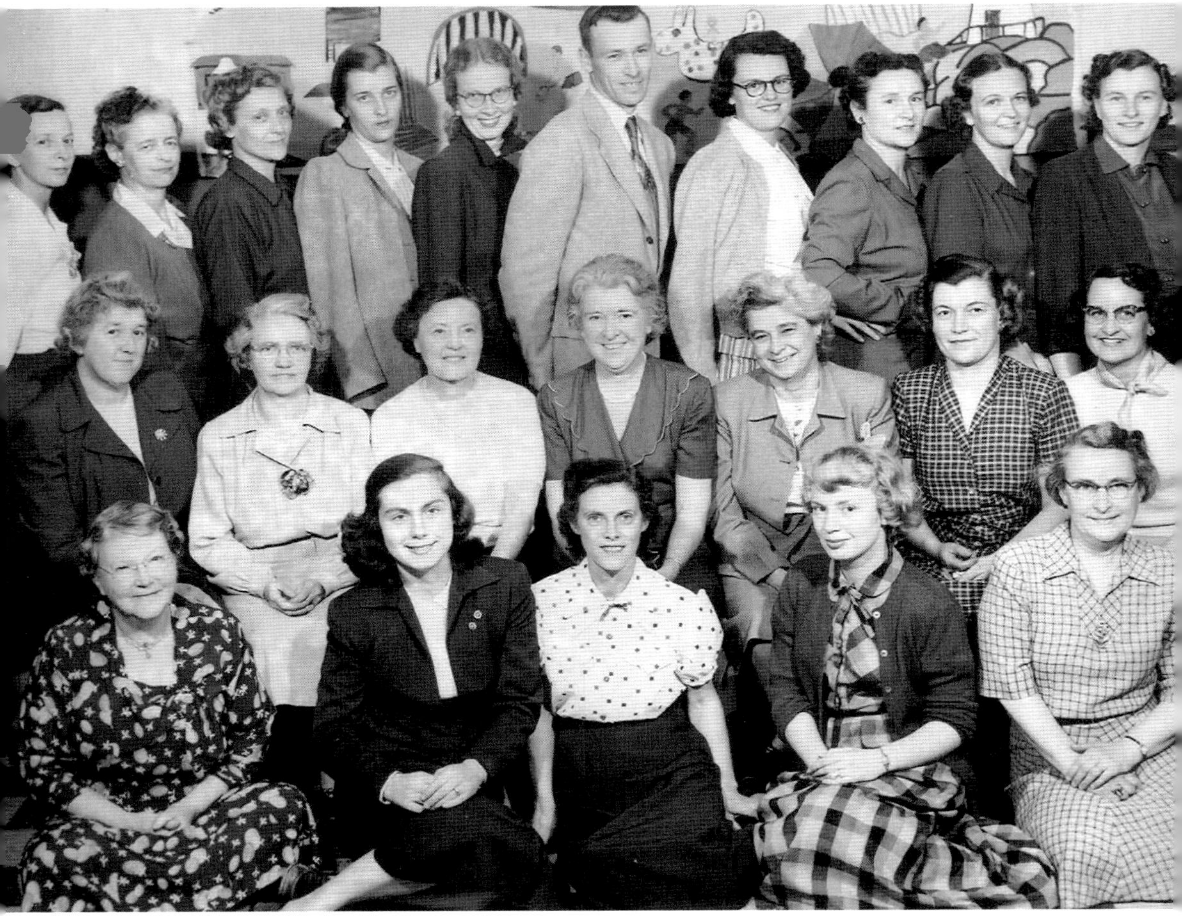

Margaret A. Mullen (1897–1990)

Margaret "Meg" Mullen was a redheaded, lively teacher and principal at the Village School, later named the Margaret A. Mullen School in 1961 after her five decades of service. She was known as an advocate of innovative ideas in teaching. Most people never know if they are appreciated, but Margaret was honored many times during her lifetime, including a community-wide reception in 1967 at her retirement. Meg Mullen is in the center in second row, among her fellow teachers, in 1955.

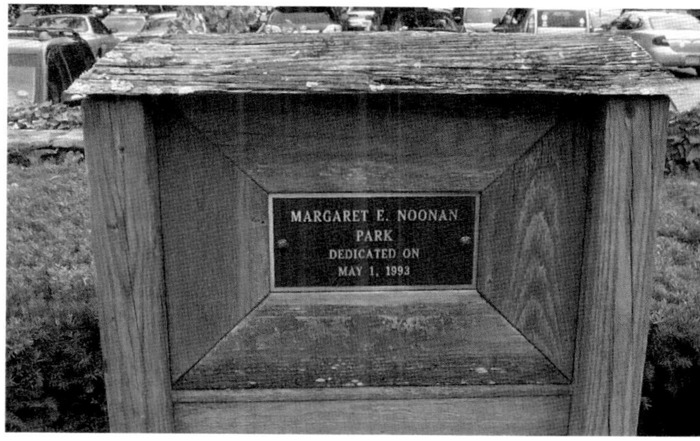

Margaret E. Noonan (1913–1990)
Margaret "Peg" Noonan came to Falmouth with her marriage to Gilbert J. Noonan in 1940. She was a secretary for the Lawrence Lynch Corp. for many years and was very involved in her church's activities at St. Patrick's. She was also a member of Falmouth's Council for Beautification. It was through this committee that Peg Noonan championed the creation of a vest-pocket park on Main Street in the space created by the demolition of the old town hall. She envisioned a mini community park for activities and events. She always proposed that the park be named in honor of Milford Lawrence, a popular selectman. The Main Street Revitalization Committee revisited Peg Noonan's idea, and the park was dedicated in 1993, with one exception—that it be named Peg Noonan Park.

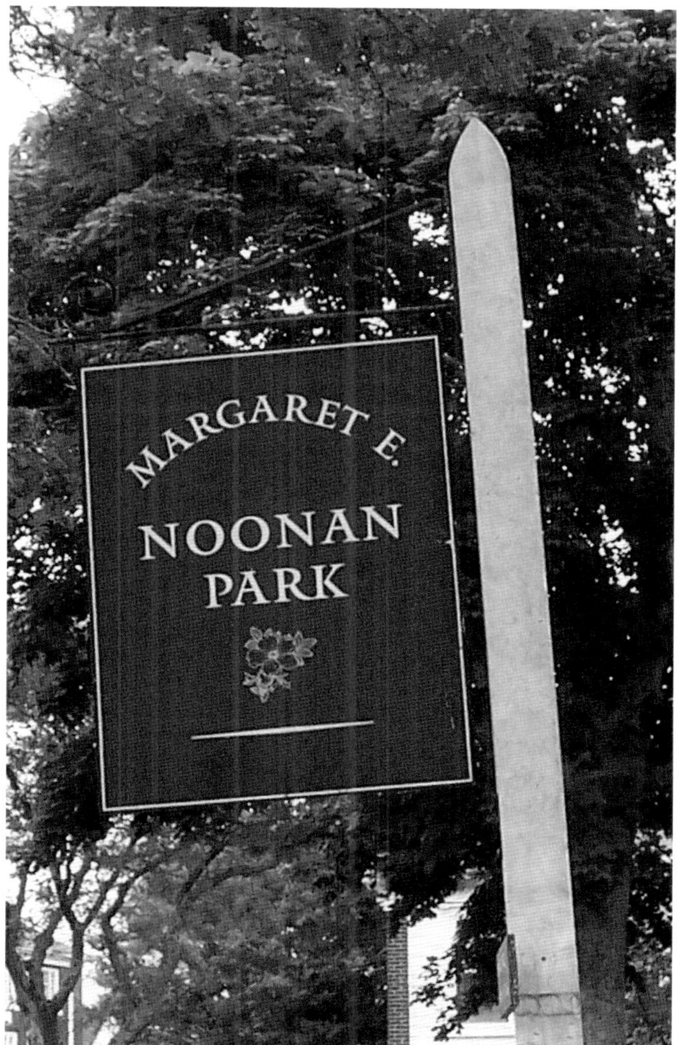

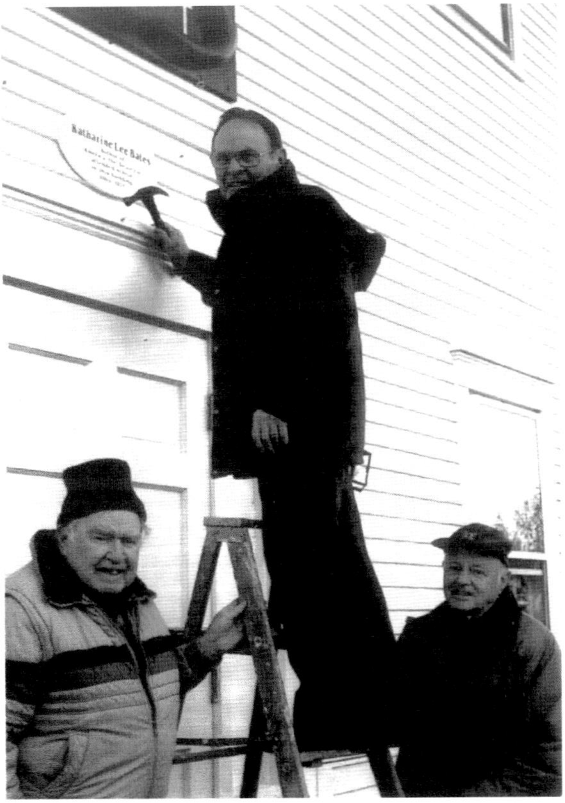

Robert H. Bidwell (1919–)

Bob Bidwell has been summering in Falmouth since the age of six. When the Davisville resident celebrated his 80th birthday, the town celebrated Robert H. Bidwell Day for his leadership and community service. He was president of the Davisville Association, the historical commission, and the Historic Highfield for 10 years, the first president of FACES, and president of the Falmouth Historical Society. In 1992, he created a public celebration for the 100th anniversary of "America the Beautiful." In 1999, he coordinated the reenactment of the Battle of Falmouth. His legacy and that of Katharine Lee Bates live on in the annual K.L. Bates Poetry Festival. He said, "Everyone who lives in this town should be proud of its history." The dedication of the Katharine Lee Bates statue on the library lawn is an event Bob Bidwell contributed to. At left, he is putting finishing touches on the Katharine Lee Bates house.

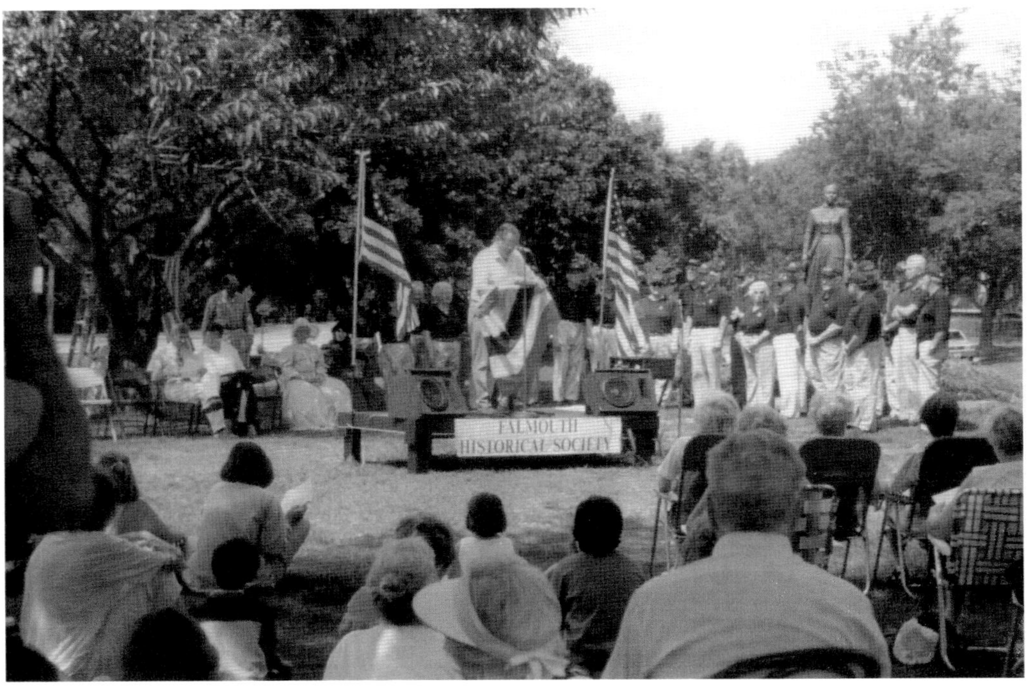

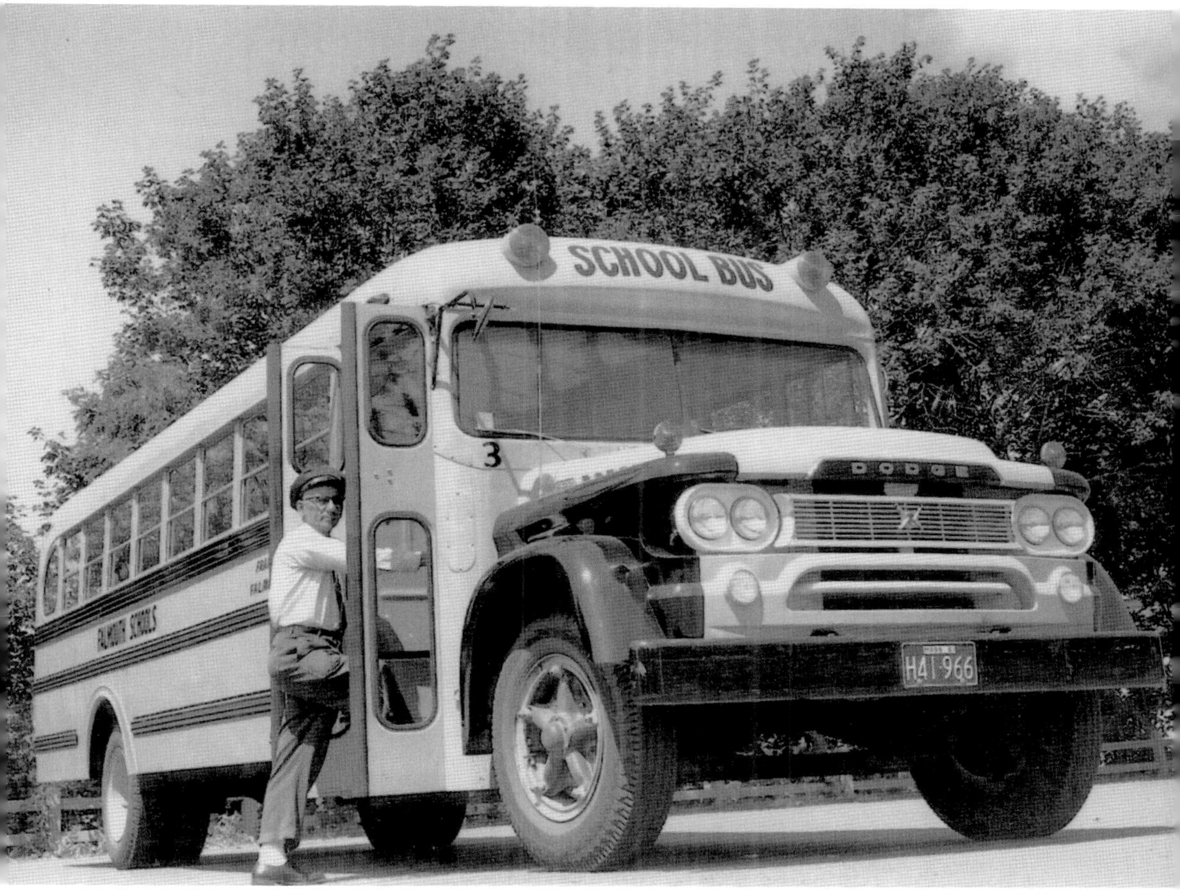

Frank Rego (1904–2008)
Frank Rego was a Falmouth school bus driver from 1923 to 1966, driving three generations safely to school. He was feted at his 100th birthday, recalling his early days of driving a converted truck and on occasion in storms, a horse and buggy. He was remembered for mentoring children on his Hatchville route and for his "heart of gold."

Kitty Baker (1925–2011)

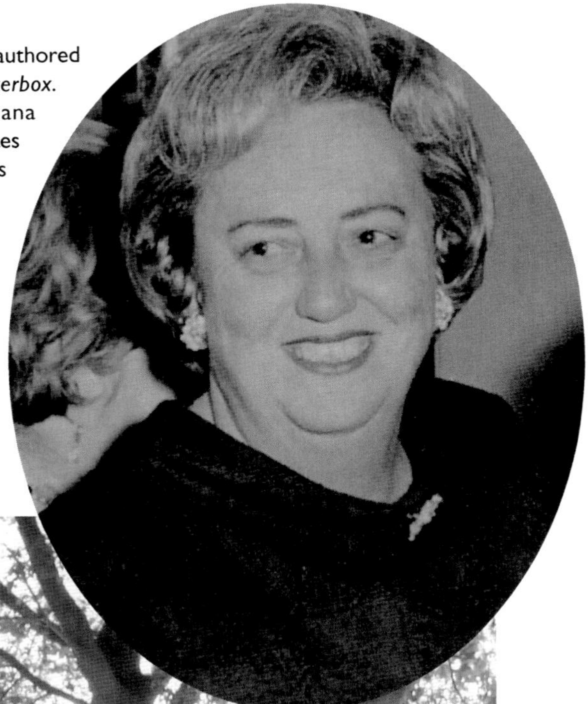

Kitty Baker, a Lawrence High School graduate, authored the weekly social newspaper column, *Chatterbox*. Once called a Norman Rockwell Americana columnist, she loved to list names of Falmouthites and wish them a Happy Birthday, as well as support every cause and bake sale in town. Earlier in her career, she was a noted theater critic, interviewing celebrities of the straw-hat theater circuit, and she played a key role in establishing the Falmouth Theater Guild. *Chatterbox* was read religiously by residents. Kitty's optimism and belief in Falmouth was widely recognized. There will never again be a *Chatterbox* and there was only one Kitty Baker.

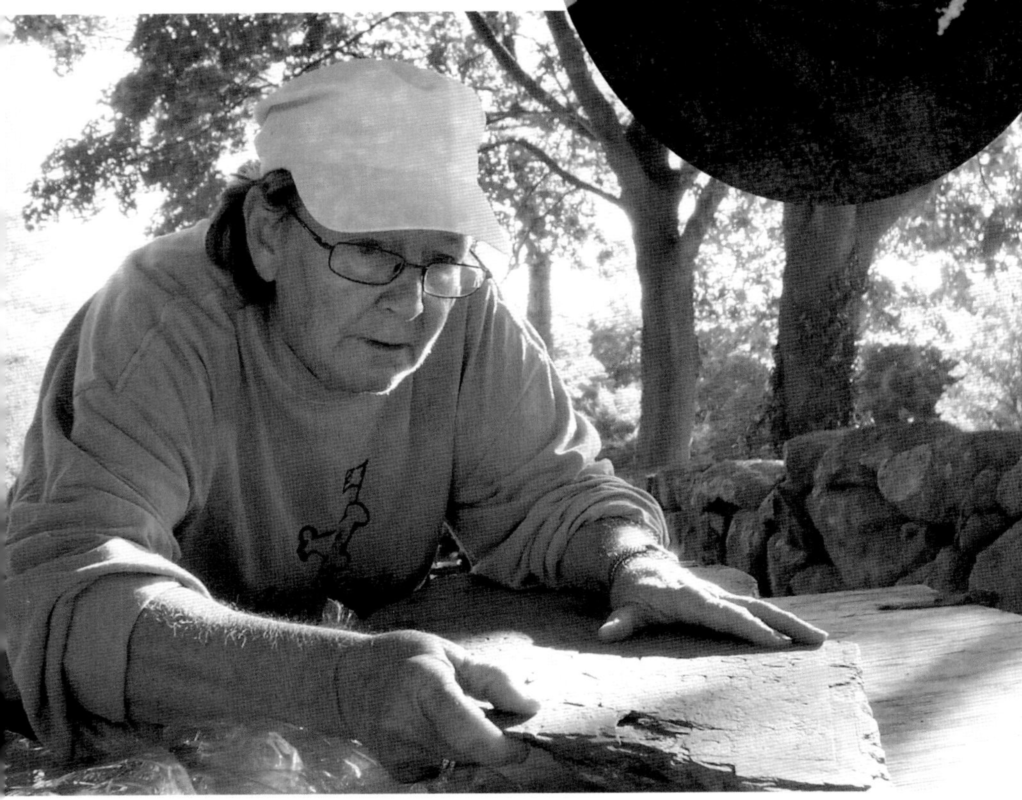

Donna Walcovy

Donna Walcovy began working in the Falmouth town cemeteries in 2001, repairing and cleaning neglected, sunken, and broken gravestones. She has worked in the Old Town Burial Ground, East Falmouth Cemetery, Methodist Cemetery, Oak Grove Cemetery, and the Village Cemetery in Woods Hole. She has raised awareness of new methods of preserving gravestones and of the precious lives commemorated and honored in the town cemeteries.

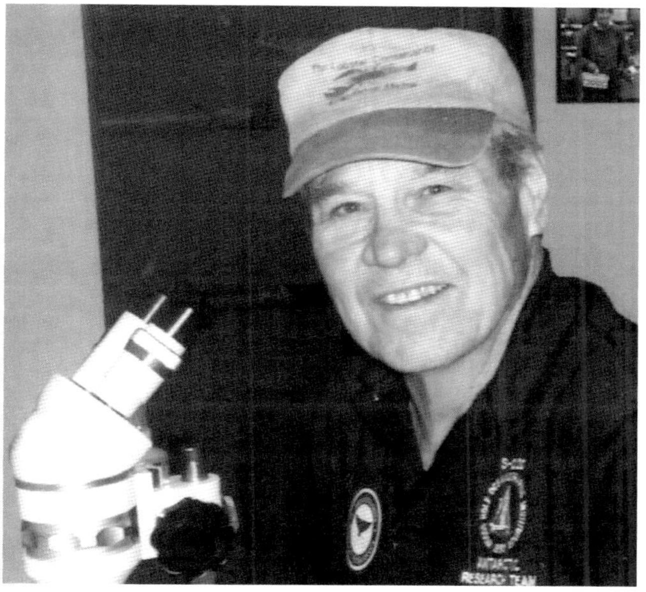

George Hampson (1937–)
George Hampson is legendary here, not only for his 37-year career at WHOI studying oil spills and identifying new species, but also for his post-WHOI activities as a mentor and environmentalist for community betterment. He was a founding member of the Coalition for Buzzards Bay, the 300 Committee, and the Massachusetts Estuaries Project. He is an advisor to Sea Lab, which brings coastal studies to kindergarten through 12-grade students and is always available for crash courses in ocean sampling. Hampson was honored by the Falmouth Historical Society with the Heritage Award in 2008.

Alfred "Al" Irish (1919–)
Al Irish graduated from Lawrence High School Class of 1937 and still has reunions with fellow classmates. He has the title of historian for the Cape Cod Baseball League's Falmouth Commodores. His love of baseball goes back to 1923 when he went to games with his grandfather at the beautiful Falmouth Heights ballpark with views of Vineyard Sound. For nine years, Irish served as director and treasurer of the Falmouth Historical Society. He is a role model for citizen volunteers. He still lives at his grandparents' King Street house and is a salt-of-the-earth Falmouthite. Al Irish received the Heritage Award in 2001. (Courtesy T. Richard Miner Jr.)

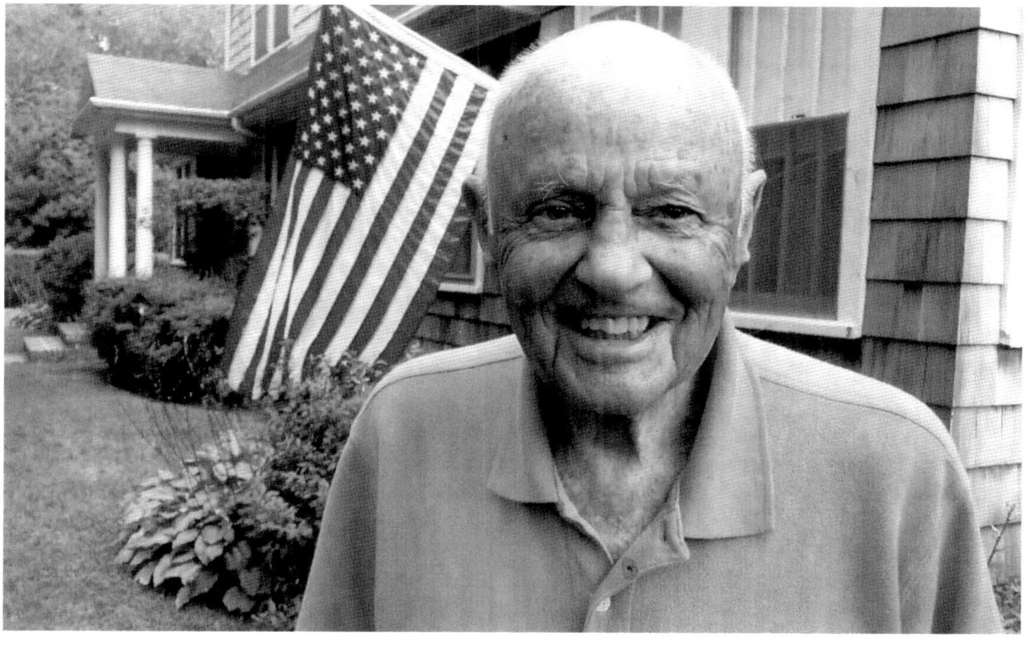

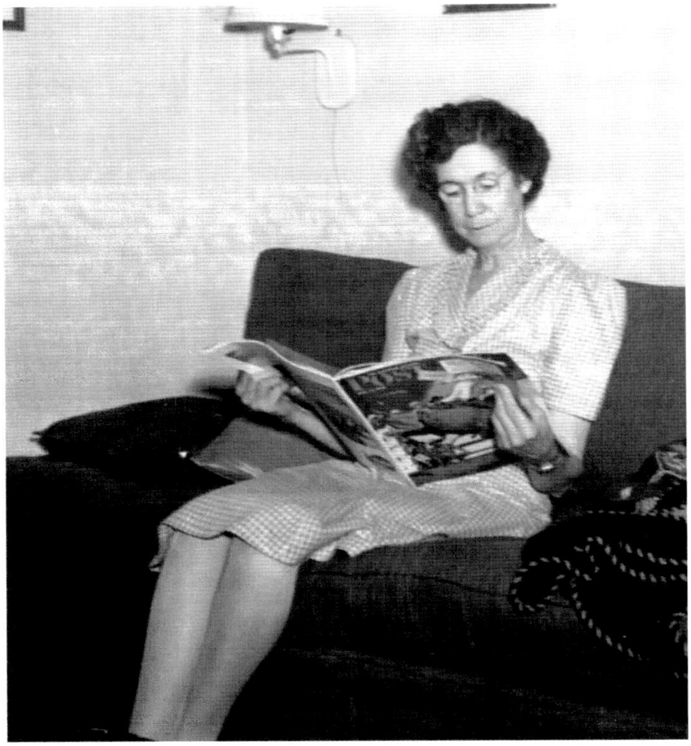

Beatrice A. Hunt (1889–1983)
Beatrice Hunt was the director of Camp Cowasset for Girls in North Falmouth from 1915 to 1962. Known as "Miss Bea," she ran this exclusive 93-acre camp overlooking Buzzards Bay near Silver Beach, offering horseback riding, sailing, and swimming. The camp closed at the end of its 50th season. Eventually, this area became Wild Harbor Estates.

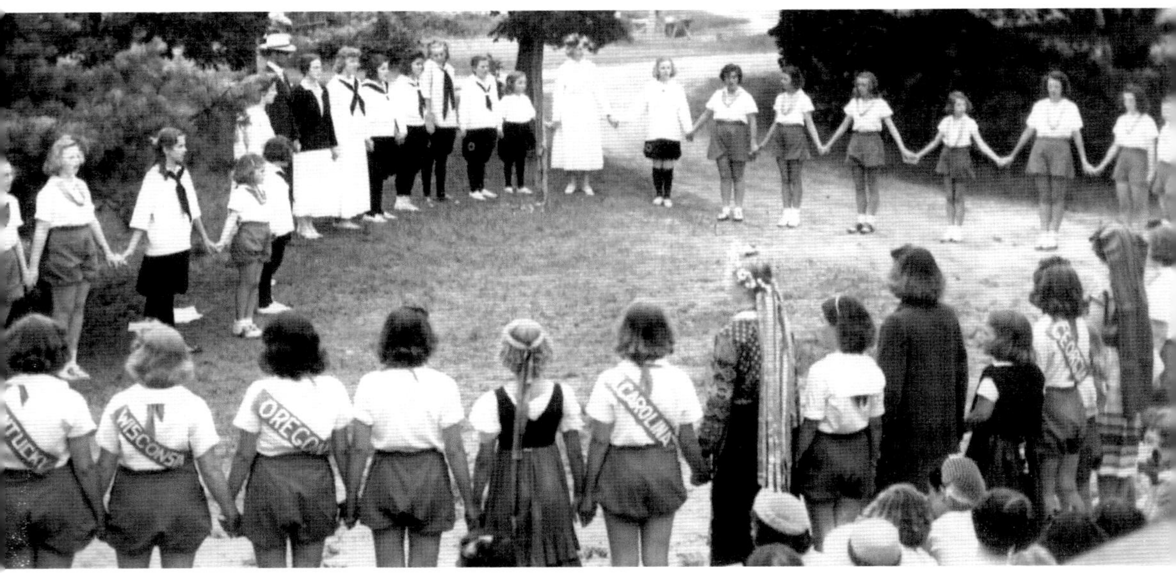

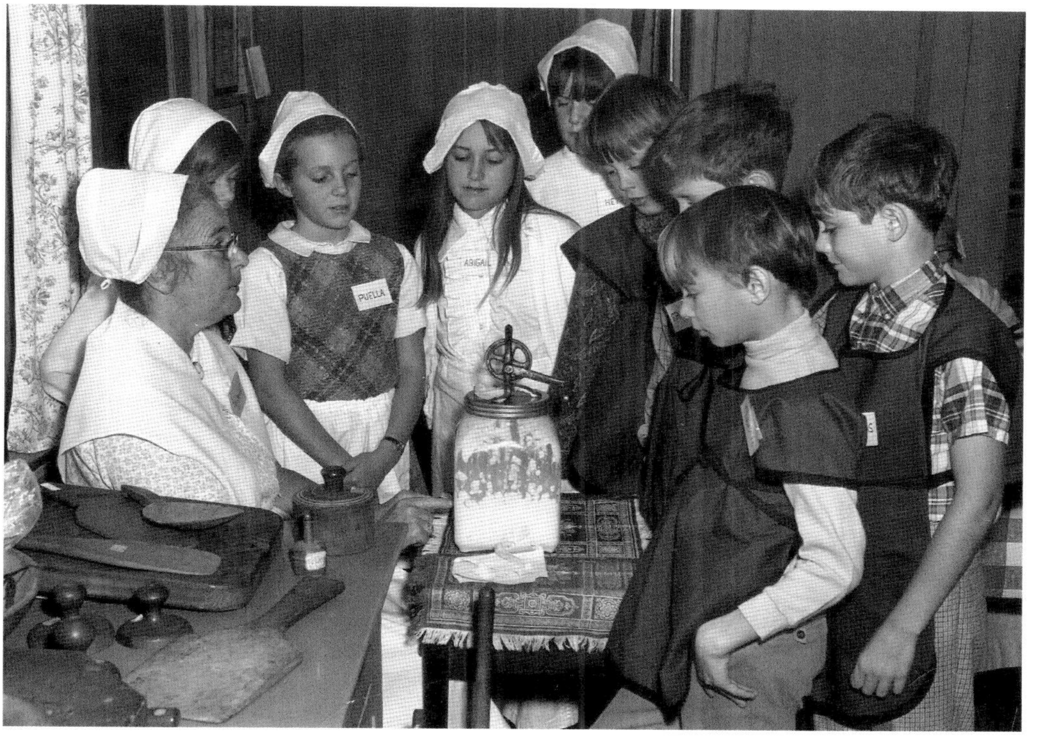

Eleanor Conant Yeager (1905–1981)

Eleanor Conant Yeager was a Falmouth native, growing up at 65 Palmer Avenue, a half-cape house later to become part of the Museums on the Green. She grew up in the 1920s and 1930s at her mother's boardinghouse and later recorded stories of small-town life in the *Falmouth Enterprise*: blueberry summers, train rides, Christmas dinners, and sometimes thinly disguised gossip of Falmouth's wealthiest residents. She was an active docent for the Falmouth Historical Society, demonstrating Colonial chores to schoolchildren, and was curator of the Katharine Lee Bates house in the 1970s.

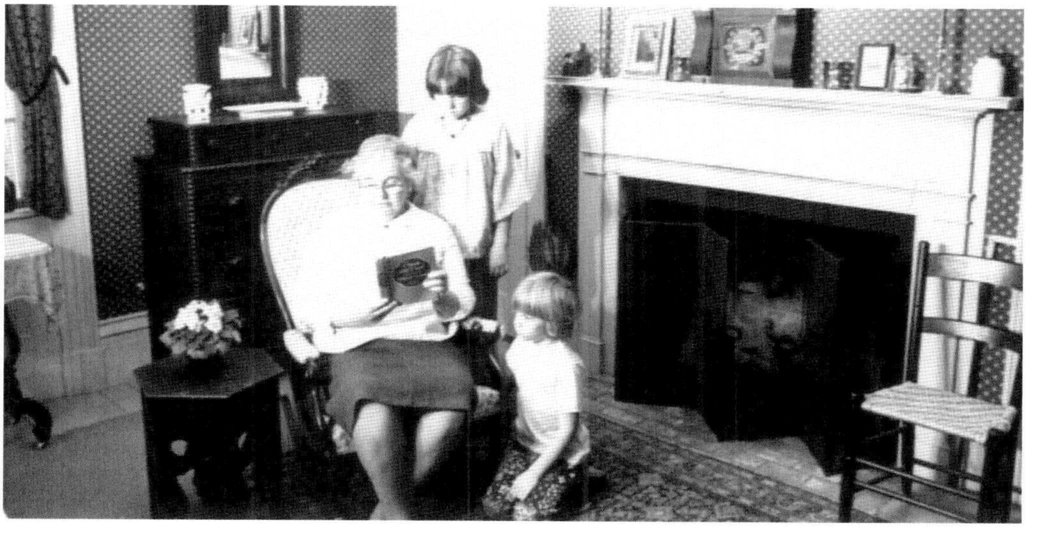

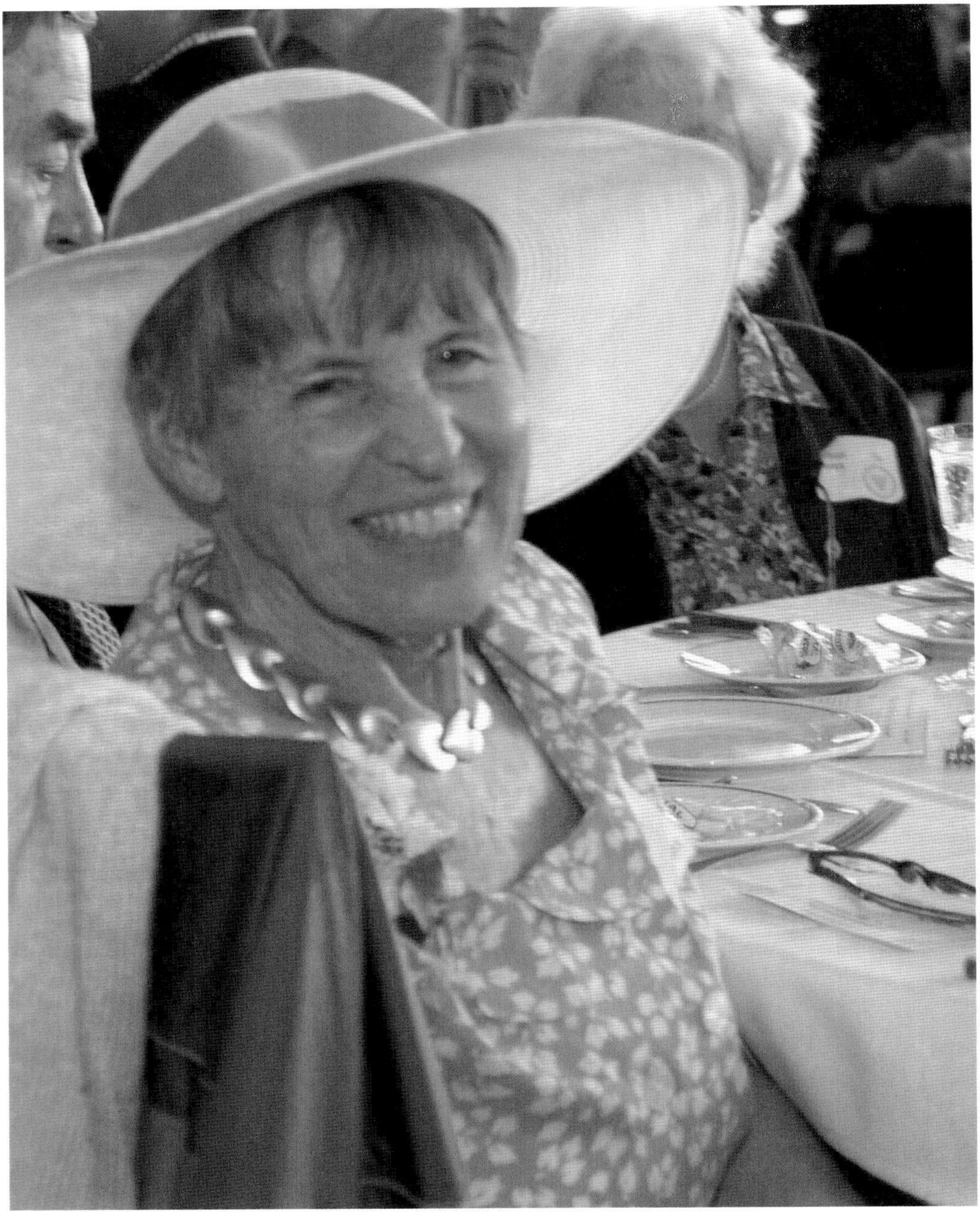

Judith G. Stetson (1933–)
Judy Stetson is a community role model and activist. She has served on the Falmouth Conservation Commission, Falmouth Finance Committee, Falmouth League of Women Voters, and as a town meeting member for 30 years. She was a founding member of the Volunteers in Public Schools and assisted in the writing and editing of the *Book of Falmouth*. Currently she is also editor for *Spritsail*, a journal that features the history of Falmouth. As a true "citizen activist," she was honored in 2011 by the Falmouth Historical Society with the Heritage Award. (Courtesy Amy Rader.)

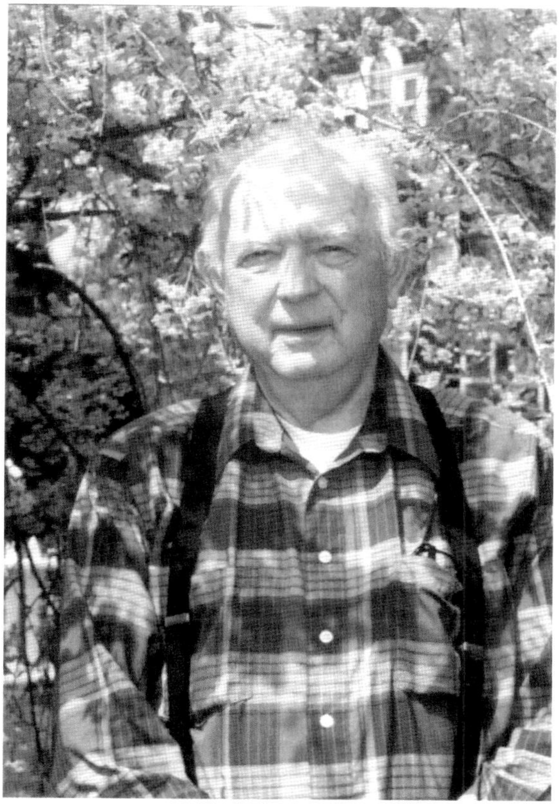

William "Bill" Dunkle (1929–2010) Bill Dunkle was employed by WHOI for 41 years, first as a draftsmen and later as an archivist and data librarian. At WHOI, he earned the title "keeper of institutional memory." His passion for local history as well as maps and photographs made him an extraordinary collector. He amassed a collection of oral histories, photographs, and memorabilia, all relating to his village of North Falmouth. He studied and listed historic houses in Falmouth for the historical commission and was a faithful volunteer at the Falmouth Historical Society. He is pictured below escorting a c. 1800 cannon onto the grounds of the Falmouth Historical Society.

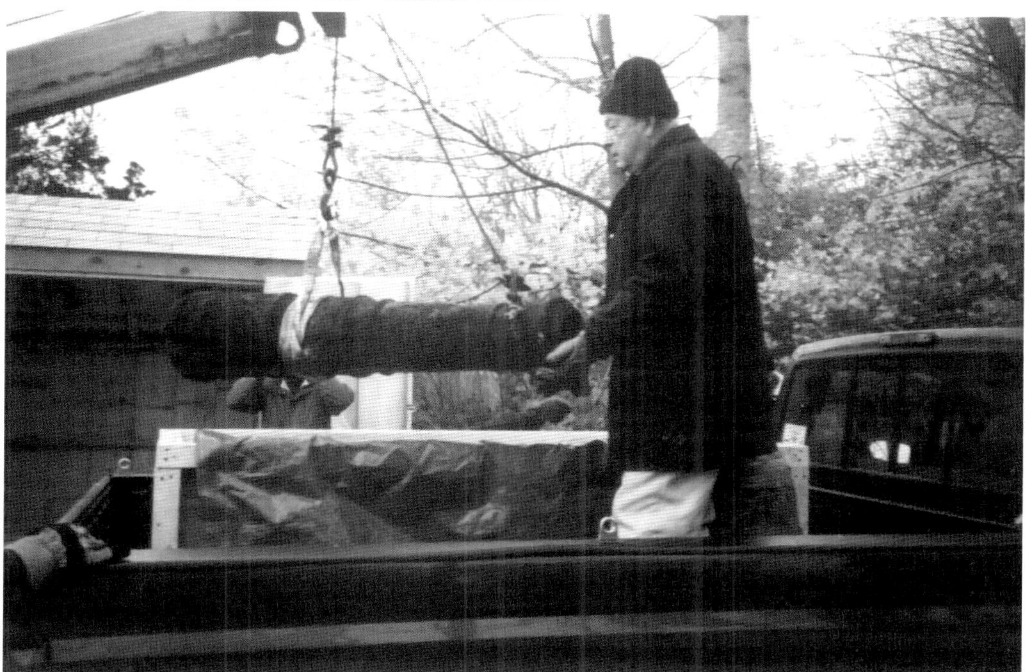

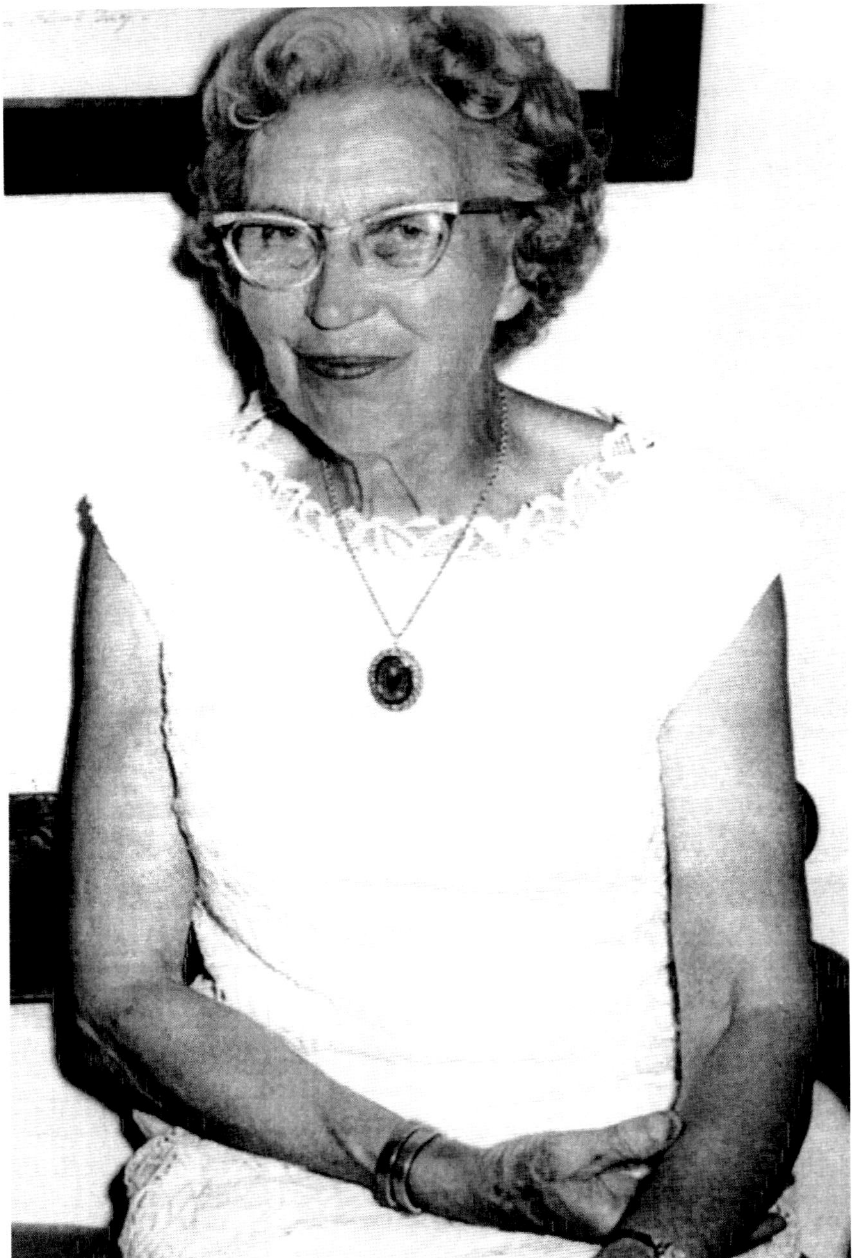

Edna Harris (1878–1967)
Edna Harris had a 50-year career in the restaurant business, beginning in 1912 with the Megansett Tea Room, a summer colony restaurant. In 1930, she opened her first Coonamessett Inn at Crane acres in Hatchville. It was part of a complex of guesthouses, riding stables, a golf course, and summer theater. In 1953, she opened the second Coonamessett Inn in Thomas Jones's 1796 barn on Jones Road. She gained a reputation of impeccable service in her pretentious year-round restaurant, one of the first on Cape Cod. She was a hard worker but never dressed fashionably, unlike her high-fashion customers.

CHAPTER EIGHT

Creative Falmouth

We catch the wind in a woven net, / A shining net.

—Katharine Lee Bates

Captured here are a few high flyers who specialized in creativity and living large. Perhaps it is the Cape Cod air or lifestyle that helped produce such productive and unique citizens.

They are scientists, authors, artists, crafters, and philosophers. It is safe to say that this is the fastest-growing population in Falmouth.

The town's creative fellows include those of high distinction in their fields. They have changed the world by inventing an underwater submersible; organizing a road race; mastering the visual arts; playing on a fledgling baseball league; searching for sacred landscapes, the lost Atlantis, and a cure for cancer; and editing the *Book of Falmouth*. Who would not admire a town that fostered the genius and flare of an Albert Szent-Györgyi or the sustained commitment of a 97-year-old poet? They are all about living in a small town with a talent for allowing its residents to follow their own pursuits.

Allyn Collins Vine (1914–1994)

Al Vine was once described as having unharnessed creative thinking. He was a tinkerer and senior scientist at WHOI for 50 years. He is credited with devising the first deep-diving, manned, research submersible, ALVIN. It was suitably christened with a contraction of his name. His lively mind and enthusiasm for life and science made him comfortable with engineers and national leaders. Here, Al (right) poses with Congressman Hastings Keith (left) in Washington, DC, in 1966. The congressman had just heard news of the new submersible that was developed in his hometown district and wanted to congratulate its inventor. (Courtesy Nickerson Archives, Cape Cod Community College.)

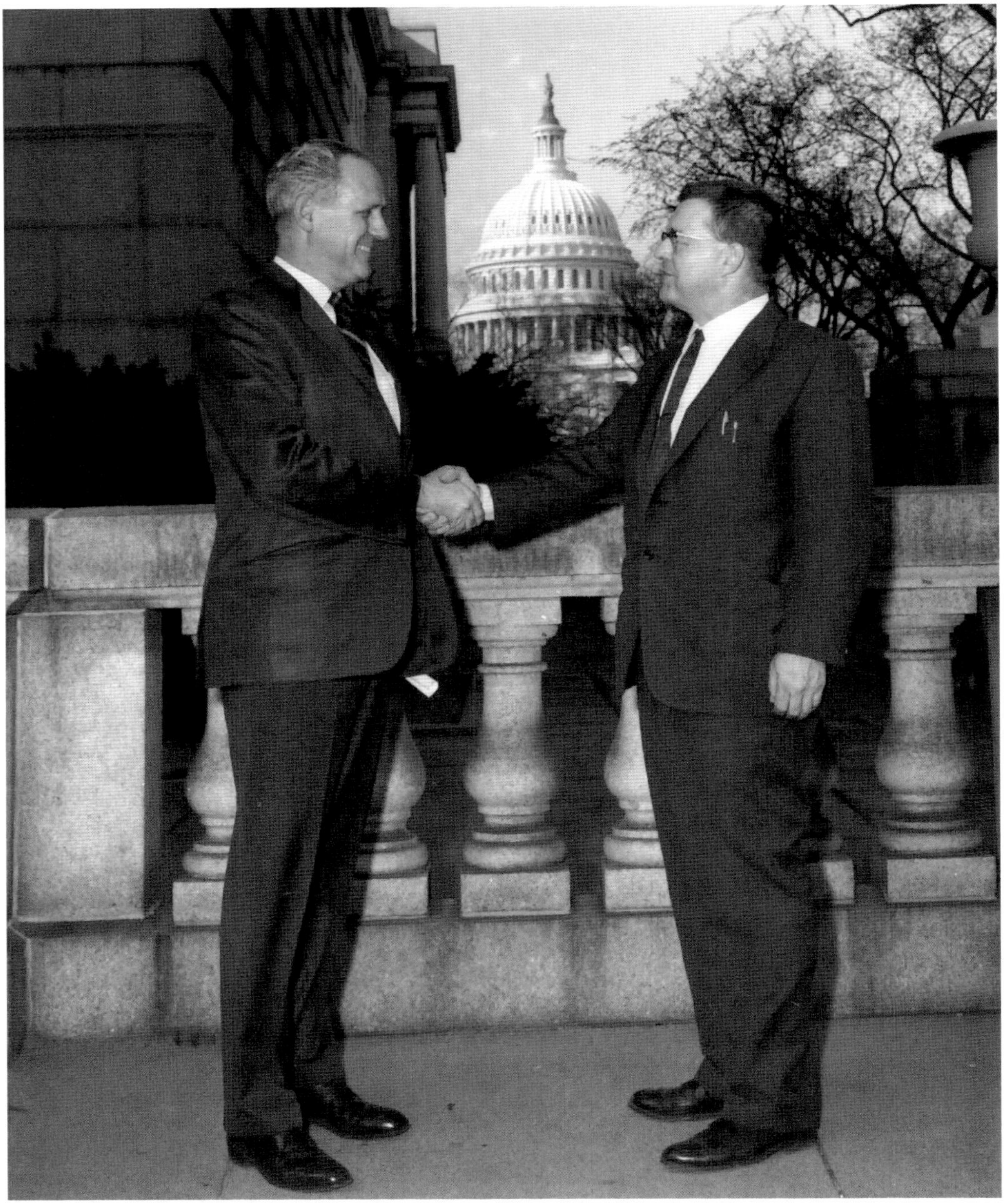

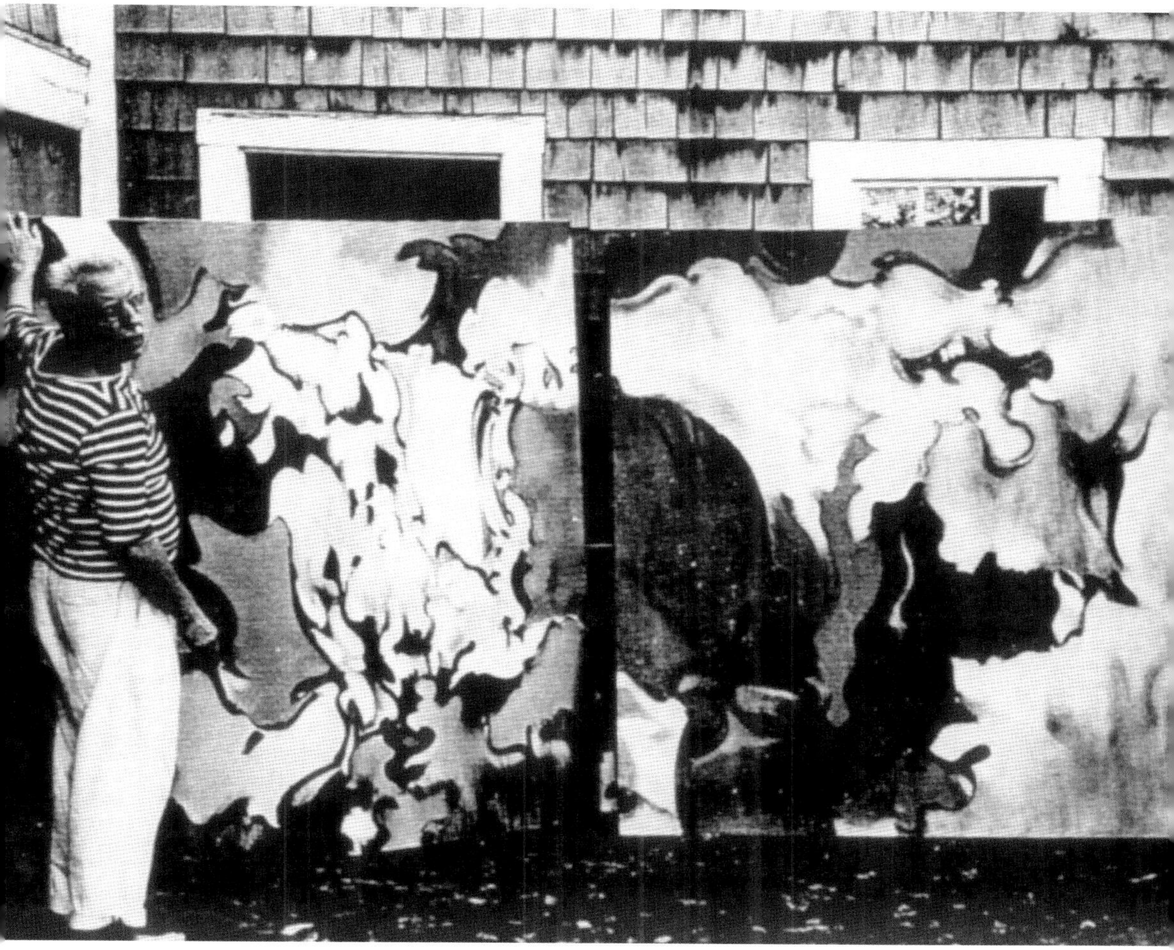

William "Bill" Littlefield (1902–1969)
William Littlefield was a recognized painter by critics, painters, and connoisseurs. He lived at his Depot Avenue studio from 1945, taking many trips to France and New York. He described himself as "a rare bird," making his living only through his art. The term might have also described his eccentric dress and sometimes-blunt honesty as an art critic for the local newspaper. He left behind his early representational art to become a leader in the abstract art movement. He was active in the Falmouth Artists' Guild and took interest in local school art projects.

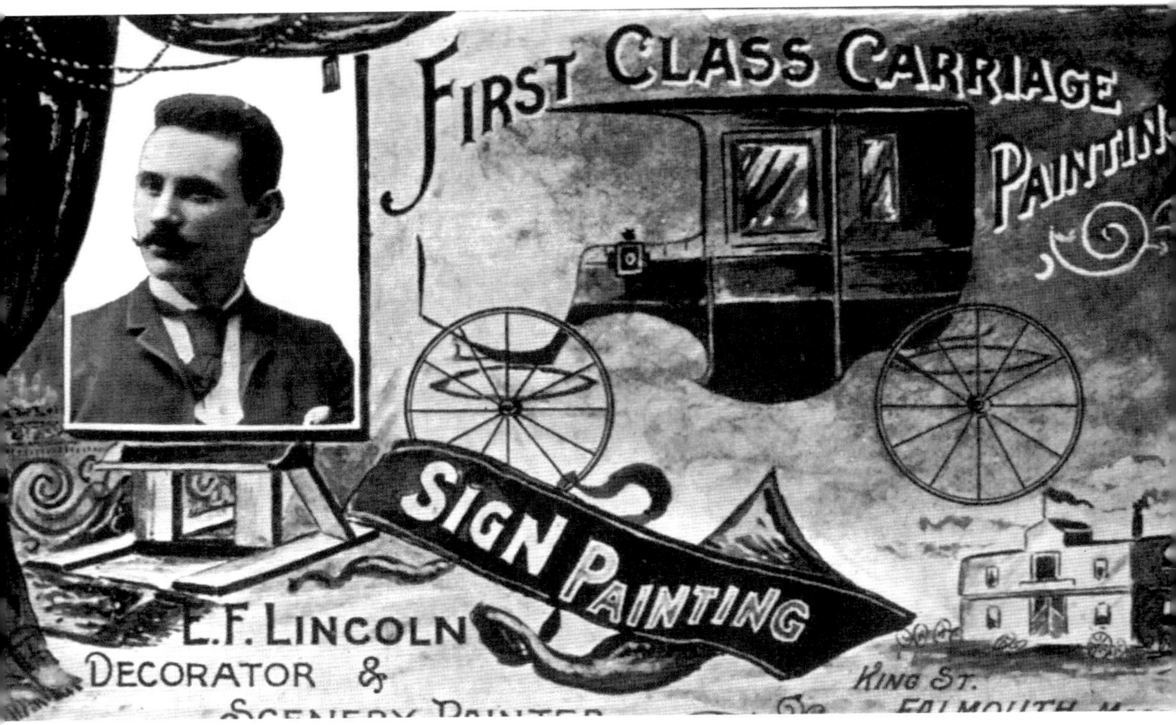

Ephraim F. Lincoln (1864–1934)

E.F. "Eph" Lincoln, a carriage builder and sign painter with a shop located on King Street, became a local marine artist. He depicted some of Falmouth's great moments including his famed HMS *Nimrod* painting. His clipper ships and maritime views are locally prized. He is also credited with designing Falmouth's own town seal. He instructed many in his studio and was praised by William H. Littlefield for his design and craft. (Image from *Falmouth by the Sea.*)

James W. Mavor Jr. (1923–2006)

Jim Mavor was a longtime summer resident of Woods Hole, moving there permanently in 1961. He was a graduate from the Massachusetts Institute of Technology (MIT) Naval Architecture School and worked on the design and construction of the submersible Alvin for the WHOI. He spent 20 years in the study of archaeology and published a work on the sacred landscapes of New England. His love of sailing and folk dancing rounded out his time in Woods Hole.

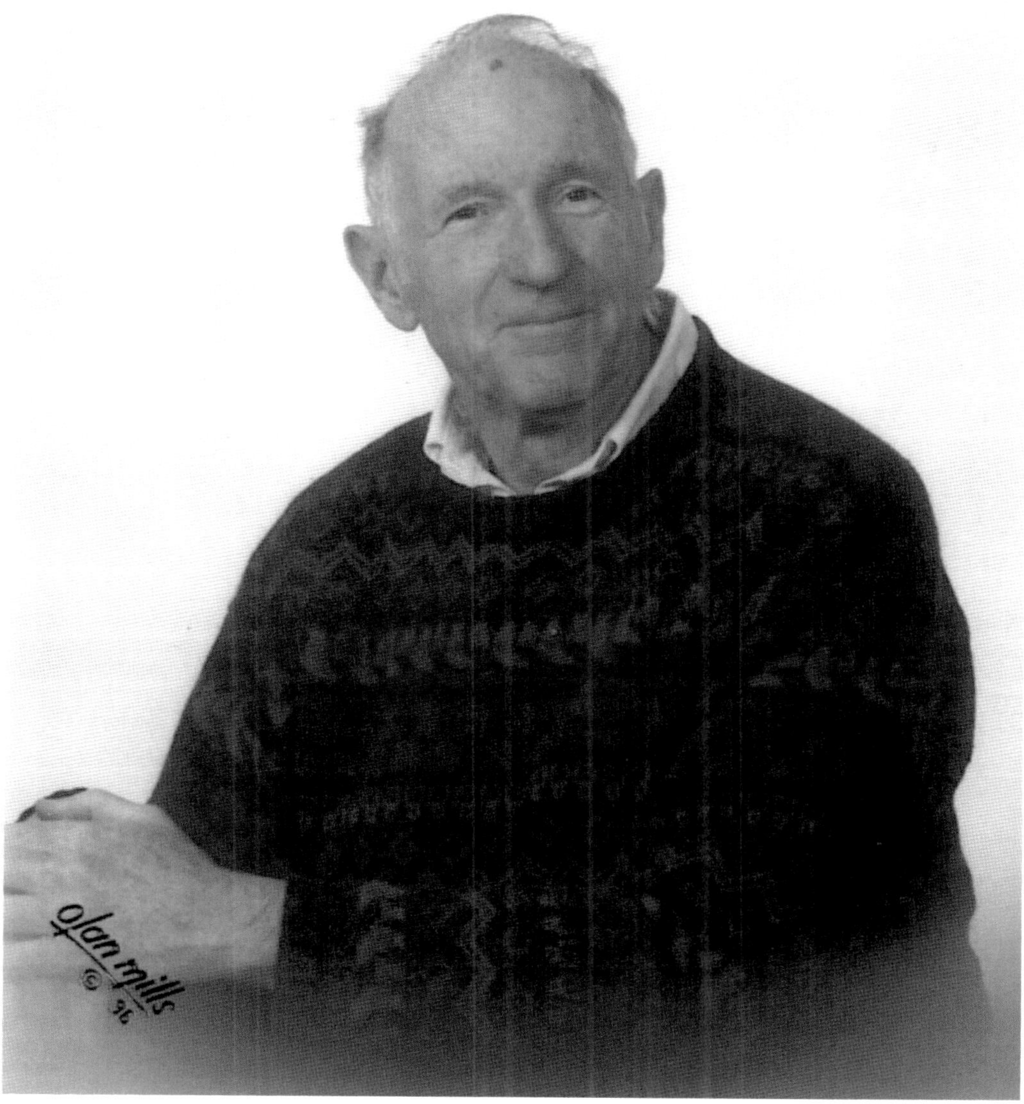

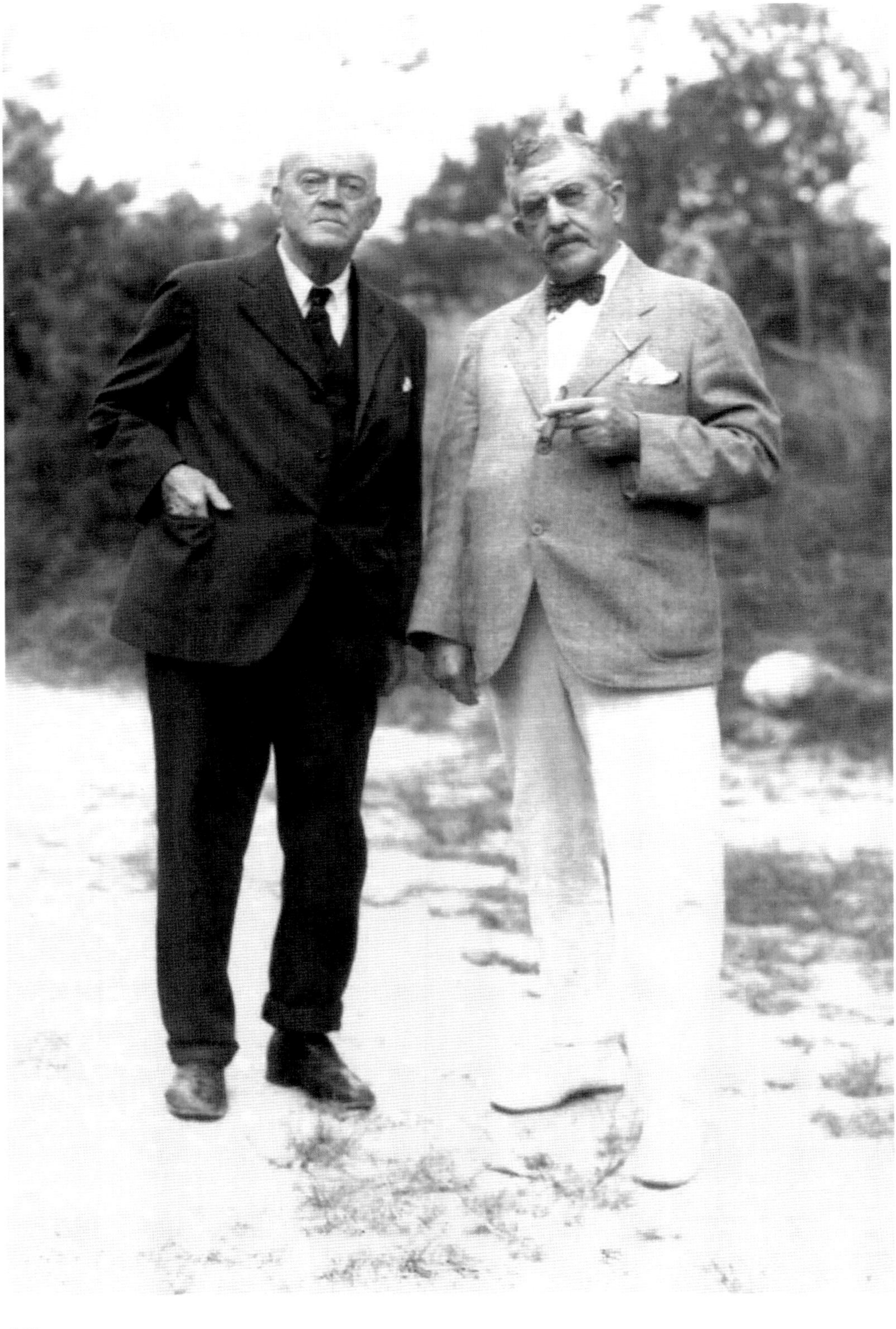

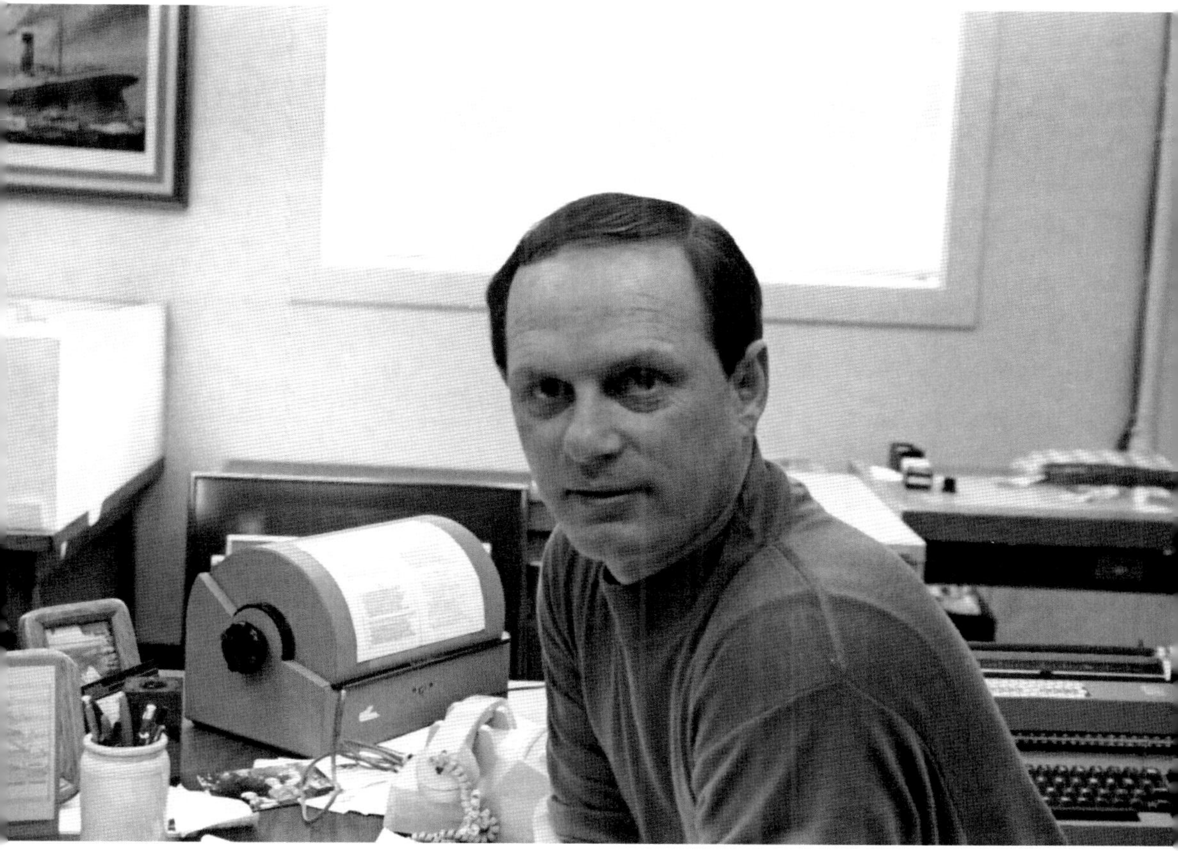

Robert Ballard (1942–)
Robert "Bob" Ballard was a research fellow at WHOI, and in 1974, he became a fulltime marine scientist there. His daring and charisma led him to mapping the sea floor and discovering the deep-sea thermal vents of the Galapagos Islands. ALVIN and the JASON Project aided Ballard with his greatest discovery: the HMS *Titanic* in 1985. He was to go on to many more underwater archeological finds such as the battleship Bismarck and the PT–109. His JASON Project sent live telecasts to students throughout the world inspiring them to envision the ocean as a place for exploration. He is currently a scientist emeritus of WHOI. Seated in his office at WHOI, Ballard has a photograph of the *Titanic* clearly in his radar. (Courtesy WHOI/MBL archives.)

Edward H. Thompson (1857–1935) (OPPOSITE PAGE)
Edward Thompson has a striking epitaph at the Oak Grove Cemetery "Soul Unafraid." This academic spent much of his life in the Yucatan peninsula studying the Mayan culture. He was appointed as US consul to Mexico. He always maintained a house in West Falmouth where he found solace for studying and writing. His findings on the lost Atlantis might have been conjured up from his cabin property. Edward Thompson (left) shares a conversation with George Jones.

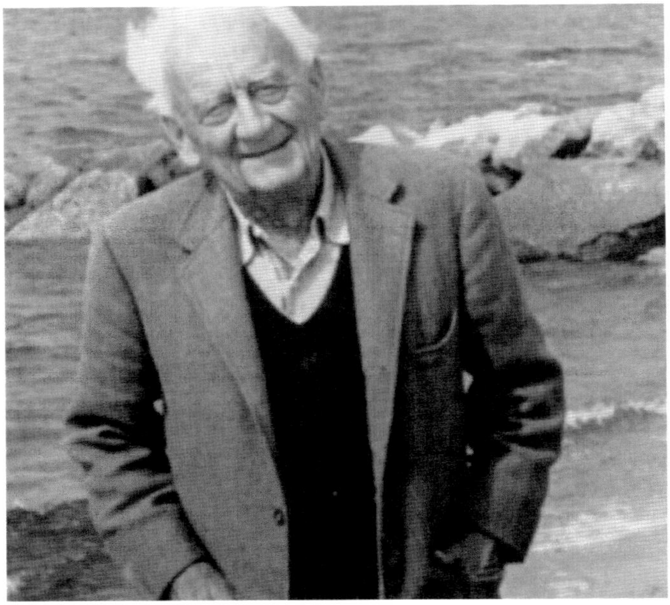

Albert Szent-Györgyi (1893–1986)

Albert Szent-Györgyi, a Nobel Prize–winning scientist, was associated with the Marine Biological Laboratory (MBL) since 1947 and lived in a fabulous house on Penzance Road in Woods Hole. His work at the MBL was important cancer research, but he always maintained a personal charm and playfulness. He supported anti-Vietnam petitions and saved Woods Hole from a proposed Atomic Park. He was known to participate in Woods Hole Day and remained a popular lecturer and hero to young researchers who admired his unique perspectives and unorthodox style. (Both courtesy MBL/WHOI archives.)

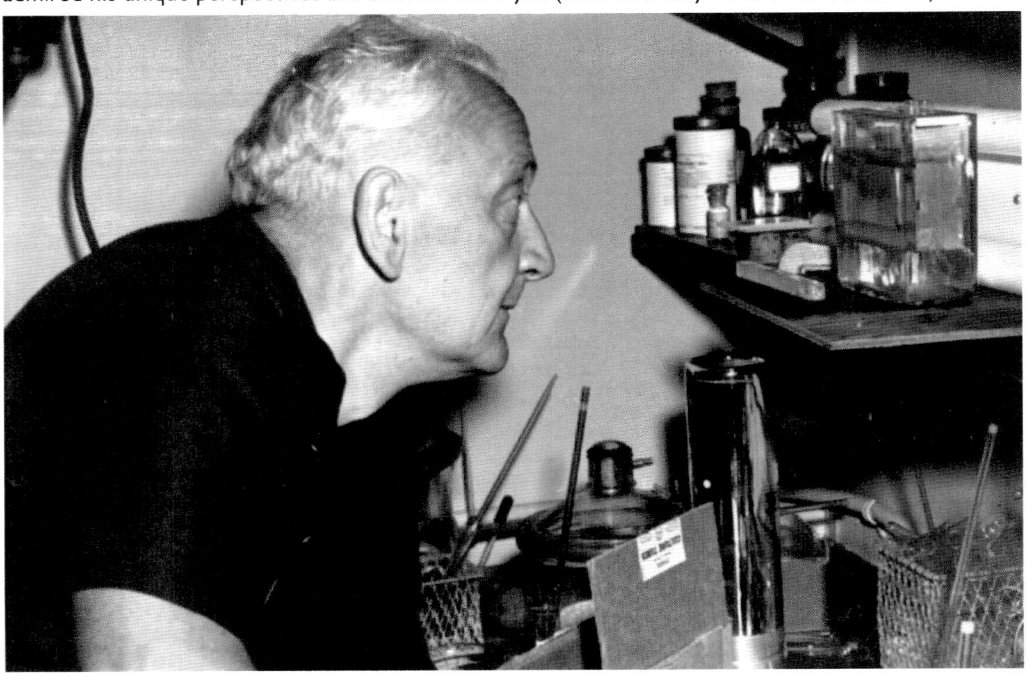

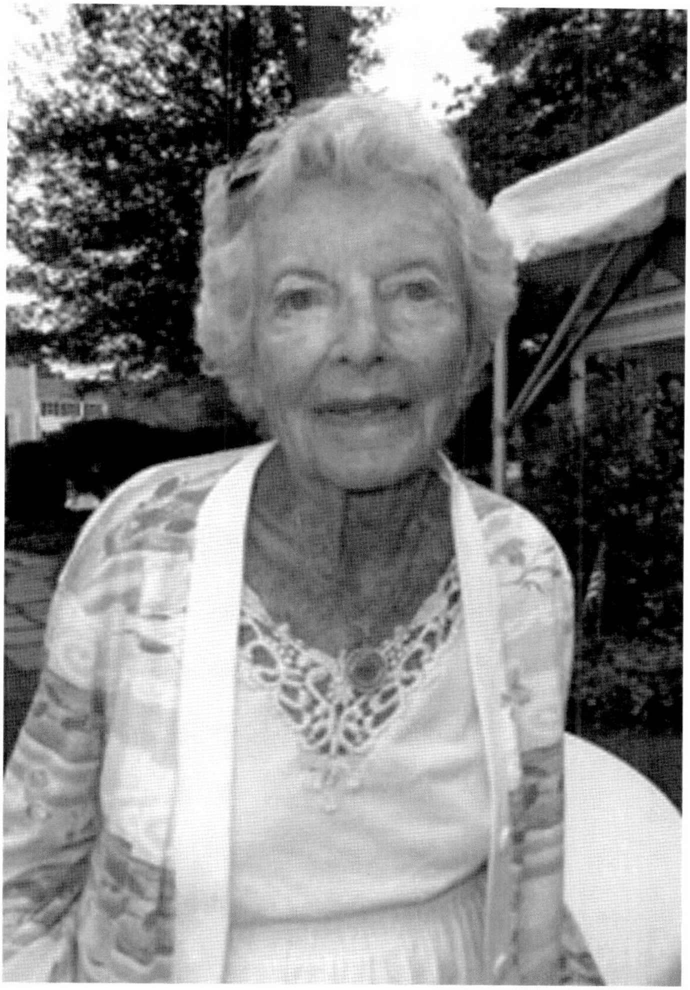

Adelaide Cummings (1914–)
Adelaide was named the first poet laureate of Falmouth in May 2012 at the age of 97. She has written seven books of poetry, the first when she was 89. After graduating from Radcliffe College at 19, she began a remarkable career as a journalist and photographer for *Life* magazine and as the editor-in-chief of *Child Life* magazine for 13 years. Memorable events of her life include having lunch with Franklin and Eleanor Roosevelt, being at LeBourget Field awaiting Lindbergh's landing in Paris in 1927, and reporting in Lakehurst, New Jersey, in 1937 when the German airship *Hindenburg* exploded and burst into flames. A passionate tennis player all her life, she was ranked the fifth national singles player in her 80s and won her last competitive match when she was 90. (Courtesy Len Miele.)

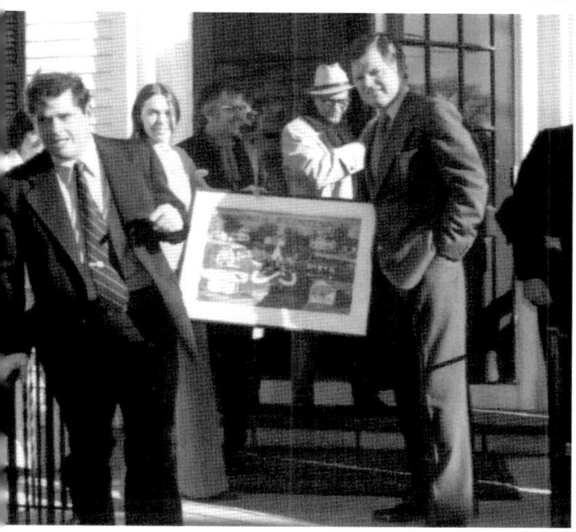

Karen Rinaldo (1952–)
Karen was born in Worcester but quickly adopted Falmouth and has been painting Falmouth's history since the 1976 bicentennial. Karen has designed posters for the bicentennial and tercentennial by sketching historical buildings and sites of Falmouth. She also celebrated the anniversary of "America the Beautiful" with a pictorial of all landmarks in Falmouth connected to Katharine Lee Bates. Her studio by Falmouth Harbor inspires many with her seascapes and Cape Cod–themed paintings. The spectacular Fourth of July fireworks in Falmouth are usually supported by the sale of her patriotic T-shirts. Here, Sen. Edward M. Kennedy (right) is presented with a bicentennial poster created by Karen Rinaldo (left, holding poster).

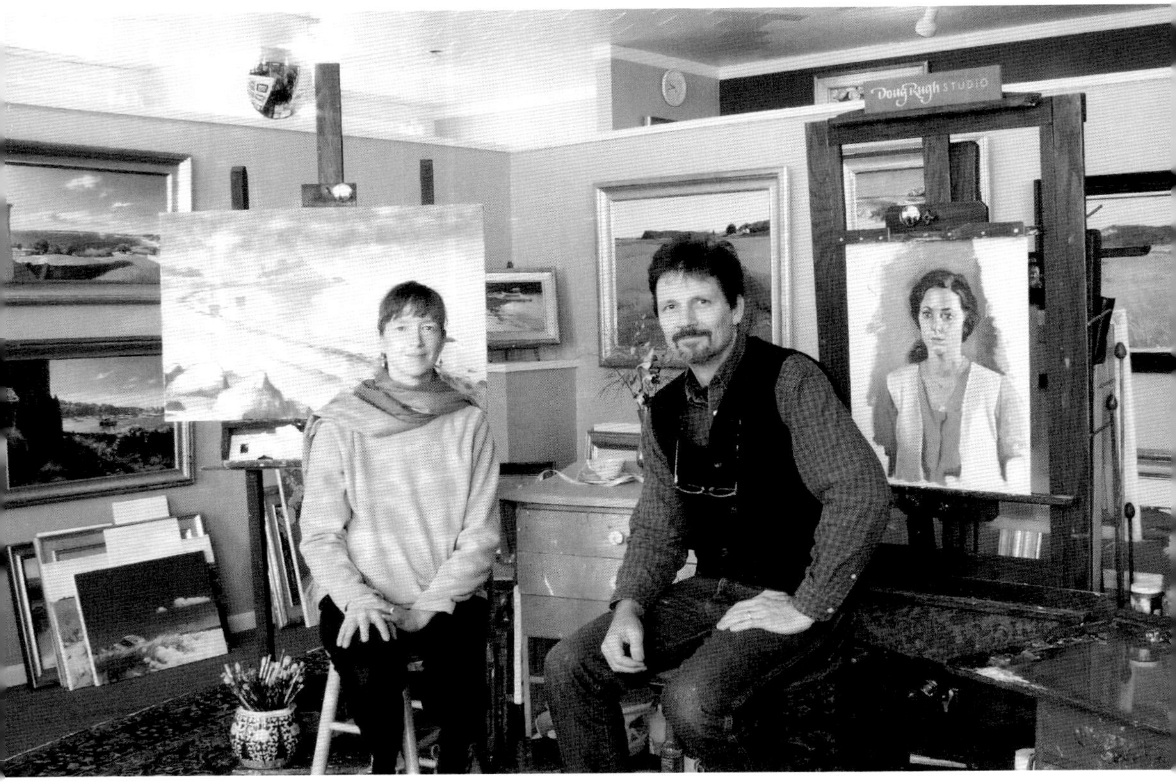

Hillary Osborn and Doug Rugh
Hillary Osborn (with a master of fine arts degree from the University of North Carolina at Greensboro) and Doug Rugh (a graduate of Rhode Island School of Design and 2006 recipient of the Copley Master award) met in 1995 at a figure painting session at the Falmouth Artists' Guild when the guild occupied the town poor house. Shortly thereafter, the two oil painters started painting together en plein air throughout Falmouth and the Upper Cape. They married and became full-time artists in 2000, moving to their current studio and gallery space at Queen's Buyway in 2008, where they create landscapes and still lifes. (Courtesy Hillary Osborn and Doug Rugh.)

George Moses

George Moses is a longtime resident of Davisville. He parlayed his successful advertising writing career in New York with an encore as the newspaper column writer of "Sound Breezes" and "Slightly Salty." His wisecracking Cape Codder style, love of local history and lore, and storytelling genius made his columns a must-read for visitors and locals. He served as town moderator for 20 years, announcing his personal opinion only once during a town meeting session to advocate for the purchase of Washburn Island. His best seller was the book *Ring Around the Punch Bowl* that gave a rare look at the lifestyles of Falmouth's wealthiest residents, including the Beebe, Lillie, and Morse families.

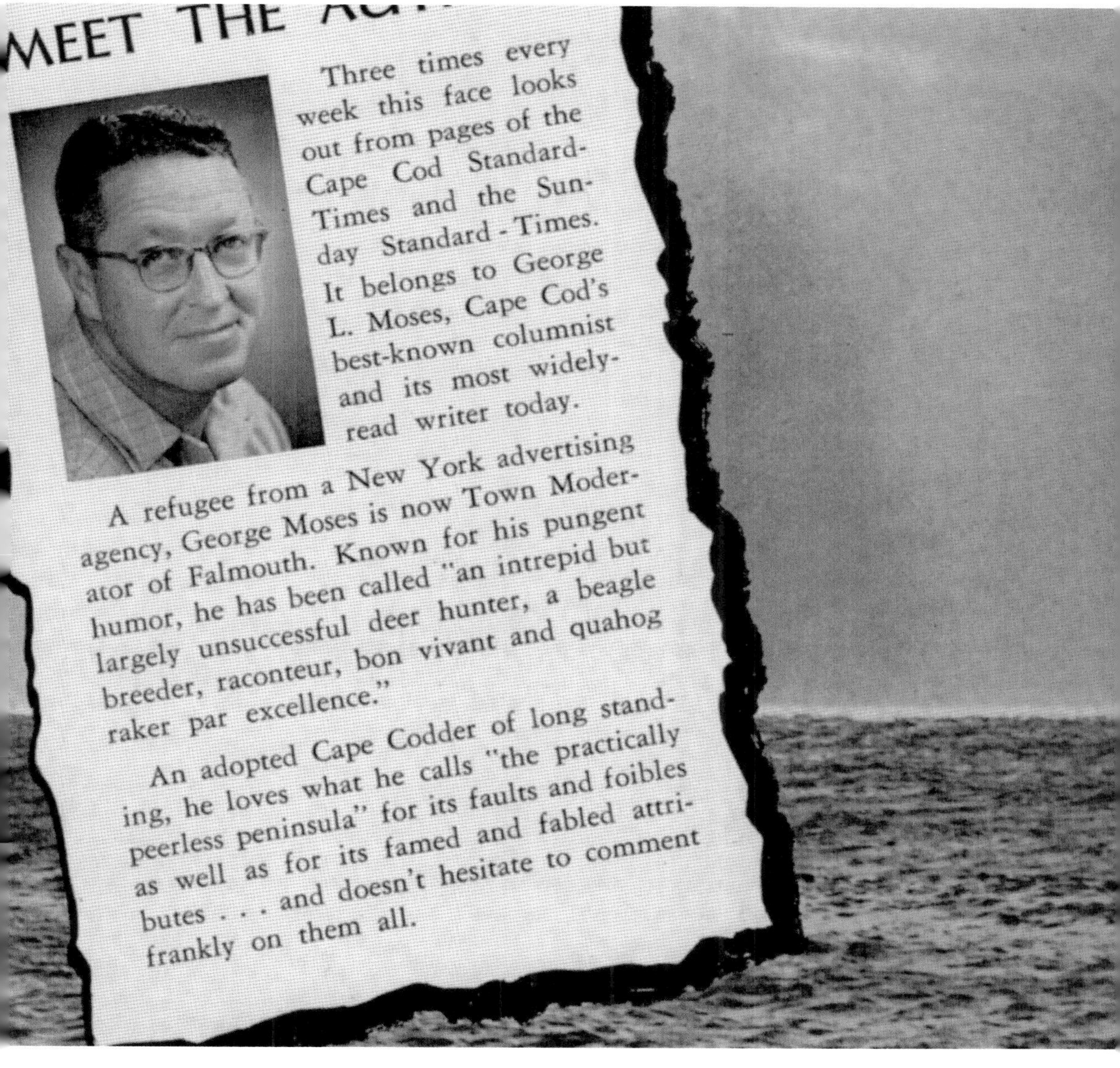

MEET THE

Three times every week this face looks out from pages of the Cape Cod Standard-Times and the Sunday Standard-Times. It belongs to George L. Moses, Cape Cod's best-known columnist and its most widely-read writer today.

A refugee from a New York advertising agency, George Moses is now Town Moderator of Falmouth. Known for his pungent humor, he has been called "an intrepid but largely unsuccessful deer hunter, a beagle breeder, raconteur, bon vivant and quahog raker par excellence."

An adopted Cape Codder of long standing, he loves what he calls "the practically peerless peninsula" for its faults and foibles as well as for its famed and fabled attributes . . . and doesn't hesitate to comment frankly on them all.

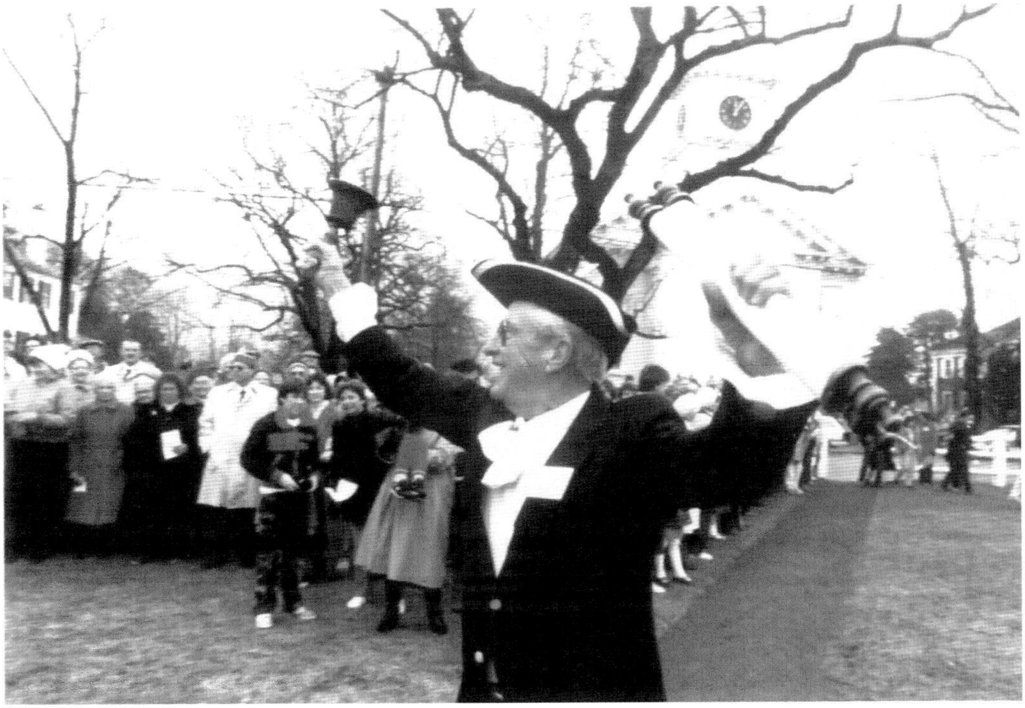

T. Burke McHugh (1917–1994)
T. Burke McHugh lived some of his finest public moments as the town crier for Falmouth's tercentennial. He was ever available to read proclamations and sport a tricornered hat with enthusiasm and style. His theatrical background—from Greenwich Village and Broadway to the Falmouth Theater Guild—helped make his appearances memorable. McHugh was a restaurateur working at the Boat House. He once said that people were his hobby, and his gregarious, outgoing manner proved it.

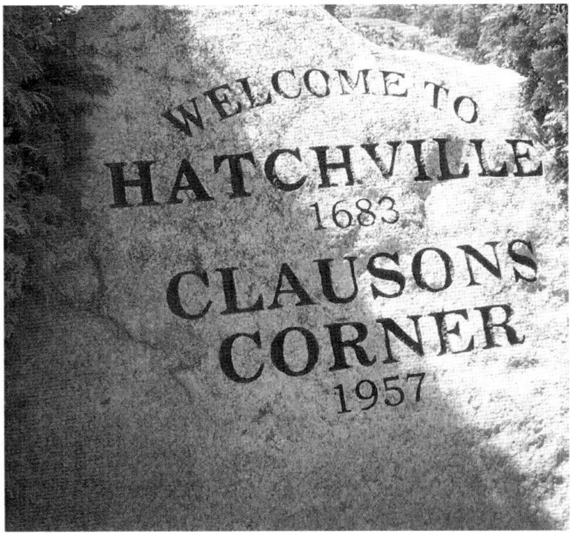

Harvey Clauson Jr. (1926–2007)
Harvey Clauson Jr. was a successful businessman in Falmouth. He was owner of Clauson's Chrysler/Plymouth car dealership in East Falmouth and Clauson's Inn and Country Club Resort and Golf Course. Clauson's Corner in Hatchville is named for Harvey. He did his civic duty as a town meeting member from 1946 to 1954 and served on the first board of trustees for the new Cape Cod Community College. Harvey was called a force to be reckoned with, doing it his way, and excited by life and its possibilities. Many baby boomers remember jazz nights at Clauson's.

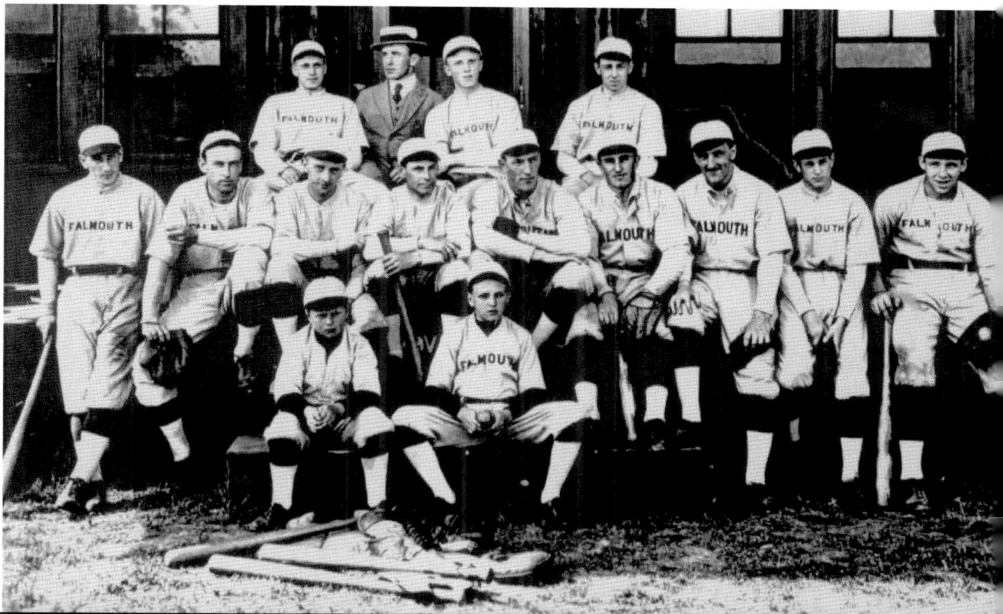

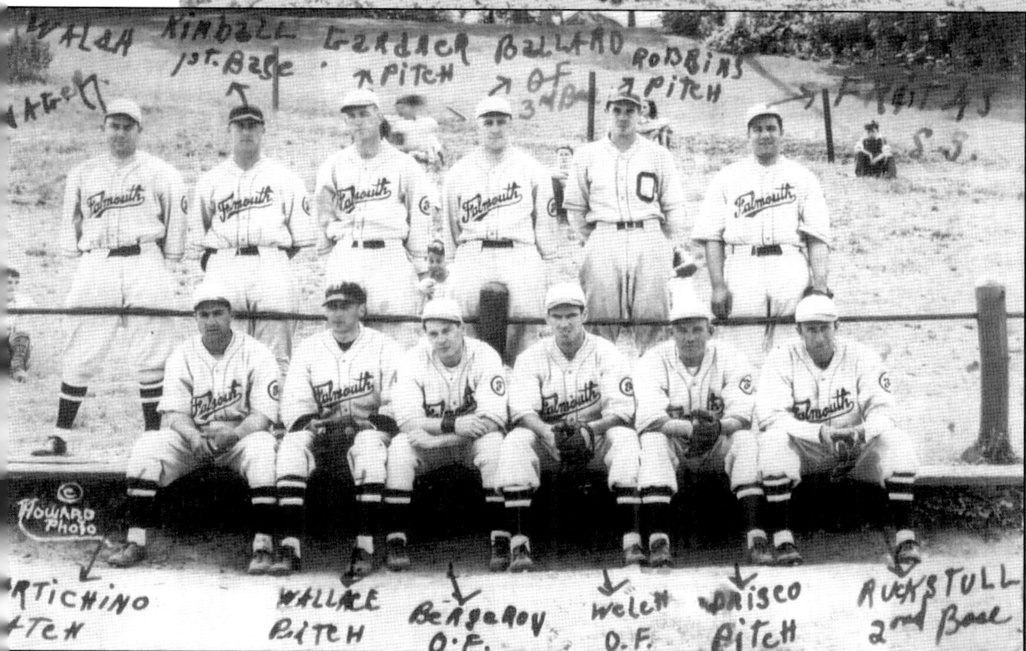

Cape Cod Baseball League

The Cape Cod Baseball League, sometimes called the Cottage Club, was highlighted by players like Myron Ruckstall, who played all 14 seasons of this early predecessor of the current Cape Cod Baseball League. Harold "Pie" Traynor played shortstop for Falmouth in the 1919 team and was later elected to the Cape Cod Baseball League Hall of Fame in 1948. "Deacon" Dan MacFayden pitched for Falmouth in 1925. The games were played then at Central Park overlooking the Falmouth Heights beach. It was a delight for locals and tourists and the start of a wonderful tradition of baseball by the sea.

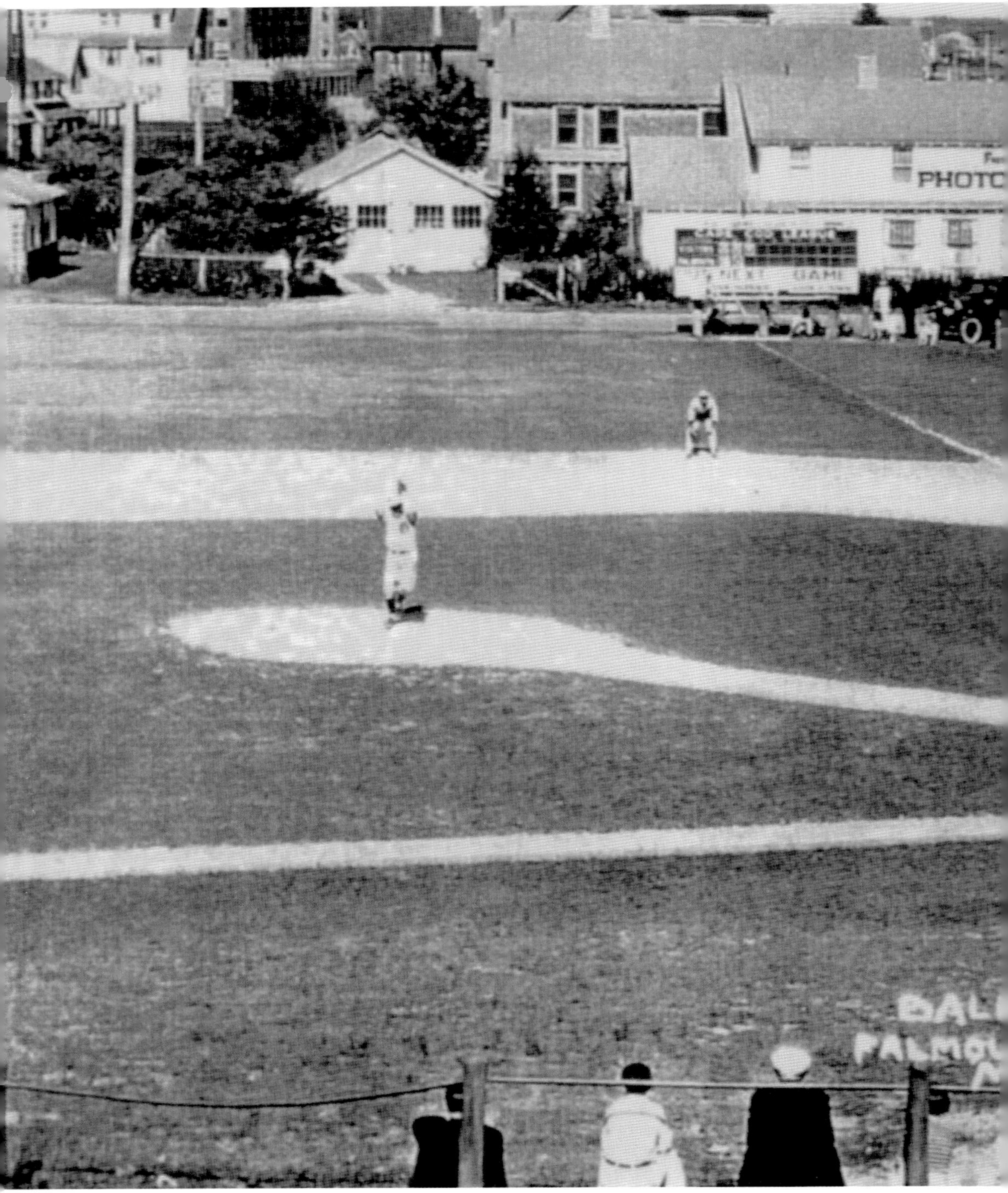

Falmouth Heights Ball Park

Shown here is a vista view of the Falmouth Heights ball park, called one of the most beautiful ball parks on the East Coast. This 1930 photograph was taken at the height of the games of the Old Cape Cod

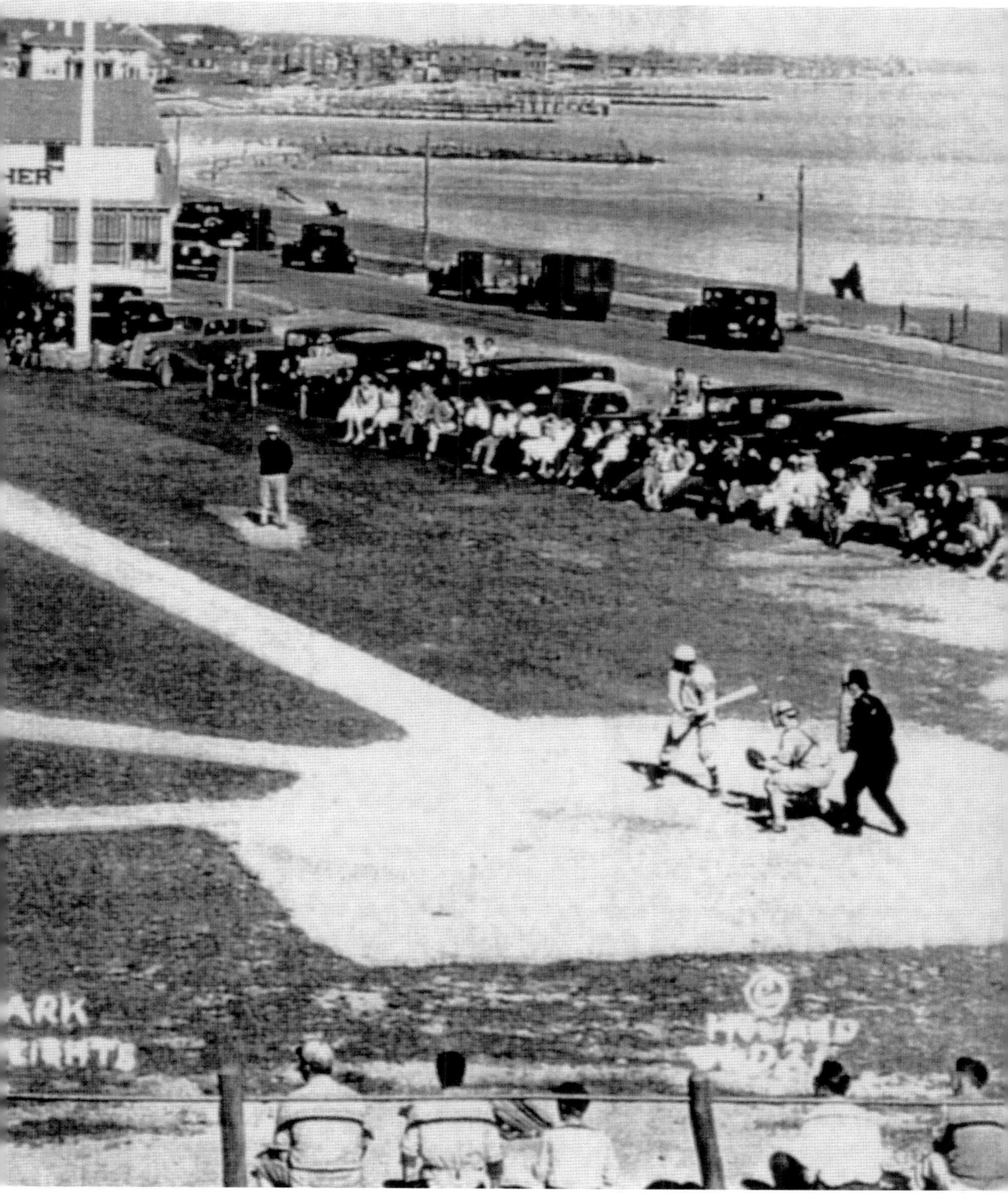

Baseball League. The ocean edge and breeze made for a spectacular backdrop for the games. However, the proximity to nearby houses led to the move away from this idyllic setting. Central Park is the official name of the park that is so associated with the beauty of Falmouth Heights.

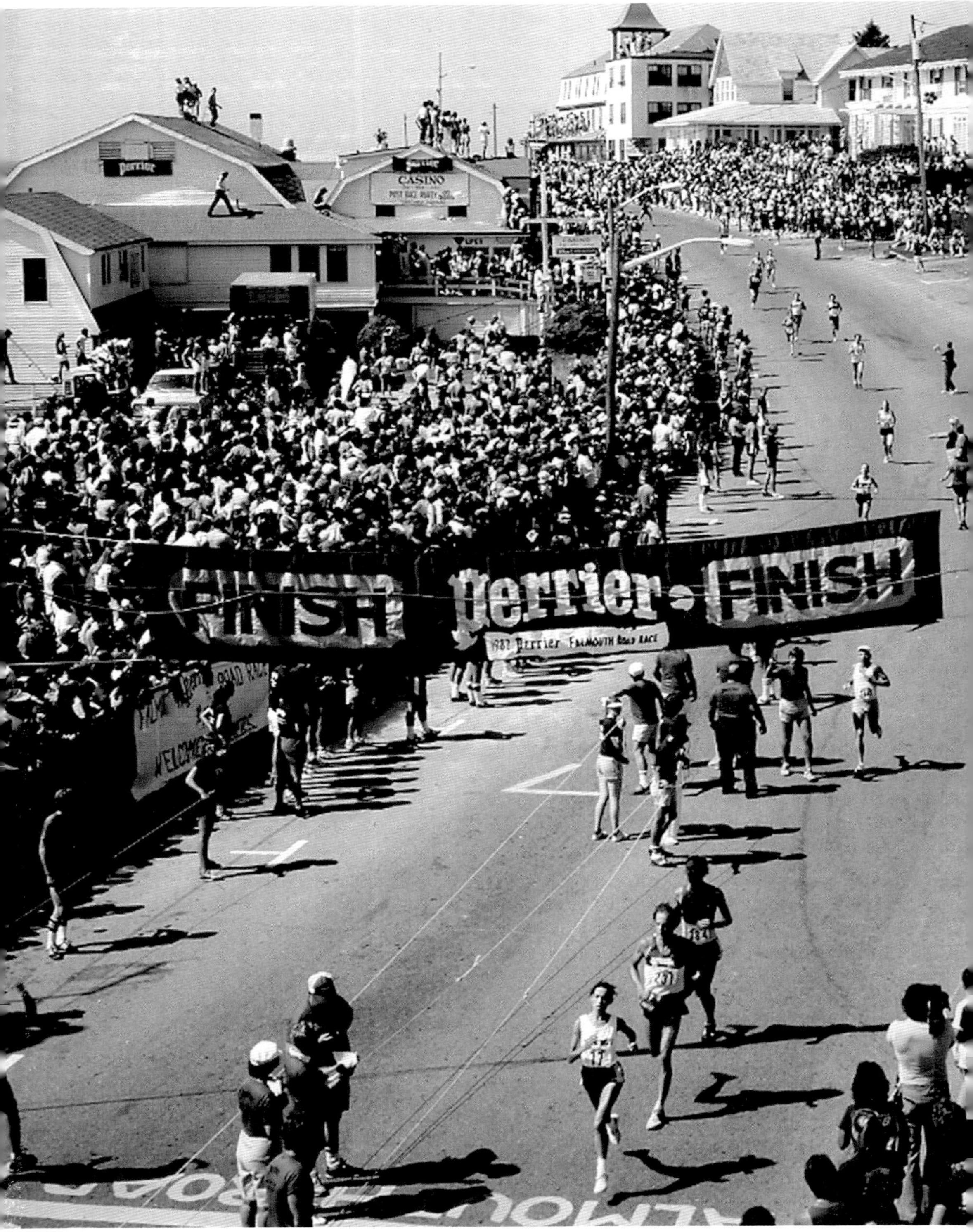

CASINO
FINISH
Perrier
FINISH
1982 Perrier FALMOUTH ROAD RACE

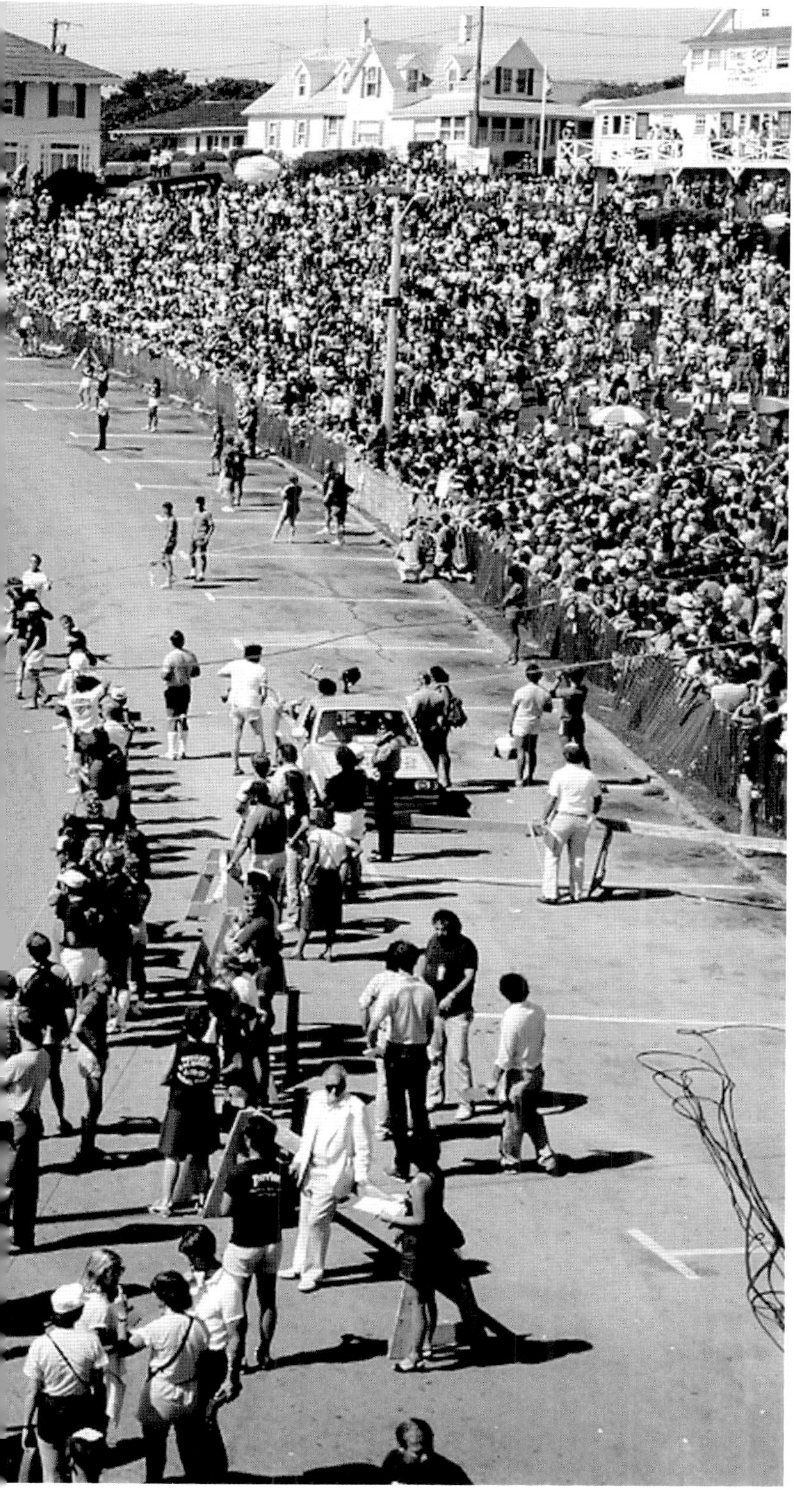

Falmouth Road Race Finish Line (1983)
This photograph of the finish line of the Falmouth Road Race shows the runners as they came downhill from the bluffs at Falmouth Heights. The scale of this popular road race, with over 10,000 runners participating annually, contrasts with the winding country roads of the course. It is both an achievement and a thrill to compete in Falmouth. (Photograph by Hugo Poisson, courtesy Falmouth Historical Society Collections.)

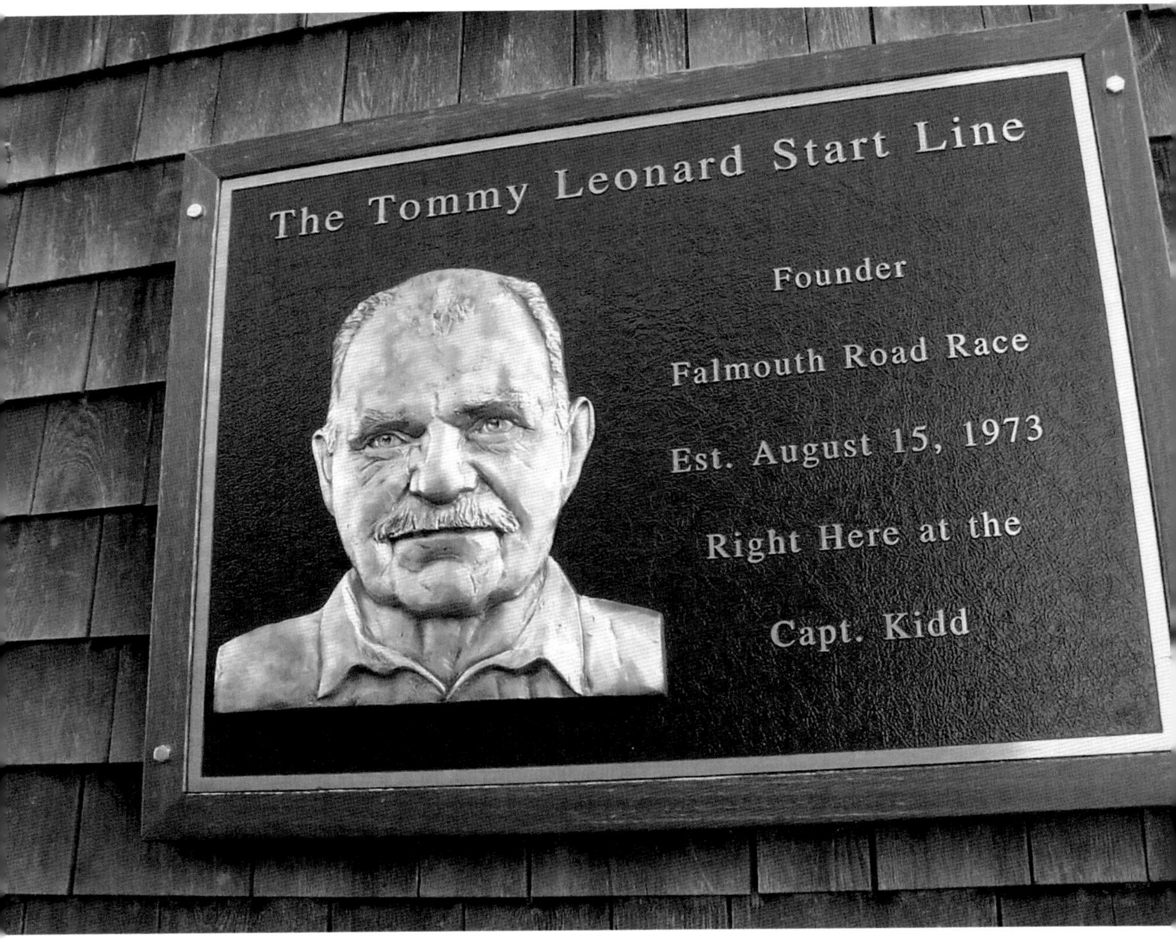

Tommy Leonard (1933–)
Tommy Leonard was the inventor and hero of the Falmouth Road Race. It all began in 1973 with a simple 7.3-mile race from the Captain Kidd Restaurant in Woods Hole to Brothers Four in Falmouth Heights. The racecourse is noted for its views of Nobska Lighthouse and Vineyard Sound. It is a phenomenon, and thousands of runners and spectators participate in Leonard's wild idea. (Courtesy Falmouth Road Race website.)

Falmouth Road Race Starting Line (OPPOSITE PAGE)
This aerial photograph shows the starting line of the Falmouth Road Race, with Water Street in Woods Hole, the WHOI buildings, Eel Pond, and Woods Hole Harbor. In the upper left is the legendary Captain Kidd Restaurant and filling all the space in between are the runners that continue to participate in this event every year. (Photograph by Hugo Poisson, courtesy Falmouth Historical Society Collections.)

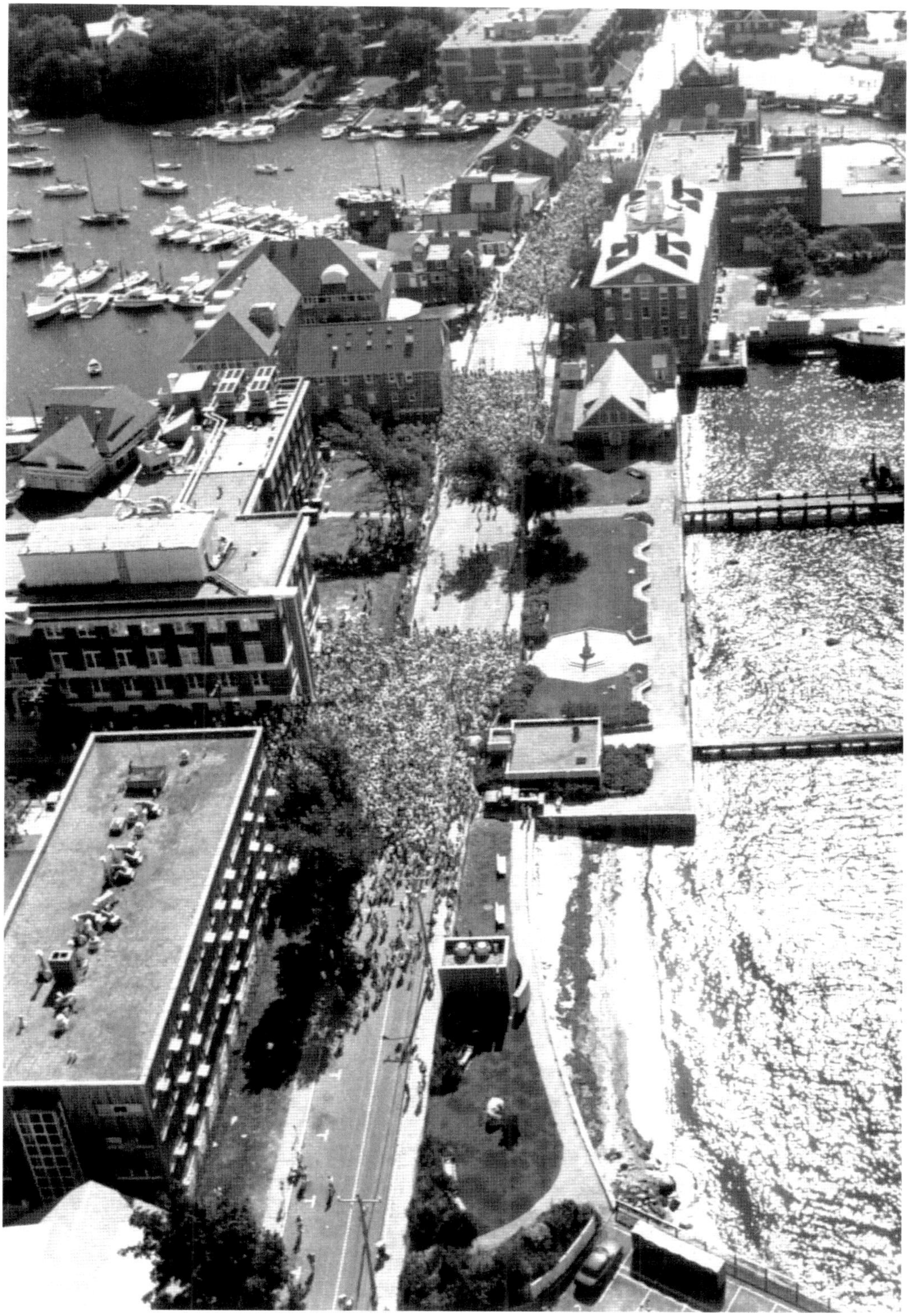

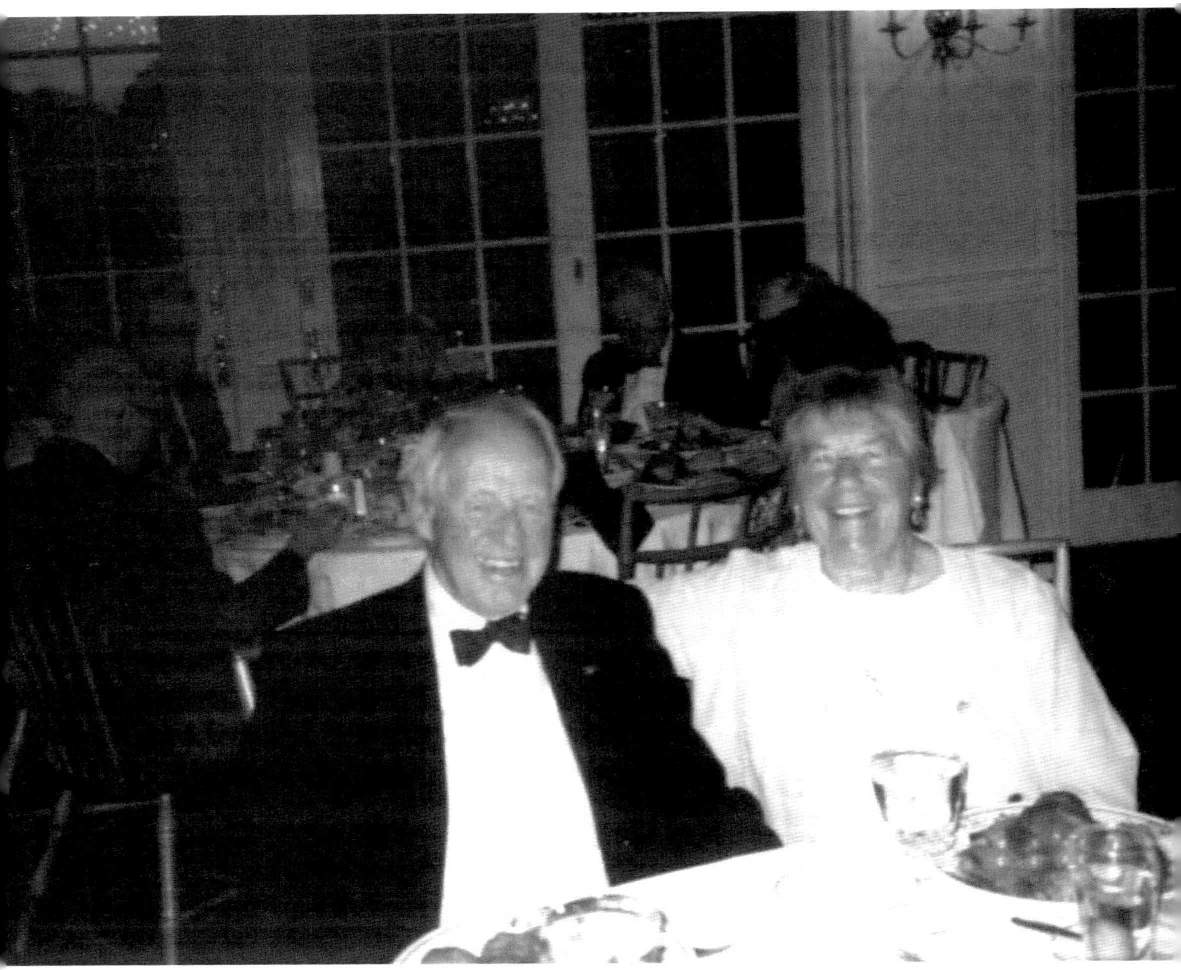

Mary Lou Smith (1942–)
Mary Lou Smith has been a historical publishing and preservation force in Woods Hole and Falmouth since the 1980s. Appropriately, her first editing achievement was *Woods Hole Reflections* in 1982, followed very closely by the imposing, unmatched *Book of Falmouth* in 1986. Not to rest of those laurels, Mary Lou Smith, together with a small committee, launched the unrivaled historical journal *Spritsail*, which has been published twice a year since 1987. Adding to this was her editing efforts in *Diary of Ruth Ann Hatch* and *New England Views*. She was the first recipient of the Heritage Award at the Falmouth Historical Society in 2000, and the Sunken Gardens at Highfield Hall were dedicated in her name in 2011. Mary Lou Smith is pictured here with her husband, Paul, at a Heritage Dinner. (Courtesy Woods Hole Historical Collections.)

INDEX